Wilderness Tracks

How to Sleuth Out Wild Creatures and Wayward Humans

by
Barbara Butler

hancock

house

ISBN 0-88839-410-1
Copyright © 1997 Barbara Butler

Cataloging in Publication Data
Butler, Barbara, 1924-
  Wilderness tracks

  Includes bibliographical references.
  ISBN 0-88839-410-1

  1. Tracking and trailing. 2. Animal tracks. I. Title.
  SK282.B87 1997   796.5   C97-910523-4

Printed in Hong Kong—Colorcraft

Production: Sharon Boglari and Nancy Miller
Editing: Nancy Miller

Published simultaneously in Canada and the United States by

HANCOCK HOUSE PUBLISHERS LTD.
19313 Zero Avenue, Surrey, B.C. V4P 1M7
(604) 538-1114 Fax (604) 538-2262

HANCOCK HOUSE PUBLISHERS
1431 Harrison Avenue, Blaine, WA 98230
(604) 538-1114 Fax (604) 538-2262
email address: *hancockhouse.com*

Contents

*For all wildlife, and those who work on their behalf.
My gratitude particularly goes out to Deschutes County
Search and Rescue in Bend, Oregon, forgiving me the opportunity to leaarn from border patrolmen Ab Taylor and Joel
Hardin, whose tracking was sheer inspiration. I also owe
much to tracker Tom Brown, Jr., whose love of wildlife I
absorbed and carry with me.*

Foreword

As a child I spent time outside observing wild creatures in Flossmoor, Illinois. I eventually became a clinical psychologist, but with every opportunity I sought the outdoors. Before my graduate work in Missouri, I lived and worked in Alaska as an airline stewardess, which took me into remote areas full of wildlife. Finally, later in life, tracking, which had been a casual endeavor, became a passion. It suited my loner personality; and I became more intimately acquainted with wildlife, enough to give workshops on tracking in Bend, Oregon and at the Glacier Institute in Glacier National Park, Montana. To this day I travel the Pacific Northwest and Canada seeking these hidden wild creatures I love. At home in Oregon I am constantly aware of what wildlife are pursuing their quiet lives, which they unwittingly share with me. I am very happy with that. I have a son, a daughter and a granddaughter. Alas, they are city dwellers.

A sense of mystery surrounds the track of an animal on a dusty road. What species was this, what was the creature doing, when was it here? Is it male or female, young or old, and where did it go? Tracking is detective work and you must be totally unprejudiced about what the living creature was doing. You cannot surmise, you must observe what the ground tells you rather than hypothesize about what you think happened.

Tracking began seriously for me on the dusty road to my land, Wildhaunt, although at the time I didn't realize it. After any absence, when I drove off the pavement onto the four-mile stretch of back road, my heart would begin to pound as I nervously noted signs of recent activity along the way. I was most anxious at the old wooden gate, for I always left it shut and I always found it open. As I drove, I scanned the dirt road for car and human tracks to tell me something about who had come through my land, why and when they had been there. I became quite proficient in tracking from an automobile, especially with such a keen motivation—the love of my land and the wildlife there. This began in 1967, and Wildhaunt became the center of my life and future.

The lush vitality of wild nature in its mystery and complexity is so intriguing it is hard to concentrate on just one aspect. Indeed, the enormous whole is interrelated in all facets; the plant and animal life all need each other to survive, to hold together in their elaborate cycles. The omission of just one ingredient can put the whole out of balance. I learned this through tracking and observing wildlife. It can be a lifetime endeavor, and one of sincere respect.

Although in 1967 I first started tracking the wildlife at Wildhaunt, it wasn't until more than ten years later that I trained with U.S. border patrolmen Ab Taylor and Joel Hardin, both retired and both originally from the El Cajon station in California. These two trackers of humans have impressive skills. The way they read the ground was an inspiration. I also went to Seattle for workshops given by Tom Brown, Jr., a nationally known survivalist and tracker; and I gleaned much from him about wildlife tracking. My lot is not to become like these men, but to learn and share with others the intimacy with nature I experience. I hope to open for others the doors through which I so joyously leapt. During my treks I photographed many of the tracks I found, and my slides and video are used in teaching wildlife workshops.

Wildhaunt lies just east of the central Oregon Cascade Mountain Range by about a dozen miles. The Three Sisters Mountains, Broken Top and Tam McArthur Rim lie boldly within my sight on clear days. The juniper and pine between my cabin and the mountains are a perpetual sea of wind noise, and cover the comings and goings of land and air creatures as they work to survive each day. The ground is sand and pumice from ancient volcanic eruptions, and the climate is dry most of the year. There is only moderate ground cover. This includes sagebrush, bitterbrush, rabbit brush, Russian thistle, wild currant, bunch grass, wild rye, granite Gilia, buckwheat, subalpine lupine, an occasional Mariposa lily, and other wildflowers and grasses. Thus the ground is open and the movement of the wildlife is temporarily recorded there. As the elevation increases toward the Cascades, the Ponderosa pines increase; and the noble fir, Douglas fir, hemlock, lodgepole pine, balsam and spruce become prolific, and on the high windswept ridges whitebark pine occurs.

Fleeting glimpses of the wildlife are not sufficient for me. I trudge on foot many miles each day to learn what bobcat denned beside my land, what badger crossed it, and in which coyote territory I reside. I come alive as each piece of evidence on the ground or in the bush reveals the presence and activity of the wildlife. I want to share with you some of these times.

Glossary

BOUND—a gait which places the rear feet of the animal either parallel and behind the front feet or exactly in the front feet tracks.

DEW TRAIL—absence of dew on grass, fields of crops, or any thick vegetation, creating a darkened area.

DIAGONAL WALKERS—animals who move their diagonal feet at the same time.

DISTURBANCE—any alteration of the natural state of the area.

GAIT—the manner a wild animal moves its feet, resulting in specialized patterns of foot tracks upon the ground.

GALLOP—fast gait in which the animal's feet all leave the ground once or twice.

JUMP—an exercise slower than a gallop with a variety of track patterns.

LOPE—a gallop of slower speed.

PACE—a gait wherein an animal moves the legs on one side of its body at the same time.

PITCH—the angle a foot makes from the direction of travel when placed on the ground, either toward or away from the body.

SHINE—flattening of dirt by a foot, creating a reflective surface noticeable primarily from twenty to fifty feet away.

SIGN-CUTTING—looking for sign in order to begin tracking.

SIGN—any evidence of alteration of the natural state made by an animal, most is noticeable within eight feet.

SINGLEFOOT—gait where each foot of the animal strikes the ground singly.

STEP TRACKING—identifying all tracks in sequence to verify that they all belong to the same subject.

STRADDLE—the measurement of the distance between the left and right tracks of an animal, front or rear. When track measurements include the feet, it is called the trail width.

STRIDE—the measurement of the distance from the rear track to the next track of an animal, measured from heel to next heel.

TRACKING—following a subject by establishing a continuous, uninterrupted chain of evidence from each step to the next.

TROT—fast gait of a diagonal walker.

WALK—movement in which the feet move at different times.

Tracking Locations Mentioned in the Book

ALASKA—Fairbanks: Tok Junction.

CANADA—Burwash Landing, Yukon Territory. Downie Creek, B.C. North Fork, Flathead River, B.C.

IDAHO—Panhandle National Forest: Blueberry Lake; Upper Priest Lake. Thierrault Lakes.

MONTANA—Cabinet Mts.: McKay Creek, Swamp Creek, Vermillion River. Flathead National Forest: Hay Creek; Trail Creek. Glacier National Park: Akokala Creek; Avalanche Lake; Big Prairie; Dutch Creek; Flathead River, North Fork; Kintla Creek; Kintla Lake; Kishenehn Creek; Logging Creek; McGee Creek; Moose City; Quartz Creek; Round Prairie. Purcell Mts.: Yaak River.

OREGON—Cascade Head, Otis. Cascade Mts.; Cherry Creek, Mitchell. Crooked River National Grasslands: Alder Springs. Deschutes National Forest: Black Butte; Green Ridge; Little Deschutes River; Metolius River; Suttle Lake; Squaw Creek; Three Sisters Wilderness. John Day River; Mitchell. Ochoco National Forest. Smith Rocks State Park. Tumalo Winter Deer Range. Wildhaunt. Willamette Valley.

WASHINGTON—Ft. Worden Coast Beach. Gibbs Lake, Olympic National Park. NorthwesTrek Wildlife Park. Okanogan National Forest: Pasayten Wilderness. Tahola.

Chapter One

The Elements of Tracking

The ground is alive where wild things write their lives over and over, telling those of us who track about their comings and goings, showing us their behavior and the inclination of their minds. The ground and surrounding brush are the novels from which we can decipher their stories, the only place where we can study the largely hidden lives that surround us. We track for pleasure and survival, to learn about wildlife and their habitat, to become intimate with nature, to read a chapter in a wild being's life, to stalk and perhaps to touch a wild creature, and so to study, enjoy and learn. We can backtrack ourselves if we get lost, find water holes and trails which wildlife use, track lost persons and wounded deer. Next to the ground, studying the subtle signs around us, we are closer to the natural order than when we walk looking far above those lives, unaware of our own footprints and those of others. Tracking gives us a clearer picture of wildlife activity than any other form of observation. As trackers we see more than we could ever sight from a stationary blind or winding on a familiar path. We catch a glimpse of scattered seeds where some creature has been feeding, we find the bed in wild grasses which a deer used the night before, we break open the scat and find what the coyote ate, and we see where the raccoon and her young drank.

With tracking, experience is the best teacher, still this book will acquaint the reader with the basic techniques. And, may it inspire you to explore your own world more thoroughly.

The tracker thinks of the ground as flat, with every depression a possible track, whether it is the impression of a paw, a hoof or even a stream. Wind, rain, sun, dew and changes of temperature are transformations that smooth the soils. Look for any disturbances in the ground: any flattening created by the weight of a living creature, any color contrast which might be a footprint, and any sheen. Keep the area you are searching between you and the sun, this way any flattened surface will reflect the light and appear brighter in contrast to the other ground. This is termed "shine." If there is no sun, keeping the sun's direction in mind will still aid in finding tracks. In contrast, in the early morning, the absence of dew on grass, fields of grain or lush vegetation creates a darkened area, called a "dew trail."

The expert tracker tests his own foot on the ground next to the track to compare the freshness. Aging a track depends upon many variables and their combinations. It really cannot be taught, it must be experienced by the tracker. Wind, sun, heat, cold and moisture all combine to influence the conditions of various soils in different ways; and as the weather changes, the tracks continue to alter. A fresh track has more clean-cut walls, sharper edges, a flatter, shinier surface and a more definite shape than an older one. As time passes, sand grains fall into the track, the breeze rounds the edges, the flattened area covers with additional dirt and the sheen changes to the color of the aged, surrounding ground. Fissures, rises and mounds caused by the upheaval of disturbance crumble, slopes flatten out, depressions fill in, mounds scatter, animals track over, the sun dries and smooths, and gravity works on it all the time. The first thing a tracker inquires about a new area is what the weather has been during the last week.

Soils can be considered in three broad categories: clay, sand and average soil, comparable to the garden variety. Clay, dense and sticky if wet, holds a track three times as long as sand. Sand is so loose in structure a track can disintegrate almost as you watch it. Average soil will hold a track for a period of time roughly equal between these two. Observing the speed and quality of disintegration from weather will teach you how to age a track. Learning how to read the story some wild creature writes on the ground takes hours upon hours of observation during all weather conditions, in all kinds of soils, all year around. Wind rapidly erases signs. I once rode a motorcycle along my dirt road in very high wind. When I returned eight hours later, only the faintest suggestion of tracks remained. The wind from automobiles can destroy tracks very quickly. Light mist can almost erase tracks in dirt and sand, and rain eventually obliterates them. Snow can enlarge tracks, while the sun melts away their details. At

40°F in direct sunlight, my boot tracks lost all tread pattern in snow in three to four hours, one December afternoon.

Differing types of snow, different amounts of wind, and changes of temperature combine to make tracking anywhere from easy to impossible. Damp snow once iced turns gray. Sleet can be detrimental to tracks unless it is merely a thin coating which will break easily. Keep in mind, also, that in winter the light from the sun is from the south, and southern slopes age tracks more rapidly than flat ground or northern slopes. The same tracks will look older on the south side than on the north side.

A track leaves characteristics that shape the soil in and around it. The contortions of the foot deform the ground as it hits and then lifts off again. These pressure releases vary with the speed of the animal and are good clues to learn. The greater the speed, the more disturbance of the ground. Track yourself, observing the differences. The greater your speed, the more explosion on the ground as more pressure is applied. All sides will push out and away. There will be more forward carry of dirt beyond the track as well, and you will first notice turns of your quarry by the direction of this trail of evidence. Different pressure patterns will be produced in the heel, toe and ball of the foot with different gaits. As the body turns to look left or right, this will be reflected in the tracks, too.

Trackers also learn to interpret an animal's activities by reading the stride, straddle and pitch of its tracks. They all vary with differing speeds. With greater speed the stride, or length between the prints, will lengthen. Increased speed also narrows the straddle, or trail width, and may alter the pitch, the angle the foot makes in relation to the direction the animal is traveling. Time spent on reading difficult tracks will teach you more than tracking good tracks all day long. If the ground is read accurately, it will tell you the truth of the story, revealing a mystery which can be solved. The tracks will tell you what species the animal was, when it was there, its size, mood and in some cases its age and sex. A track changes with every important change of impulse, movement and feeling. As the animal behaves differently, this is reflected in the ground. Sightings of wild creatures are usually short lived, and your very presence alerts the animals and alters their normal behavior. Tracks, however, reveal their natural ways.

In dense cover, vegetation breaks may be the only clues by which to track an animal. Here again, as when you test your own footprint on the ground to compare its freshness with the tracks you are following, you should experiment with different plants and trees to learn how they age when broken in passage. You should also know the various signs animals leave on plants when they have been feeding. It can be crucial to your tracking to detect the difference between a branch broken in flight and one that has been bitten by a browsing deer. Injured vegetation turns color. A trail through short grass will show lighter than the surrounding area, whereas a trail through tall grass will show darker. The underside of leaves are lighter and become more noticeable when turned by any disturbance. Large leaves or tall grass crushed in the ground turn dark and are moist from breaks. With sufficient pressure, dirt grains become embedded into the underside.

In general, the more unnatural the position of leafy plants, the more recent the injury, as live vegetation begins righting itself immediately. Test a break on the same bush and compare it with the break in question. The taller the trampled grass, the harder for it to stand up straight, so the longer it takes to right itself. The wetter the ground, the poorer the footing of the plant, and the longer the healing process. In dry grass, older trails look darker than fresher ones since night dew expands stems and reduces light reflection, and accumulations of dust interfere with shine. Heat is beneficial and does not affect the aging process radically, unless it is severe. Extreme heat increases withering, and then a break a few hours old may look like it is as much as a day old. Dense vegetation returns to its normal position with the passage of time and can totally obliterate a trail. In the ground below, however, the indentation of a hoof may remain. Light rains encourage vegetation to right itself quickly as the flattened stems expand and colors become more uniform. In general, broken branches have a lighter color when freshly broken, but they eventually darken.

Identifying and aging scat is important. Color and size are derived from diet and the bulk of the ingested material. Differences in color may also be due to heat and bacteria. Flies are attracted to fresh scat, and in the first few hours numerous flies will remain on a summer scat. Before twenty-four hours there will be half as many flies, and none beyond that time. After twenty-four hours, the moisture disappears and a crust begins to thicken. If a bear, for example, has eaten flesh, the scat may be runny black. If green vegetation was consumed it may be black but will be fibrous. Scat of flesh smells, that of vegetation does not. The condition of the area underneath the scat assists in aging it. The presence of insects, larvae or eggs indicate the scat is several days old.

In tracking, the terrain has to be considered as well. Downhill tracking is easier than sidehill and uphill tracking, for more sign is made. The steeper the slope, the more sign is left since there are many more foot placements. Sidehill tracking leaves far more sign than flat ground, but less than downhill slopes. In uphill tracking the more sandy the soil, the more difficulty there is in determining the difference between animal and human tracks. In reality, the trail may change often as the animal picks the easiest way. Slides occur in uphill and downhill walking, leaving obvious clues.

Tracking enhances one's inner resources, patience and concentration, and teaches the use of all senses, including the sixth sense, intuition. Noticing detail is important. The touch and feel of a track or vegetation helps to age it. Smell indicates the freshness of the porcupine's debarking of the tree or a recent scat deposit. Experience stores the minutiae of the weather and soil variables as you note the disintegration of the track, the crumbling of the soil particles from its walls and the blown debris accumulation. Attitude is important as you track since you need to learn the cues from nature rather than projecting your expectations onto the ground. Objectivity prepares you to be open to any changes of behavior in the animal you track. Relax and accept what you see, thus learning what the creature does. Go slowly and do not skip a track. Move step by step as the animal did, thus when the line of tracks disappear you will have learned to find the obscure ones. Spend time on difficult tracks; wait and try an hour or two later when the light is different, if you cannot discern where a track should be. Difficult tracks are your true teachers.

Relax, take your time, observe, concentrate and persevere when it is difficult. Then you will be become a tracker.

I keep a journal of my tracking endeavors. I list the species, locale, date, time, measurements of the tracks, weather, age of the tracks, the distance I tracked and the behavior of the animal. I sometimes use a stick with movable washers fitting snugly to measure the length and width of the foot, the stride, straddle and normal jump of the animal. This helps my eye set to its pattern. By placing the stick on the last track to be found, I can detect the next one by measured eye expectation. I carry tweezers to lift debris from a track so I can see its clear impression in the ground beneath. I also have used a mirror to reflect light into a dark track. A ruler or tape measure will quickly reveal the length of the animal's stride, the size of its tracks and its straddle. I may take along vials to collect unidentified scat, a survey tape to locate tracks in ascertaining its trails, a compass for my own orientation, a monocular for distance viewing, scotch tape to collect hair samples, plaster of Paris for casts, a flashlight with a red lens for night tracking, and a magnifying glass. The last is probably the tool I use most. If you become very expert at judging ground by temperature you may use a thermometer for aging tracks. I also take survival items when going far. Camera and film are important.

There is a growing fascination with tracking by the outdoorsman. Where you cannot see wildlife, tracks tell you of their passing, and this awareness adds another dimension of quality experience to the solitude, beauty and adventure of wilderness experience.

Tracking is a lifetime adventure as you become more and more expert in enjoying it. It is a skill that should be kept alive in our country. So as you put your feet down, glance at the ground.

Chapter Two

The Cat Family
Felidae

BOBCAT
Felis rufus

In the silence of desert peace, if you track ever so carefully, the padded echoes of the bobcat circle close by. Although the cat is gone, its presence is felt. Where it has roamed, sharp claws have dug into a tree; a rabbit has screamed. And somewhere on a lonely rock outcrop, a leg-hold trap lies rusted, clamped upon a bobcat paw—a grim reminder of its deserted soul.

Bobcats live in coniferous, mountainous areas typified by cool, moist winters and hot, dry summers. Terrain can be relatively moderate, rolling topography; gentle to moderate slopes with steep canyons and talus slopes; or extremely steep, rugged terrain. They can also live in hot, flat, desert land with mild winters. In sagebrush and grassland habitats, these cats favor the microenvironment of rocky ledge country, field edges, trails, roads and natural or manmade travel routes, especially if these routes or edges are lined with heavy growth, such as grasses, vines or briars. All these areas provide good habitat for their main prey of mice and rabbits.

Strange, perhaps, that it was the bobcat that entered my tracking life first, for the coyotes were more numerous in my home area. I love the felines, and the bob is the most fun for me to track. I still feel the excitement of finding its tiny, careful prints daintily imprinted in the dust, and have to follow it at least part way whenever I encounter its sign. When I stop, I always wonder where the soft, furry creature with sharp claws went, and how close I came to it.

Dusty logging roads were the places I first began searching for bobcat tracks. The tracks are round and smaller than those of a coyote, which mark more oblong and show claw marks. The bobcat stride is shorter and its movement much slower and more cautious. Bobcats use the roads for nocturnal hunting because mice are easy to find as they run across the road. The bobcat uses the edge of cover for hunting; the road becomes the open field and somewhere it will mark upon it. Bobcats have even been known to bait small mammals with a scrap of meat, lying in wait for the taker of the bait.

These cat tracks are light and soft in central Oregon sand, and tracking across pine needles is a real challenge. Knowing the speed and gait of the cat as it enters difficult ground is helpful, for if it did not change gait, you already have the mental set of its stride length to see the next track more easily. You are almost always already looking at it. Keeping this mental set aids tremendously in continuing your tracking. Once distracted from this set due to its change of direction, the older age of the track or many depressions in the duff (partly decayed organic matter on forest floors) can make tracking frustrating. A tracking stick marked with the cat's normal walking stride can help you concentrate again. You may have to go around the area if all else fails, and cut for sign on a ninety-degree angle on soil more conducive to receiving and holding track. Then back-tracking will assist you in learning to spot the tracks you could not find at first. Spending your time on the difficult tracks helps you learn the cues which will in the future be necessary, when, instead of another track ahead, there seem to be no other tracks. Bobcats frequently utilize rock outcroppings where tracks may be impossible to see. As you track, you learn automatically the habits of the animal, and when rock presents itself as a barrier you often intuit where the cat has gone, and so can easily cut sign ahead.

When I moved to my place in 1975, many bobcats lived on and near my land. Since then people have moved in, trappers have depleted the population, and now very few bobs live here. At one time I could start onto bobtail track within a quarter-mile from home and continue to track all day long. I have tracked them with kittens, seen their dens and found tracks of breeding males and females. I have tracked males seeking new territory, identified different cats and learned their territories, but I have spent days and weeks and months doing it. I have even had a bobcat ahead of me so close it made fresh tracks while I cut for sign in the other direction.

The land in this Oregon country is crossed with old logging roads. Second growth and stumps from turn of the century logging dot the rises and canyons on the desert floor. Juniper and pine throng together, and their sap scent the western winds. I used the old logging roads.

Denning females lie at least a mile from each other's territory. Where I found tracks, I surveyed the area for likely den sites, looking for many tracks in one area, and more frequent scat deposits. I then tracked and backtracked away from the likely den area. Where I found tracks in an area repeatedly, I returned a few times to establish residence activity, always making a wide perimeter of the probable den area. If I accidentally stumbled across a den, I left quickly to avoid disturbance. Then I regularly checked during the following weeks to look for kitten tracks along with adult ones.

In 1980, in an eight-month period, I was able to identify the number of females denning with kittens within a two- to three-mile radius of my home. It took many miles of tracking, almost daily. After identifying dens, I was able to save some time by using a few old logging roads to ride a small, quiet trail bike within a reasonable distance of the bobs' home ranges without frightening the cats. Going slowly, many tracks can be identified from a small bike.

What I found were four females. Each had only one kitten. I found the tracks of only one male during the month of March, the most frequent breeding month. The dens the females dug were large and deep, judging from the amount of sand excavated. One cat used an old coyote den, adding another opening. I observed these cats for several years. They would use the same den some years, or construct new dens. During intense summer heat one year, a bob dug a den on my land in the open sand, not too deep, quite close to my cabin. I thought it must be quite cool down there. It was not used very long, and there was no evidence of a kitten.

After a winter illness, I found a complex of dens dug about 150 feet from the cabin...I wish I still shared my land with as many bobs as I did then.

Often I left home in late afternoon or early evening and made a long journey by foot, or went early in the morning hoping to see the bob I had been tracking. I kept tabs on one den this time. One bob had made a den beside an old overgrown logging road near the peak of a rise. It had excavated a considerable amount of sand, and I would like to have known how deep and far it had dug. Other dens were nearby, some obviously abandoned in the making, some old and sanded in, and one or two waiting, likely safe alternatives. The bobcat always knew when I was there, of course, for it was only once I saw it.

Not far from its active den one morning I tracked it. It was hunting, carefully, slowly through the brush, tracks shining in the early sun, clean of any fine dust, very fresh. It had moved with hesitation, listening and looking, going on and on. I felt it had just been there. And of course it had. It was not far ahead. I tired a little, stopping now and then to look around, and then I saw it. It was a flash, ahead 100 feet, and it moved across my vision in an opening between the brush. That was all. I stalked then toward the spot, and intermittently picked up its tracks, for my eyes were ahead of me and not on the ground. It knew, of course, where I was. Where it went, I never knew. It left its fresher tracks there for me, but that was all. I never caught up.

I came closer to another bob in the 1970s. I had discovered a series of dens in the shoulder of an old logging road, one of which this cat was using frequently for a short period of time, but there were no kittens. I took up its track one day when it had been made within the hour and tracked it across the road and into some large rocks where I lost the track. I circled around but there was no more sign. So I left it in the rocks, secure again.

More exciting was the closeness when I tracked another time, the same cat, I believe. It was the same year and territory. There was patchy snow upon the ground. I tracked it over snow and frozen ground early one morning for a long way. I felt it was headed home from a night's hunting. I was able to track rather quickly, and its tracks told me I was not too far behind. I was excited, yet concerned about troubling a cat. I thought they knew me by then as innocuous, for my spoor had been there and nothing terrible had happened while I lived here. As I rarely came close, it seemed innocent enough in the scheme of things to try to see the cat.

As I got close, not only the tracks but a feel for the cat pervaded me. It chose a rock outcrop to enter, tracks showing a slight slip as it dropped into them where I could not see. I felt it was down there. But I needed to know. I cut carefully around the outcrop, making sure it could not have jumped out on the other side, and I returned in jubilation upon coming on to the spot where I began the circle. Ah, clever cat. While I was gone that short time, new tracks led away and they crossed a road. I sat down and laughed at being outwitted. And was that bob laughing too?

Since those years, bobcat tracks are fewer in the northern portion of the Tumalo Winter Deer Range, and their dens have disintegrated. Occasionally one passes through, however. In 1992 a bob did make several dens near the cabin. It might have stayed had I not been so eager to learn about her. After my trespass it left.

In the winter of 1992–93 we had a snowfall totaling seven feet. When it melted down to three feet in March, I was lying on my deck in the sun, exhausted from shoveling. Two Stellar jays squawked loudly 200 feet away. As their shrieks came closer, I knew they were following some creature on the ground. I glanced to catch a slight movement behind the brush. Expecting a coyote, I searched the brush at the next opening. To my surprise a bobcat appeared.

It was medium in size, very relaxed, moving slowly, turning its head from side to side in its hunting mode. I was able to watch it from seventy-five feet away, as it was unaware of my presence. I watched until a gentle slope hid the cat's movement, and waited thirty long moments so I would not disturb it, giving it enough time to get ahead of me. The cat's weight put its tracks only slightly into the packed snow. It had moved behind my cabin, and then continued back in the direction from which it had come. Without snowshoes I tired quickly in the snow. It is easier if the bobcat comes to you.

***

Soft-footed and a nocturnal hunter, the bobcat conceals itself well and is seldom seen. It shows different color variations depending upon the climate it inhabits. In the desert it is buff; in the mountains, gray-black. Seasonally its coat changes from grayer in the winter to lighter in the summer. Some individuals are melanistic with black or very dark brown coats. Albinism may occur, too. The tip of its tail is black, and it has some short ear tufts. Its body length is somewhere between twenty-five and thirty inches, with a tail from around four inches to seven inches. A sixty-eight-pound bobcat has been recorded; however, the average weight is between fifteen and thirty-five pounds.

As with all the feline family, the bobcat is a solitary creature, with, of course, the exception of the breeding season. The bobcat can breed and conceive at any time of the year. However, most breeding takes place between December and August, with the peak occurring in March or April. Studies have shown that kittens are rarely born in the months of December, January or February. Somehow nature avoids the disadvantages of hard winter births. The female may breed when she reaches a year of age, and males are sexually mature at two years. The female estrus cycle is normally between forty-four and forty-six days. Breeding with domestic cats has been known, and the offspring are mixed, some with ear tufts and bobbed tails.

Bobcat dens are found in rock caves, logs or dug into the sand, often at the base of a tree or sagebrush. Bobs may use the same area each year to den, often in a den very close to one previously used. They have been known to use an abandoned coyote den, but usually dig their own. The openings, and there are usually more than one, are just large enough, as a rule, to accommodate their body. Very little bedding is used.

Although in southern climes two litters a year are possible, most bobs produce a yearly litter of two to three kittens, even six, after a gestation of fifty to seventy days. When the female licks off the placental sac she identifies her young by taste imprint. The kittens weigh four to eight ounces at birth, open their eyes at about ten days and use their senses in reverse order of their later acuity: smell, hearing and sight. The mother is very protective of her young—male bobcats will devour them. When a mother with young has been frightened by humans, she has been known to desert or kill her young. The kittens leave their mother in autumn or the following spring.

Home ranges for the bobcat depend upon the food supply. Males may hunt in an area twenty-five to fifty square miles in a poor area, overlapping female territories. However, a female with kittens may not go more than five miles, more likely one or two, if the food supply is good. Females have exclusive territories which do not overlap other females' territories. Bobcats mark their territories with scat and urine, and the more important the area is, e.g., the den area, the more heavily and frequently it is marked. The bob uses trees to sharpen its claws and stretch its muscles. Naturalists have debated how much this relates to territorial marking. At the very least it is a sign indicating their presence. The bob covers food which it has not consumed, and marks it with its scent. A young male has been known to have traveled as far as 100 miles to find his own territory, and young kits easily go eighteen miles for their own range. Territorial habits include climbing trees, swimming if necessary, and using the same trails in both directions, but with varying consistency. The cat's great curiosity makes it very vulnerable to trapping, for although it will note a human invader, it will still return to the same spot. The bobcat has been eradicated from some areas through hunting and trapping. They need privacy and can't adapt to human intrusion into their habitat. Densities vary extremely, from one cat per one and a half to seven square miles. Starvation is the prime killer of kittens, for in times of need the mother feeds only herself.

Killing must be learned, and there must be an intense enough stimulus from prey to elicit a kill in the learning process. Bobcats have a biological need to hunt, not just the desire for fresh food. The bobcat will not eat carrion unless it is very hungry, and never eats tainted meat. It preys primarily on the cottontail, mice, birds and rodents. It can and will take a weakened deer, one which would probably die within a short time of other causes. A very small proportion of the bobcat population is older cats, and some of these may have learned the vulnerability of livestock; however, studies indicate that this constitutes very little of the bobcat diet.

Bobcats live, on the average, ten to fourteen years in the wild; surviving the first five years of life is difficult and crucial. Records of bobcats in captivity indicate life spans of twenty-five to thirty-two years. In the wilds they die from injury, starvation, hunting, trapping and other man-related causes such as electrocution.

COUGAR
Felis concolor

For eons the cougar's screams and those of its prey have resounded throughout our vast timbered reaches. How many have passed this way without the intrusion of man? Will we be able to hear their low grumbles and purrs and catch their eye-shine tomorrow? Will their fast flicking tails stir the ground and their wide paw pads still leave their mark for us to see?

The cougar's microenvironment is the yearly habitat of the mule deer, high in elevation, or on the desert canyon reaches. I track cougar primarily in coniferous forest from 3,500 feet and higher, primarily where snow runoff streams or rivers exist. Manzanita, rabbit brush and sagebrush thrive in the high desert and lava outcrop is everywhere. I have also tracked cougar in steep mountainous terrain at 6,000–8,000 feet in the Cascades of Oregon and northern Washington. In Washington, I found where a cougar killed a deer, dragged it across a road then back again, and then down the road and up a grade into a steep meadow, crushing the grass. The kill was barely two days old, so I did not venture up there, since the cougar was likely still close. It had left its scent, scratching up a pile of dirt to cover its urination. One partial paw track was there, definitely the size and shape of a cougar paw. Only a bloody spot remained of the deer, and many bees and its odor attested to its freshness. That was in the steep ruggedness of the northern Cascades near the Pasayten Wilderness.

In Oregon, cougar inhabit the Three Sisters Wilderness, eastern Oregon, the Ochocos and the Wallowas.

Cougar, like bobcats, often travel a road. I easily pick up track there from the shine and disturbance of the ground. I backtracked one cougar a half-mile from the point I found its spoor. It had traveled on the shoulder of the road, likely when dark, and I first saw its tracks as noticeable depressions in the red cinders of the ground. It at times padded on the pavement. Before it came to the road it had climbed up a long, steep embankment from Squaw Creek, near Sisters, Oregon. I decided to track it in its direction of travel, as the manzanita shrubs below were very high and thick, and the day would be getting hotter. This cougar left the pavement area and chose a dusty road I knew well. For two miles it padded down the road, never off, only finding something once to break its stride when it slowed in very soft sand, dried from a rain wash. Here it shortened its stride and yet never leaped, and then continued on, after missing some opportunity for the squirrel or rabbit it might have heard. Perhaps it even heard a deer. Where the tracks ended, it left some scat and turned around. The boundary of its territory having been marked, it returned along the same road to the pavement again.

I have tracked cougar in snow, but snow tracking is difficult. In central Oregon, the snow melts in large areas or the crusts harden from weather, and tracks may be hard to find. When there is snow, the ground is usually frozen, and so tracks are difficult to discern past the snow patch. I tracked two young cougar by Black Butte near Sisters one winter. They traveled almost neck to neck. In a mile they never found even a mouse, although one nosed a log hopefully. That they traveled together is unusual, as it was not a female with a young offspring, nor was it breeding season. These were probably two cubs from the same litter still together from a spring birth, judging from their small tracks (less than three inches).

One day along Swamp Creek in Northwest Montana I meandered off the trail. Throughout the years I have become more of a wanderer than a hiker. At times sitting and observing reveal more than you can imagine. A scat pile caught my attention. Cougar. Its abrupt, broken segments and size were typical. Across the trail I noticed further cougar sign. A tree five to six inches in diameter was covered with scratches. From about a six-foot height the tree was deeply scarred with claw marks for about a foot and a half. I measured the width between the claw marks, too narrow for the claws of a bear and too fine a claw mark. The marks were old, and the tree was healing itself. Below the upper marks was a separate lower group about three feet long. This group appeared older, indicating the cougar had used the tree upon at least two occasions. Finding trees like this is a real challenge, for the home range of the cougar is both a vast area and rough in terrain. I consider myself fortunate when I come across one.

The most intriguing tracking experience I have had with cougar was in the Three Sisters Wilderness. I was meandering along an old logging road one evening. My dog suddenly focused intently on one area and became nervous and frightened, so frightened that I had to repeat the command to heel frequently. She wanted to turn and go home. We carried on, and she continued to glance behind her as we left the area, still noticeably disturbed. We returned the same route, and at the same area she again became unnerved, and I became uneasy owing to her behavior.

Later that evening very near camp I found two-day-old cougar track. I scouted the area for the next few days and discovered that the cougar had gone in the same direction from a certain area several times over a period of a few days. It was not fast tracking in the duff and debris of the area, many of the tracks being a muss rather than definitive in shape. The tracks were three inches wide and about three inches long, too small to say which sex the cougar was. The front heel pad of a male cougar would measure more than two and a quarter inches wide, the rear heel pad more than two inches wide; less than that size, the cougar would be a young male or a female. The tracks were not indicating a heel pad of those large widths. However, there was no question of its maker. I surmised it might be a female, but a scratch mark I found led me to believe it was more likely male, this being more of a male habit. The tracks were medium in size for cougar, with a thirty-inch walking stride. I sat out the heat that afternoon and at seven in the evening intuited the probable location of the cougar. Lava rock uprisings formed many canyons nearby, and I took the dog on a lead for better ears and nose. Bonanza!

We were nearly through a canyon. The ground was pockmarked with the tracks of deer, still low in elevation for May after a mild winter and warm temperatures. My dog stopped, looking at the high lava rock to our left. Her head was high, her eyes wide and intent, her nose working and body tense. She stepped a pace forward, nervous, raising a paw. She glanced at me for some indication of my feeling or intent. I had no explanation. It was neither coyote nor elk, for I had seen no fear from her on those. She had not lived near bobcat long, and never bear, but I felt it must be the cougar. We walked a few steps more, and the wind, gusting to thirty miles per hour, brought her stronger scent. As we moved on she would stop to glance in all directions, behind her as well. She was very nervous. And I was happy. Six days had passed since I had found the cougar tracks.

The dog and I sat outside at camp until dark. An almost full moon was going to light the partially cloudy night, and I listened and watched. Just as I was going to turn in, the dog looked east and uttered a low, quiet bark. I felt it was the cougar. A half hour later I went to bed in the van, watching out the windows until the last remnant of light disappeared. I fell asleep. After only a half hour of sleep I was abruptly awakened by the voice of the cougar. A ten-second, melancholy moan broke the stillness, sharp at first, deeply resonant, rising in pitch with a slight tremolo, and then falling. It was within fifty feet. I groggily looked outside, seeing nothing. I should have dashed outside perhaps, but that would have only threatened the cougar and been detrimental to any future rapport. It was only three hours prior that we had invaded its space, and it had come to tell us of its displeasure. It was a call of protest and I heeded the request. The next morning there were fresh tracks close by.

As cougar rarely sleep in the same spot at night, unless denning with kittens, I chose to avoid disturbing the cougar and did not return to the area until the next week. It seemed that the cougar had been using one specific area at night, which might have meant a den with cubs. She, or possibly a young male, however, had moved on. Either she had moved her young if she had had some, or the cougar had worked its territory to a natural threshold, and found it was time to move on. Some tracks told me the cougar had not left the area right after our encounter.

In the same area in February, 1996, I came across a freshly killed adult doe covered with debris, and running cougar tracks so fresh I realized I had spooked it, but I saw not even a tail as it left.

In 1997 on an early spring morning I was headed for a long walk. I had gotten only 200 feet from my cabin with my dog, when I crossed fresh cougar tracks. They were in pine-needle-covered sand, and I bent closely to assess their age. In a few yards the sand, still damp from the night's dew, showed clear definitions of the track. The three lobes on the posterior of the heel pad showed clearly. It had been windy the previous days, and none of these tracks showed wind debris. I started looking around, and put my dog on down a distance behind me as I went a little further. She had reacted by scenting the tracks as well. However, the scent can remain some hours, and these tracks looked as though they could even have been made within the hour.

I worked my way slowly along for several hundred feet. I was not only sorting out the track, measuring it (a male which had been coming through all winter), but looking carefully ahead. My dog was obeying her instructions. As I came within fifty feet of a large juniper with a dead juniper lying horizontally beneath it, I glanced back at a track where my dog was. She was looking at the junipers ahead, then lowered her head, and gave a low woof, and backed up about two yards. I looked ahead to see a small dark shadow cross between two limbs of the dead juniper, nothing I could identity. I thought that if I had not had my dog with me, I certainly might have seen a cougar. (Perhaps too close?) I slowly went back toward home. I couldn't believe it was anything but the cougar ahead. But I thought it was prudent to leave it alone. We continued our walk. About a mile beyond, having crossed two sets of fresh male boot tracks coming from the direction of a nearby ranch, they appeared again going back toward the ranch. There, also, were cougar tracks headed in the direction of my cabin. The tracks indicated that the cougar had come upon the men's tracks, slowed and stopped, and likely sniffed at the brush where they had passed, then continued on.

When I returned home, I began to walk around the spot where the cougar had been at about a 200-foot distance, but my dog refused to go. I saw no more of the tracks then. That evening I went again to the area, my dog still refusing to join me, although she would have gone if I insisted. She is a good indicator to me that something lies ahead. When I got to the junipers, the tracks led to the exact spot, a shady, sheltered, grassy area. But in my impatience to go on, I apparently wiped out further tracks, something I always caution others not to do. Frustrated, I decided to wait until I was able to concentrate better. The next morning it poured rain, and I had no inclination to track in that—a lesson for me.

I thought this cougar could have been one I first saw tracks of in 1992 at my home. At that time the tracks were under the size for an adult male, and thus it could have been a female or young male. In later years, the tracks in this same territory indicated a male. Even considering the possibility it was the same cat, I could not be certain. But my dog was doing her job again.

I remembered the evening that one year when walking near home when my dog behaved in such a frightened way. It was no longer a mystery. Now when she looks up at me with such behavior, I can say, "cougar."

***

The cougar is heavy and long, lithe and fast. Its coordinated grace and stalk surprise both the mule deer and the elk. Its strength is such that it can carry a carcass away after a kill. Its weight ranges from 70 to 270 pounds. From nose tip to tail tip the cougar may span to ninety inches or more. Its smooth coat of hair varies from reddish to brown, slate-gray or yellow. The tips of its tail and ears, and the backs of its ears and sides of its nose are dark. Its greenish gold eyeshine comes from its yellow irises and green pupils.

The cougar is a solitary creature whose fatal claws rarely seek the flesh of its own kind in combat. It is as though it knows it would not survive with such injury from another cat, and thus it avoids encounters. It marks its 100 square miles or more of territory with scent and scat so it will not meet its kind. Its use of trails, though not exactly regular, makes it vulnerable to man, as does its curiosity.

The cougar has adapted to many types of terrain: rocky deserts, mountains, cliffs, chaparral, and swamps from the subtropics to the tropics. They are dispersed throughout western North America, including Wyoming, British Columbia and southern Alberta, to Mexico and southern Texas, and east into Louisiana, southern Alabama and southern Florida, and into Tennessee and Maine. Their habitat is constantly threatened by the intrusion of man, and they are frequently hunted.

Cougars find dens in thickets, concealed logs and brush, and in isolated caves. The female alone rears her one to six cubs, usually two, for two or three years. The size of her litter depends upon the amount of her food supply. Males remain solitary and a threat to the young, and the mother is most protective of her cubs. With young cubs her home range is much reduced in size, perhaps only five square miles, if adequate food is available. She may give birth at any time of year, but most births are recorded in the spring in colder climes. If a female lives ten years, she may possibly rear only four successful litters.

After eighty-eight to ninety-seven days of gestation, spotted cubs are born. Newborn open their eyes at about ten days of age, suckle at least four to five weeks, and often for a long time. They are seven to twelve inches long at birth, eight to sixteen ounces in weight, weigh ten pounds by eight weeks, thirty to forty-five pounds at six months, and a yearling will double its weight from six months. They have a ringed, spotted tail, and some are black, a melanistic stage in which spots are somewhat visible, too.

The cougar stalks its prey to within thirty feet if possible, and uses a short, fast burst of speed to reach its kill. It can outrun a deer for only short bursts. It bites the rear, neck or back of its prey to bring it down. A female with kits old enough to eat meat will lead them to her kill. What a cougar eats depends upon what it is fed as a cub. An adult cougar requires meat equivalent in amount to a mule deer a week. It will eat insects, birds or small mammals, but no carrion unless it is starving, and never tainted meat. It eats eight to nine pounds of meat at a sitting, caches the remains and marks the kill with urine. Only 75 percent of the time can a cougar successfully find food. Its senses are excellent, best in order of hearing, smell and sight. It can hear probably a mile away, and its smell is keener than that of the bobcat, but not as keen as the coyote. The cougar has phenomenal strength. It can swing a deer onto its back and dash off, or drag a kill by its brisket a long way. It has been known to carry a large calf over its back across a four-foot fence, and thence up a large ledge of rocks, jumping fifteen feet in height along the way. It can also swim a mile.

The cougar's temperament can be a feisty one, but in the wild it appears docile to humans unless cornered. It may follow humans out of curiosity, yet there have been some authenticated records of attacks on humans. Older cougar unable to hunt from loss of teeth may be a threat to humans; the danger also exists where new housing developments encroach on its hunting territory, or when cougar populations increase thus reducing food supply. Its ears are a signal to its intent. If they are half-way down and back it is in a threatening mood. If its ears are all the way back and its feet beneath it braced for a spring, an attack is imminent. If it is confused, its ears may wander. With pleasure, its ears are peaked upright parallel to each other. It is a very patient animal, and when caught in a trap it is usually very quiet and subdued.

The population densities of cougar vary, of course. The sex ratio is normally 120 to 130 males per 100 females. A breeding population density is fixed by genetic tolerance for space and interaction and environmental conditions: cover, food and water. The longevity of a cougar is reported to be eighteen years or more in the wild. The causes of death are virus, starvation, accident, hunting, poison, tumors and old age. Critical times for their survival are the postnatal period when the cub is first independent, and advanced age.

LYNX
Felis lynx

Where have the lynx of the Pacific Northwest gone? They were in abundance in some areas of Washington in the 1950s. I can visualize the beautiful creature still, and have to do so, for there are few other views of it since man has intruded so on its former habitat. Perhaps the lynx's inherent secrecy will keep the few remaining individuals in the United States invisible.

In Fairbanks, Alaska, in the early 1950s, I saw lynx. My husband and I came slowly around the bend in a road midday. Two adult lynx were lying atop a large boulder in the warm sun. At our approach they rose cautiously, and slid back among the rocks out of sight. I remember their long ear tufts and big feet, and their full, healthy coat of hair, for I was barely thirty feet away.

Once I saw a beautiful trail of tracks in wet sand. I had risen from a nap quite near a stream and sauntered along the bank when my eyes picked up very large tracks in the wet, firm sand. As I went from track to track I was impressed with their size. Although Alaskans claim there are no cougar there, I thought at the time I had seen cougar tracks. Later, of course, I learned that lynx tracks are often larger than those of a cougar. Little did I know that more than thirty years later I would wish I had photographed those tracks.

I have photographed and cast a lynx track with the cooperation of NorthwesTrek, a wildlife park in Washington. The tracks are of a male lynx about six years old. Finding lynx track has been the most difficult of all so far, and I am excited by the search. Summer, however, is not the best time to find them, for there is little soft ground, dry or wet.

I spent two weeks in the northern Washington Cascades one summer looking for lynx tracks with no success. It was a great adventure, and the steep country is exciting, replete with wildlife. Before I could zero in on the best area, I talked to people conducting a radio-collar study on lynx. Despite their advice, I was not successful. The high prairies full of wildflowers and narrow mountain streams were an outdoor fairyland. Unfortunately none of the wet stream banks yielded lynx tracks in July, and the great wildfires of 1994 have reduced lynx territory. Some residents encouraged me to come up for snow tracks. However, riding snowmobiles to find tracks does not suit my style. I prefer to tough it out on dirt, which provides plenty of time in the day to track. Quiet and alone, not only do I not disturb nature, but I am at one with it; thus it offers more opportunity for other observations. The idea is not to just photograph tracks, but to learn lynx ways.

***

The tall, black ear tufts of the lynx and the large cheek ruffs and throat beard distinguish it quickly from the bobcat. The lynx has longer legs and hair, and often is heavier and larger than the bobcat. It is buff in color, with a slight, black hair line along its back and brownish underparts. Lynx feet are large and well-haired. The males can be twenty-nine to almost forty-two inches long, and weigh eleven to forty pounds. They are two feet tall at the shoulder. The lynx tail is two to five and a half inches long, slightly bushy, with a black tip both on top and underneath, which also distinguishes it from the bobcat.

The lynx lives in dense boreal forests with thickets and rocky out-crops, usually above 4,500 feet, in the habitat of the snowshoe hare, its primary prey. It ranges throughout most of Canada and Alaska into the north-central Cascades of Washington and extreme northwest of Montana, with a few in the Garnet Mountains of Montana. In the northern Washington Cascades in 1989 there was a stable population of about twenty-five lynx. There are some in the Rocky Mountain areas and in the very northern part of New England, Michigan and Wisconsin.

Dens are in logs, timber clumps, roots and caves. Breeding season is January into the first part of April, although lynx can breed at any time of year. Gestation is about two months. The birth of two to four young occurs in May into July. When the young are born they weigh four to eight ounces and in two months are out eating solid food, and are weaned at twelve weeks. The young may den with the mother the first winter.

Lynx prey primarily on snowshoe hare. Studies show they some-times eat tree squirrels, deer carrion, mice and birds. In northern latitudes the lynx population cycles with the snowshoe hare population, but in marginal areas these hare do not cycle, and so the lynx population seems to remain noncyclical there, too. Studies have shown that if necessary, lynx go 300 miles for food, but usually have a territory of forty-seven to ninety-four square miles. Some have been known to cover as much as 430 miles in order to find sufficient food, due to high lynx density or poor food supply. If prey is sufficient, however, one square mile would serve. Lynx hunt familiar areas, lying in wait at prey activity places. Their sight, hearing and smell are used in about that order of superiority. They may hunt in pairs. One out of five attempts at catching a hare succeed. During the day the lynx, primarily nocturnal and crepuscular, lies in a thicket. It beds down only in the most severe winter. Lynx have lived fifteen to eighteen years in captivity. Starvation in the wild is the usual cause of death.

Chapter Three

The Dog Family
Canidae

COYOTE
Canis latrans

The coyote is a wild and wary canine indigenous to North America, with a long-standing reputation for cleverness, intelligence and survival. In Indian myths, it is usually depicted as a wise but manipulative being, always laying traps for the unwary. It must possess considerable wisdom to have survived so well.

The microenvironment the coyote prefers includes areas of good ground cover, although it inhabits open areas of desert as well. Coyotes are so adaptable they even live in urban areas in various parts of the Southwest.

I live in coyote country and enjoy observing and tracking coyotes. As I live with them and do not molest them, they accept me from a close flight distance, about fifty feet. They are aware that my dogs are fenced unless walking with me, and behave accordingly. They hunt past the house, and follow a well-worn trail across my place. It is habitual for the coyote to use certain trails, and often quite by clockwork. My property lies in an overlap area of two families, one on top of the ridge and another from the flat to the south. I learned this by extensive tracking of individual coyotes over a period of time, and by studying how they mark their territory with scat.

In my beginning tracking days, a yearling male came limping across my land, and I saw him from my deck. I recognized he was a yearling from his tracks, more pointed toe pads than those of older coyotes. He used his left rear leg only when coming to a halt. I think he had been in a leg-hold trap. Tracking a three-legged coyote is good experience, for he is easily identified. I learned his route and trails. Not long after I became familiar with him, I spotted him by my house, bloody from a fight. I persuaded a veterinarian to prescribe an antibiotic, and left it for him in hamburger, at his usual time and place of travel. This began four years of friendship. We would sit and look at each other, fifty to 100 feet apart. He had his usual spots where he would lie in the fragrant sage cover, watching me. I always looked for him but never attempted to tame him, for wild animals should be wild. But track him I did, although never as far as a den, for he needed his privacy and space. His leg finally healed enough so that he only rarely and momentarily held it up when running.

My dogs were jealous and they occasionally chased him when we would chance upon him. Early in our relationship, he needed to check everything out, and as I sat quietly upon my deck, he came cautiously up the drive to within twenty feet of the deck, and I looked into the most beautiful yellow eyes I have ever seen. He sniffed around and, satisfied, never came that close in my view again. But we knew each other's habits, and where one went the other would certainly know. I would occasionally bring road-killed rabbits for him.

One year this special coyote disappeared at denning time, and much later he brought a six- or seven-month old pup back with him. Late that fall and winter I saw and tracked the pup, but his father never returned. I remember him well, and often still see him in my mind on the trail behind some sage. His pup was taller, thinner and a very anxious, high-strung canine, whereas the father had been relaxed and casual. I felt such grief over his father's disappearance that I had no heart to track his offspring after that, and I have not seen him past that year. It is difficult to make attachments to wildlife, for their disappearances engender keen grief, especially when you don't know what exactly happened to them. The joy of the relationship, however, is beyond belief.

I tracked another coyote well known to me near my home once for about five miles. I had been curious about his extended range and I pursued his fresh tracks through the heat for most of a summer day. For all my efforts nothing spectacular occurred. He never even caught a mouse or chased a rabbit in all those steps. I was thinking that the next time I would backtrack him to get an idea of the circumference of his travels. So I decided on another fifteen minutes or so of tracking and then I was going to head for home. After all these miles of walking this coyote finally did something different. He sat down. There must have been a reason and I wondered what it was. I looked at the muss in the dirt. His rear had swiveled in the dirt. His paw prints on his front feet had spread apart, the right one pointing forward and wide, the left front track was close to his body and back toward the rear. The right leg track showed, with a half-hearted paw track, and there was no left rear print. Then there were rear tracks and front tracks which had been made after the sitting position as he left the spot and walked on. Time in the past spent watching my dog sit and scratch his ear, and then checking the ground after he left, paid off. The coyote had scratched his left ear.

One crisp and sunny day in February south of Wildhaunt I was on snowshoes. The snow was a foot and a half deep, and pockmarked with small rodent and rabbit tracks. All at once, just ahead of me, came the calls of coyotes. I stood still, breathing quietly, waiting for a rush of movement or sound. None came, and I waited longer, in anticipation and excitement. All was still. I slowly moved forward toward the spot, hoping for a glimpse of a coyote. I came to the spot, and the snow still sparkled with coyote tracks. It was the mating season, and this was displayed on the layer of snow. Two coyotes had greeted each other, mated and then ran off away from my direction, not 100 feet from where I had stood. I tracked them for a short while. They parted about 100 feet ahead, came together closer in places, and then moved further apart, no doubt to rejoin ahead somewhere. Tracking two coyotes is more time consuming, especially when they move apart for any distance. Snowshoes are far superior to skis when tracking as the brush and low limbs are more easily circumvented, and there are no poles to tie up one's hands.

So much of tracking is uneventful. It is the slow accumulation of sign converting to knowledge; familiarity within the context of nature. Sights, sounds, smells and feelings blend the tracker into the paths of nature, sometimes gentle, sometimes violent, all committed to the surfaces of the forest world. For a time these inscriptions are there for us to divine, to absorb into our minds. Then they are effaced, and their residual sign are only in our souls. Wild lives are innocent and so temporal, as fragile as their marks are illusive. How satisfying to nurture wild spirits whose brief span in time so enhances the earth with their mysteries.

I have spent most of my spare time walking as far and in as many different directions as I could as often as possible. It began long ago as a world of experiences and surprises, and it still is, learning new places and trails. Even approaching a familiar place from a new direction is different, and I notice other things. Oft I do not recognize a familiar spot until I look back.

As I walked, I became more and more aware of the presence of coyote. I chanced upon scattered leg bones of deer, obviously predated, some still bloody. At times quantities of deer hair were strewn across the land, where a deer had met its demise. Tracks came into focus, and so did the coyote. My kinship, however, with the coyote really came before I knew its tracks. My sporadic views of it left a keen curiosity, but what prompted my closeness was its voice. I sit many an evening beneath flying bats and listen to the songs of coyotes. I track them by voice without ever leaving my deck. Some nights the horizon is afire with coyote songs, and often they happen by very near. Voices of the wild capture primitive callings from my unconscious, unidentifiable and totally hypnotizing, a touch of the intrinsic power of the coyote.

One evening I walked near my cabin, quiet but intent, and glanced to the side to see a coyote sitting unaware of me. It hesitated only a moment, and lifted its head high and howled a long note, and ended with a series of yaps. Then it got up and went into the brush.

Walking with my dog quite far from home once, in my path appeared a coyote pup, and it was rushed in half-greeting and half-aggression by my Australian shepherd. The coyote pup stood in the path looking at strangers it no doubt had never seen before, one of which resembled it. It had not time to reflect, for the Aussie nosed it and they sported around once, and the young coyote fled. I called back my dog. It all happened so fast I wished it had been a longer encounter. I never saw the coyote pup again.

The highlight of my viewing of coyotes came in the denning season in 1981. I had tracked coyotes on my ridge and flatland by this time in years past, and I was pursuing the spoor of one coyote, wondering which one it was, and where it was headed. Other tracks appeared as I approached one area and they went in both directions. It was clear that the area was well, and daily, used. It began to register: den. Many trails merged into one, and I slowly continued. I was on a gradual slope which increased in steepness just above me until it reached the crest of a ridge. The bitterbrush and sagebrush were thick and grew in sand, which was very deep in its dry condition at this time. Suddenly the den was there, fresh tracks in and out, and I did not hesitate to see which were laid upon which, for I feared disturbing the site. I went on well past the den, and past the well-used trails. I sat down and thought. It was so close to home, and

I scanned the terrain with a plan. That evening I left well enough alone, and the following evening approached the den site from over an eighth of a mile away, to assess the distance to and the visibility of the den with binoculars. It took a couple of hours to quietly find the best spot with cover where the tracks were absent and which gave me a view of the specific den area. I had had the presence of mind to note a tree as a landmark when I had passed the den. I did not want to have to relocate the den and spoil the anticipated scenario, whatever it might be.

The pups can be born over a period of time, but usually in my area it is around May first, and this was about June first. The morning I was to spend viewing the den I was careful to belly in when the area was in view. I crawled a very long way, not wanting to stand and be in sight of any coyote. I arrived late, unfortunately, and was berating myself for this, for by the time I got into position it was almost nine. I had not calculated on the amount of time it would take me to crawl up there. I was within an eighth of a mile.

I squirmed as little as possible, but not being accustomed to sitting on the ground for long periods, I was uncomfortable. However, my dreams came true. Out of a storybook it unfolded, unbelievably. Appearing quite abruptly on the steeper, higher slope, were two adult coyotes. They were affectionately licking each other and prancing around in what appeared to be joyous love. It was apparent that these were the parents and I watched through binoculars in admiration. One was obviously the female, a smaller, commonly marked coyote, and the other, the male, I recognized from a glimpse in the past. He was an enormous light gray male so much lighter in color than the usual coyote, he was unmistakable. He had run past my cabin a year or so before, so distinctive he could easily be recognized. I hardly dared to breathe, and my hands became very tired holding heavy binoculars. In a few moments, however, they went off up the hill and all was still. I contemplated the situation. If I saw no more, my summer was made. But I was in quiet expectation of any possibilities.

I waited, and looked, and sat, and thought. I looked some more. There was a pup, indeed, so small after seeing the adults. It was moving around in puplike fashion, pouncing and grabbing sticks, and flopping down. It went behind sage and disappeared, and then reappeared again a little later. I was trying to get a frame of reference to judge its size, but rabbit brush and bitterbrush come in all sizes, and the trees do, too. The pup was at what is known as a rendezvous spot. It was away from the den area, in an area with a view where the adults leave the pups when they hunt. I had read that some adult was left with the pups, and I searched and searched, but I am certain that no adult was with this pup this day. It may have been that there was no surviving pup from a previous litter which stayed with this pair, or the pair was mated for the first time, and there were no family members to assume that role.

I glassed the spots for many hours. Over this time more pups appeared, but toward the end of the day I had seen only three pups at once. I had no way of knowing how many there were because I could not identify the different pups except one. This was my day, indeed. As I had all day, I was looking at as much detail as possible, their movements, size, coloration, whatever I could think of, I saw one pup with a white-tipped tail. Now this does occur, as I learned later, rarely, as most coyotes have black-tipped tails. Here I not only was privy to the family life of coyotes in all this detail, but I was seeing a coyote which I could identify in future years as knowing its natal den. My heart was flying high.

The pups would occasionally nap. Once I was able to see three napping at the same time close to each other. I became aware of a doe browsing above them, and quite close. I looked intently at this, thinking the doe would approach the pups and wondering what the reaction would be. She did, indeed, browse to the spot of the sleeping pups. She stopped, looked at them, staring for a minute or two, and browsed by. The pups slept on.

By 7:00 P.M. I hadn't seen the adults. I could see four pups asleep on the slope. One picked up its head to look uphill, then another, and then all of them. They all rose, looking uphill. I expected an adult. Then the large gray male appeared. The pups ran up to him as fast as they could, nuzzling his muzzle, bumping into each other and wagging their tails, reaching for his mouth until the male regurgitated some food. The pups were in a little frenzy. And they looked so small. The male stood there for a short while and disappeared, and I was not to see him again. It was not long before I saw the female come into view quite a distance off to my left. She stood and looked around, sensing the lay of the land. Almost immediately the pups became aware of her presence, and they all rushed to her as she headed downhill. As I put the glasses to my eyes, I counted five pups, no more. The female looked as large as a lion next to the tiny pups I had spent so many hours watching. As I looked at her through the glasses, she looked so close I thought she was heading directly toward me, and I would be discovered. But she headed straight for the den, the pups practically nursing along the way. I sat for awhile, visualizing it all over again, hardly believing I had seen the ways of a coyote family as I had.

Although I looked for the next five years as closely as I could ,at all the coyote in my area that I could see, and searched as well, I never was to see a coyote that I could identify as having a white-tipped tail.

***

The coyote inhabits everything from open plains to brushy areas and open woodlands, and lives in all areas of the Pacific Northwest, north and west of western Canada and eastern Alaska. Lithe and graceful, its full, variably colored coat may be gray, reddish or bluish in tinge, with buff underparts, yellow legs and a black-tipped tail. Although its winter coat gives it the appearance of heaviness, its frame is slight, its legs are slender, its muzzle long and narrow, and its weight in the Northwest is usually perhaps twenty-five or thirty pounds. It is twenty-three to twenty-six inches high at the shoulder, and thirty-two to thirty-seven inches long with a tail of twelve to fifteen inches. Its eyes are yellow and they shine at night as greenish gold.

The coyote is a social animal, its social structure is the family as opposed to the large pack of the wolf. It relies on its sense of smell above its hearing and sight, but all senses are keen. Its prey is primarily small mammals; and jackrabbit, mice, squirrels, insects, fruit, birds and carrion are among its versatile diet. It may wait motionless at a point, its paw raised, staring, for ten minutes for a mouse to move under the snow, and its success at a pounce is very high. It can and does cull out weak deer as opportunity may dictate. Sometimes a family will team up to down the larger prey. The coyote's speed is from twenty miles per hour at a trot to thirty miles per hour running, and as fast as forty miles per hour for short bursts.

The coyote litter varies from one to a possible twelve pups, as evidenced by uterine scars, but the average size is five pups. The parents breed anywhere from January through March, and their young, depending on elevation and latitude, are born in April or May. These furred pups open their eyes at nine to fourteen days, cut teeth at three weeks, and are out of their den at two weeks. They establish dominance hierarchy at one month, and howl very young in response to the adults, initiating howls before six weeks. Their ability to discriminate the meaning of communications from adults comes very early, and they are very obedient to their mother, or they might not survive. The coyote is very patient and learns quickly, although it may take a generation or more to instill new learning into the species.

Coyotes dig many dens, in anticipation of whelping, widely spread over their territory. They might excavate new dens or remodel old badger holes. Dens vary, but most have only one tunnel entrance, which may drop perpendicularly for two or three feet before leveling off. Seldom do they have a second opening. The entrance is just large enough for a coyote to squeeze through. The chamber may vary in size; one was recorded to have been found after a thirty-foot tunnel. An older opening in a den may be plugged, and a new one formed. Its home range may extend from five to 100 square miles, but is usually about sixteen to twenty-five square miles.

The coyote may live much longer in captivity but in the wild, life is usually at best five years. It may die of malnutrition when the population becomes oversized. High population density also expedites the spread of disease and infertility and creates social stress. This in turn may lead to inadequate breeding, poor maternal care and infant mortality. When decimated by trapping, shooting or poison, lower-ranking females breed, creating an increase in population. The coyote is a prey species for the cougar, bear and man. It may die from the same diseases as does the domestic dog: hepatitis, distemper and parasites.

The coyote can mate with domestic dogs and produce fertile offspring. However, both sexes of coyotes breed only in late winter, but dogs can mate throughout the year. Thus a first coyote-dog union is possible. The coy-dog offspring of such a union inherits an annual breeding pattern from its wild side except both sexes come into heat in the fall, several months before the pure-blood coyotes. Thus, they cannot mate back to the wild coyote, and the coyote strain remains pure. The mongrel generation can breed to a domestic dog, but if the female lives in the wild, the litter is born in midwinter, and neither the male coy-dog nor domestic male assists the female in the rearing of the young, as does the purebred coyote, and this usually prevents survival of the litter.

The coyote's voice is renowned. It has varied vocalizations, most often sounded in the evening or at dawn. The calls are melodious and also consist of barks, howls and yaps. Their variations of notes frequently give the listener the impression he is hearing many more coyotes than are actually there.

RED FOX
Vulpes fulva

The red fox is part dog, part cat in its ways. Its rear feet step into its front tracks like a cat, but it looks like a dog. What were its origins to be so mixed? It stands on its hind feet, too, to reach grapes from the vines. With its color so bright, how can it hide?

The microenvironment for the red fox is most often a bed of grass in an open field, perhaps near a mouse hole. In the near distance are the woods where it will spend some of its time.

In the Northwest the red fox inhabits coastal Washington and western Oregon and northern California. It is also found throughout most of Canada and Alaska. It resides in wetter, more timbered regions rather than in dry desert where the coyote holds sway. The exuberance of this fox is apparent in tracking it. Although it is careful, there is sometimes the flavor of abandonment in its behavior. I think of this fox as imaginative and inventive, not just intelligent. Its tracks often lead off easy trails into curious bypaths as though it were seeking variety in its day. I tracked a fox in northern California one day. It led me around its area in great circuitous fashion. It is difficult to know for sure to what smells and noises a predator responds to guide his activity, and we must be careful not to interpret human attributes from the behavior of wild creatures, for we may never understand all of their dynamics. These fox tracks led me up a brushy slope, weaving back and forth twenty to fifty feet from side to side as it climbed, slowing now and then, but keeping a rather even pace, the only hint of purposeful behavior. In its search or enjoyment it continued a rather random trail which broadened out in longer semicircles as it proceeded on. Loose, dry leaves made its tracks visible in the soft soil beneath quite frequently, and where they did not push aside, slightly broken ground cover told of its earlier presence. It went on across the hills beyond long after I turned for home, disappointed that I had human limitations. In my mind I tracked it on and on. I readily remember the points where I have had to part trails with wildlife.

Early one morning as I walked along a northern Washington beach at Ft. Worden, a line of fresh tracks attracted my attention. A red fox's tracks were plainly evident in the smooth sand. The characteristic heel pad protrusion and the resulting large space between the toe pads and the heel pad showed, and the long claws marked clearly. This red fox had run down the beach the night before for about a mile, directly along the foot of the cliff by the water. Eventually it climbed the steep, grassy grade. I saw places where it had flattened the grasses. I chose to track no further because somewhere up there it lay at rest, and I did not need to disturb it. In the Willamette Valley of Oregon, red fox have lived among the farms and can be seen at midday lying in open fields. As the farmland becomes more extensive, and the red fox habitat becomes more populated, they disperse into the foothills where they may be adapting to a somewhat different environment. Occasionally there are reports of red fox on the eastern slopes of the Cascades in Oregon, and they do inhabit the Crater Lake area in southern Oregon. Researchers report a possible rare member of the *macroura* subspecies in Montana, and also a high elevation western mountain fox.

One summer near Corvallis, Oregon, I searched for red fox tracks. It was difficult as most of the land is private. I spent time following streams where the land was wetter and would hold track. I climbed hills looking for older track just to find the presence of fox, for I knew they were there. I spent two days in this endeavor without success. Finally I looked on the shoulders of the roads where the crops stopped and the dirt areas remained. I found two tracks, one of which was identifiable as red fox. But that was not all I got for my trouble. I acquired an excellent case of poison oak. I do not track west of the Cascades any more.

When I lived in Fairbanks, Alaska, I saw a red fox crossing my path about 100 feet ahead of me one day. It did not see me, so I stood still to watch from beside a tree, savoring the opportunity to view it. It immediately caught my scent and came directly toward me, mouth open. I was not sure of its intent as it approached within ten feet of me. I shot a .22 next to it to frighten it away, but that bothered it not the least, and it circled me and the tree. Its unusual behavior made me worry that it might be in the initial stages of rabies, so I cautiously backed off and it followed me only a short way. The only other possible explanation for its curious behavior might be that he had been tamed by some of the local gold miners at one time.

***

This well known, shy and nervous fox inhabits all of the Northwest U.S., except the Rockies and the Southwest and most of Canada and Alaska. It primarily seeks a mix of wooded and open country, hunting the open areas, and finding refuge in the brushlands. Cultivated areas are preferred. The red fox ranges usually one to two miles, but sometimes it travels up to five miles a night. Its total territory is probably a ten-square-mile section.

Its reddish yellow coat is quite visible in open areas. Its fur is darkest on its back, and its belly is white, with a bushy tail with some black hairs and white tip. Its legs and feet are black. There are black and silver phases in the red fox coloration, and variations of these. The red fox body extends twenty-two to twenty-five inches in length, fifteen to sixteen inches at shoulder height, and it weighs about seven to fifteen pounds. Its fluffy tail is fourteen to sixteen inches in length, and may brush the snow on the downhill side of its trail. It is a careful walker, and no drag marks register in the snow as might with coyote tracks. The red fox usually sleeps in the same general area, and has fairly consistent habits. It roams when food is scarce, and the population is usually widely scattered throughout an area. Like other canines, it marks its territory with scat. It stalks and pounces like a cat, and is omnivorous, eating vegetables, fruit, nuts, birds, small mammals, invertebrates, crayfish, insects, caterpillars, grasses in the summer and domestic chickens if it can get to them. It consumes a pound of food daily. Its hearing is excellent, its smell is good, and it relies least upon its sight. This fox is primarily nocturnal but also exhibits diurnal behavior. It lives near human habitat at times, but stays clear of humans. However, red foxes can be easily tamed.

The red fox, unlike the gray fox, only dens if with kits. It uses logs, abandoned woodchuck holes, hillside burrows or a place of barren ground with a view, for a den site. It rarely digs its own den. In January through mid-February they breed. A pair may mate for the year, and in subsequent years. A monestrus period of fourteen days in the female results in a fifty-one- to fifty-three-day gestation when bred. Thus in March to May, depending upon latitude, a litter of one to ten kits is born. Occasionally litters have been born in the winter, but this is rare. The usually solitary male fox may bring some food to a denning female. The four-ounce newborn are blind at birth, open their eyes in nine days, are weaned in two months, play above ground in four to five weeks, and at that age eat predigested food brought home to them. They disperse at four months of age, or by fall. Coyote, cougar, bobcat and man prey upon the red fox. The female may let off a pungent odor when afraid or in an emergency situation. Twelve years is their potential wild life, but captive reports of longevity estimate from sixteen to eighteen years.

GRAY FOX
Urocyon cinerecargenteus

This fox hides very well in the dense forest. Humans very seldom find it. It hunts by night when we are all asleep. If we venture out into the night in the darkness where it might be, we will never see its elliptical eye pupils, but its eyes may reflect a shine for us. The shine may even come from above in a tree.

The microenvironment for the gray fox is thick cover in mountainous interior or even coastal ranges. Its dens are used all year around, so darkness is its comfort.

Gray fox tracks are so small, it is hard to believe that they are canine tracks. The few gray fox tracks I have seen were a surprise, and I only saw the eye shine from one in a tree at night in northern California. The tracks I have seen were in mud near the head of the Little Deschutes River in central Oregon. I had seen the bare, wet mud beside a backwash the evening before, and found tracks there in the morning. The fox had moved slowly and cautiously among the reeds and grasses of the swampy river edge. It was ready, no doubt, to pounce upon an insect or snatch a mouse. Its well-defined tracks proceeded on top of the wet mud. It was too spongy for my weight so I sank into the water and could not follow further. I turned around to retrace my steps, and in attempting to cross a wet, mossy log, fell into the river up to my waist. I managed to save my camera, but certainly not my dignity.

A student once asked me how to differentiate between the tracks of a gray fox and those of a small dog. The gray fox track could be identified by tracking it over a distance, as a fox and dog behave quite differently. Also, the fox track would be very narrow, much narrower probably than any dog's, and his straddle would be much narrower. Gray fox are not as plentiful in the Northwest as in the east, and as they live in more heavily forested areas, and are much more sensitive to people than red fox, they are harder to find.

I did chance upon gray fox track on the northern Oregon coast at Cascade Head near Otis one year. A beautiful natural area has been set aside there, but one cannot leave the trail. Thus I did not venture very far into the brush to follow this fox. The understory is so thick with foliage it would have taken many hours to track it. The one-and-a-half-inch tracks were so small I thought at first they were those of a young bobcat or domestic cat. They were in mud where the fox had come to drink from a rain puddle. The muss revealed unmistakable canine claw marks, not feline. The toe lobes and the heel pad were distinctively canine too. Thus I had no doubts about my identification. The tracks showed its careful movement. Indeed, almost feline in its caution.

***

This small and unusual canine is secretive and docile in temperament. It has a salt and pepper coat of gray with buffy underfur. Its long, bushy tail has a median black stripe along its total length to its tip. A rusty yellow neck and white throat contrast against its gray face. Smallest of the Pacific Northwest canines, it weighs seven to thirteen pounds, is fifteen inches high at the shoulder, and its body is twenty-one to twenty-nine inches in length, with an eleven to sixteen inch tail.

The gray fox is different from the other canines in that it climbs trees straight up. Its claws are long and curved like the felines, but are not retractable, and it is not only able to climb trees, but readily does. Its eyeshine may be reflected from a tree limb. Its tracks in the front measure about 1⅝ inches in length, and 1⅜ inches in width, and its rear paws tracks measure 1½ inches in length and 1¼ inches in width. It walks with an 8- to 12-inch stride. Its trail width is only 3¾ inches wide. It has been said that it has been known to backtrack in its own tracks.

Geographically gray foxes occur from the eastern edges of the Dakotas, Nebraska, Kansas, Oklahoma and Texas. They live in New Mexico, Arizona, California, Colorado, Utah, southern Nevada and western Oregon. They are not really found in Canada. The favored terrain is varied but is more associated with woods and brushy areas, swamps and heavy undergrowth.

The home range of this small and lithe creature usually is under one to two square miles. As with other canines, it marks its territory with scent and it scratches to cover its scat or urine. It also caches food in shallow heaps, or buries it near an active kit den.

The gray fox has a varied, omnivorous diet. It will prey on small mammals, eat insects, fruits and vegetables, nuts, grass and carrion. Its hearing is its most acute sense and it relies upon this and its sense of smell more than its sight.

This fox dens all year, and in February and March breeds. In sixty-three days a litter of two to seven dark brown kits are born blind. They are weaned at three months. When they are about seven pounds, at four months, they are hunting for themselves. The offspring will stay together with the mother through the summer. The male assists with the young but does not den with them.

The secretive nature of the gray fox keeps it from human sight, and its nocturnal preference also makes it usually invisible, although it may be about during the daytime. Its bark is very seldom heard. It is threatened by traps, wild and domestic dogs, and bobcats and cougar. It has lived ten years in captivity, and other than predation, disease is instrumental in its demise.

TIMBER WOLF
Canis lupus

The long, mournful, low-pitched howl of the wolf has returned to us—the incredible, unequaled and magnificent song is in the wilderness of Montana and Washington and Idaho today. You can stand in the middle of Big Prairie in Glacier National Park and hear wolves. Their tracks are found more frequently and look! There is their greenish orange eyeshine as the moonlight casts into the timber.

Is it possible to talk about a microenvironment for the wolf who ranges so many miles? The northern latitudes, with cold winters and forested terrain offer a wide variety of microenvironments. Where the prey rests, the gray wolf is there. It is far on the tundra of the Alaskan slopes, throughout Canada to the borders of the northern States. If it were not a prey for man, it would be anywhere large wildlife exist.

On a trip to Montana to track wolves, in northern Idaho one July, below Blueberry Lake near the Canadian border, it rained very heavily and continuously. I sat in my van for four days and read until I absolutely needed to get out. I donned rain gear and ventured forth. I spent much of the time beneath large trees waiting for nature's revelation, for if you wait quietly, creatures will appear. I was, however, the only living creature abroad. Further exploration led me to large canine tracks which I first thought were those of a domestic dog. I tracked them in the slick, deep mud for a quarter of a mile or so, and as I did my mind collected the steady, purposeful gait of this animal, and I took further notice. Its strides were long, its straddle narrow, and it appeared very comfortable with its surroundings. Wolf tracks are often difficult to distinguish from dog, but the clues to me began to read wolf. The tracks had been made some hour before, and there had been continual rain, so precise definition was not possible. I left two days later, but my traveling companion, an old friend

I'd met hiking in the Cascades, did not leave until the morning following my departure, when he viewed a wolf on the road.

One day in Montana I saw a black, thin wolf in a drenching summer rain. At first, from a distance, it looked like a black lab, but then a second glance told me it was wolf. Thin, long-legged, it had come from the wet, wet brush onto the road and then my car came around the bend. It looked and made a decision. It ran down the road for an eighth of a mile and broke back into the brush. I stopped and tracked in sloppy, deep clay mud, and photographed the tracks—muddy, rain-filled wolf tracks, as fresh as they could be! Down the road and into the wet brush—wet, wet until it was too wet, I tracked. Then I backtracked from where it entered the road.

Another time in Glacier, thirty to forty feet below me I saw the carcass of a white-tail doe on a gravel bar. Her haunches were missing, and her bloody ribs bared. Her forelegs were crossed in front of her head grotesquely. Death is pathetic. I shuddered and glanced at the surrounding brush. The deer remains were not covered, the ground relatively undisturbed around the body, and so my initial hypothesis was that it was a wolf kill, not bear. Nor was this the kill spot. I stood on an almost vertical ridge overlooking a flat delta bordering the North Fork of the Flathead River. It was July, 1986.

I sat down for further observation and thought. The area was too undisturbed to be the kill site. However, if it was a wolf kill I wondered why half of the doe yet remained, unless I had disturbed the event. A bear would have dragged, then covered, the kill. If I had disturbed it when feeding, it would probably still have stayed at the scent. I searched the hard, dry, heavily grassed ground and walked along the ridge edge. Here a slope had allowed fishermen and walkers a steep, loose-shaled trail, and I bent down, nose to the ground. It took but a moment. There they were, wolf tracks! I clung to the brush and rocks, avoiding the trail and tracks. I searched further on the flat, finding good tracks on the sandbars. They were about eight hours old—last night's kill. I tracked and backtracked for several hours. The deer had been killed in a grassy, willowed area and dragged about 200 yards from the kill site to the gravelbar. I diagrammed the interesting kill approach. Five wolves had descended upon the white-tail, coming in an almost star pattern to the deer.

I wanted to be there when they returned, which would be after dark. However, I was in the park confines, and camping outside of a campground was prohibited. It was a few too many miles from my campground for me to want to walk in the dark. In the morning the scene was bare, and the graveled rock gave me some cues to the wolves' return. Beyond, more wolf tracks.

Kishenehn Creek off the North Fork of the Flathead River flows a good five miles in Montana and also in Canada. A companion from Montana and I took the gorgeous, remote walk one day, perfect wolf habitat. As we proceeded on, grizzly clawing high on a snag greeted us not too far along. Further on, fresh black bear tracks formed their definitions in the muddy streambank. It was definitely bear country. We had planned to cross the creek to view an old patrol cabin, but I declined when I saw the strength of the current and the depth of the creek at the crossing area. The creek was rocky, swift and cold. I was especially afraid of submerging my camera, as well as myself. So we sojourned on the east side of the creek, and it must have been meant to be. A wolf had chosen the same easy path we had. The wolf had stepped on soft moist ground with small green growth which helped to camouflage the tracks. We walked behind this wolf some hours after it had been there for about a half mile. I had almost become so used to wolf tracks I took them in my stride, but the excitement that I could have even chanced to be here when it was, never left me. Kishenehn Creek was indeed perfect wolf country.

Kintla Creek off the North Fork of the Flathead River was another place where I tracked wolf. The creek was easily accessed from the road, and a beach ran the length from a bridge to the Flathead River. Moose and deer frequented the area. The first tracks I found of wolf in Glacier Park were here. At first I took them for large dog tracks, but the tracking revealed behavior quite dissimilar to the domestic dog. What this wolf did was come out of the brush along a path used by fishermen, run along the brush edge to the water toward the Flathead, drink at the river, and run up the beach area back to the trail and up the slope into the brush. It then ran through a place used to park cars, across the road and continued upslope into the brush again, and went on. Although the tracks were within the size limitations of a domestic dog, the animal did not run back and forth along the beach as a fisherman's dog would. Even though dogs are prohibited from running free in the park, I considered the possibility that one had. So I looked very carefully at these tracks, and photographed them. An inquiry of a ranger later revealed a recent sighting of wolf at that spot. Later in another area on the banks of the Flathead River, I tracked another wolf for a long way down the beach, it just kept going and going, striding out, undoubtedly looking for some scent of prey. I was becoming familiar with wolf behavior.

I found further wolf tracks along Trail Creek where I also found grizzly scat and diggings. This was just west of the North Fork of the Flathead River outside of the boundary of Glacier. Some houses are close to the creek and off the road in this area. The wolf tracks I discovered were in loose soil, which was sandy in texture, and in between a very rocky streambank where the winter flow covered the rocks. The tracks did not show claw marks due to the loose soil, and a three-lobed suggestion at the posterior of the heel pad looked at first quite similar to cougar track. I pondered over the three tracks I found, unable to reach a conclusion as to their maker without more careful analysis. The stride was within both animals' walking limits, and the sandy nature of the soil rolled the edges of the tracks to give me poor assessment of the shape of the tracks. The straddle was perhaps too narrow for a cougar. I was caught by the lack of claw marks, but primarily the three-lobed extrusions of the heel pad, which were indistinct in the loose soil, showed more prominently in one track over the others. The tracks measured three and a half inches long and three and three-quarters inches wide, giving it an almost rounder feline configuration than oblong like a canine. As I moved from the close, kneeling position to look from a standing position, the distance enabled me to identify the track as wolf. The three lobes were insignificant, the oblong shape of the toe pads became diagnostic. After photographs I cast the best track. Soil of this quality at high noon is deceiving, and sometimes looking too closely at detail instead of the overall configuration combined with the detail can be disconcerting. At times when not certain in the field, I have even come home to find the photographs reveal the detail enough to be clearly diagnostic—just one good reason to take many photographs from many angles of a confusing track, and in different light conditions.

While in Glacier a couple of years ago, I presented workshops on tracking. I would go out for days before a workshop to find tracks for the group, so they would have the option of seeing wildlife tracks which they might not have the opportunity to see elsewhere. I then covered them up so the weather and other creatures would not destroy them, and they would generally be in good condition for the workshop.

One year on Quartz Creek, off Road Seven in the park, I found wolf tracks for the group. The wolf had come from thick brush with tough vegetation and rocks onto the sandbar of Quartz Creek west of the creek, walked down to drink, walked along the bank toward the road, and then left across the creekbank where the winter flow covered the rocks. It was clearly wolf, and wolf behavior. No domestic canine had made the tracks, although there was a campground down the road. Nor were there human tracks in the immediate area. This technique of revealing the actual track to students carries far more value than talking all day long about tracks. They were able to see the movements in the individual tracks as well as the configuration of the tracks themselves, and see movements over the ground distinguishing it from domestic canine behavior. Glacier National Park is an exciting place, particularly when you leave the road and can evaluate what you see. What an expanded dimension such an experience can give to the outdoors. Think of the people driving the road who had no knowledge that a short 100 feet down the creek, the ground could come alive with adventure. Wolf tracks!

So the wolves had returned to Glacier National Park. East of Round Prairie in 1986, land was posted off limits to humans, in order to give a wolf den a wide berth. Many welcomed their return. Many were angry or fearful. But all felt the hypnotizing spell of their howls in the park, howls from the hills and the prairies, riverbanks and brush, in the moonlight and in the dark. I have heard the wolves' songs in Glacier National Park. I am happy with the sound.

Wolves were shot on the east side of the park that year. Wolves denned the following year across the border in Canada. Then wolves returned to Big Prairie in Glacier. I shall return, too, to track and listen to wolves. Perhaps one day I may peer into the still eyes of this predator, its head lowered in motionless gaze. I can visualize its fixed stare and long muzzle, nostrils moving with its breath, body on hold. I would wonder, then, about the workings of its mind, and its thoughts of me.

***

Wolves are white, black or grizzled gray, and their long tail is tipped with black, reaching almost twenty inches in length. They are four feet long and may stand thirty-eight inches high at the shoulder. The larger males may weigh up to 130 pounds. At a walk they travel five miles per hour and can run in excess of forty miles per hour for a thousand yards. They can trot at five miles per hour for fifty miles and jump up eight to ten feet from a sitting position. A wolf's jaws can crush the thigh bones of a moose.

Socially, wolves are very affectionate. Either sex maybe the leader of a pack, usually consisting of seven to eight wolves, but including as many as fifteen or so. The dominant of each sex mates, and those others who produce pups are banished from the pack and must survive alone. The pack hunts together, as a large number of animals is required to bring down their prey of moose, elk and caribou. Only seven out of 100 attempts to obtain prey succeeds. They will consume berries, fish, birds and insects as well as small prey. Twenty pounds of meat may be eaten at a sitting, 90 percent of their diet being meat. They can go seventeen days without food when none is available.

Wolves den only when with pups. For twelve to fourteen weeks the center of activity for the whole pack is the den. All the pack members help feed the pups, which may number fourteen, but usually there are about seven. The size of the litter depends upon the food supply available for the pregnant female, and half the litter dies in the first year of life. When born, the pups are blind and deaf, and weigh only one pound. Their eyes open in ten to fifteen days, in eighteen to twenty days they can hear, and at eight weeks they are weaned. At three months of age the pups are moved to a rendezvous site where they stay while the pack and their parents hunt, and by six months of age they join the hunt; at that time they are able to keep up any distance.

Wolves are primarily nocturnal, but they are also diurnal. They range daily for food, and may cache extra food. Their home ranges are vast. Larger packs can use 600 square miles, and smaller packs 100 square miles. The female with pups may restrict herself to only five square miles. These packs are usually extended families who mark their territory by the use of urine and scat, but separate pack territories overlap some. They may migrate with the migration of their prey. Wolves travel more often than any animal other than caribou. Population densities are quite variable, from one per forty square miles to one per 100 square miles.

The wolves vocal communications, so striking and thrilling, reminding us of the true wilderness, have different meanings. The alarm bark is short, and repeated once or twice. A challenge or warning is a more drawn out bark. The howl which calls the pack together is a deep howl, followed by a few barks. When the wolf is separated from the pack it gives a mournful and high pitched howl, dropping quickly in pitch. May these unforgettable wolf howls penetrate the hills forever.

Chapter Four

The Bear Family
Ursidae

BLACK BEAR
Ursus americanus

This smallest of all the bears is the most familiar to many. The mountains of the U.S. are home to many black bears, but far more live in all of Canada's forests and most of Alaska. In B.C. alone, 140,000 black bears are estimated to live. Our views of bears are mostly of this species. In some areas sightings are frequent and humans become too familiar with them, losing their fear of these wild animals. Bears in national parks and heavily populated areas can become overly familiar with people as well. Then chance encounters increase conflict and harm can occur to humans or bear, as each perceives the other from his own personal and inevitably different perspective.

The microenvironment of the black bear in the Northwest changes somewhat depending upon the food supply and season. It is found on alpine meadows, and interspersed between there and the lowland rivers and swamps. Most bears cover this range, but some stay at river bottoms all year. They can be highly variable. Simply put, the microenvironment for the bear is where he is!

In tracking black bear I am as cautious as when tracking grizzly. People have had as many physical encounters with blacks as with grizzlies. Both kinds of bear have been known to leave the trail ahead of someone and come up behind in ambush. Also, bears wander, and while you are tracking your particular bear, it may be ambling back in your direction. Their speed precludes outrunning them, and their tree climbing ability is better than any human's. Around bears a tracker must keep his eyes above the ground also.

One black bear I tracked, a large male, judging from the size of the tracks, wandered down from the forested areas in the Three Sisters Wilderness of central Oregon one May, when the snow still lay low in the foothills. I picked up his tracks on a dusty, back-country logging road about ten miles from the foothills. He meandered on and off the road, just far enough to collect ants from anthills in old stumps. I came upon his tracks after midday; the dust had begun to settle into them, obliterating the fresh shine. I judged them to be two to three hours old. As I tracked, I realized the hot May afternoon might be a good time for him to siesta. I became cautious, since two-hour-old tracks can bring you right smack over a log on top of a sleeping bear. This bear was a male—I would not have tracked a female with cubs on a hot, May afternoon.

Another day in an area around Tahola, Washington, I was walking alone about a mile from my car, and a quarter of a mile from the beach. I followed an old road, hoping it would take me to the beach, rather than having to climb over a rock expanse. The trees covered the road with a green canopy that was just barely over my head. I came to a steep drop along the road, where fifty- to sixty-foot firs stretched upwards. I heard a distinct, loud scratching sound from above me, and looking up, I saw a black bear cub scrambling down the fir. I made an immediate decision to turn and retrace my route. This is one of only two times I have run when in the immediate vicinity of bear. The sow was no doubt quite close and had put her cub up the tree at my approach. I imagine she was downhill, at the base of the tree her cub occupied. To go on could have meant an encounter. Nothing could be more reassuring to a mother bear than to have danger move away. Under almost all circumstances, however, running is contraindicated. Running away from a bear is advised only if you are next to a car, a house or some structure that will protect you and is well within reach. However, running can provoke a chase, one the bear will probably win. If the bear has spotted you, it may be safest to slowly move backwards.

The other time I deliberately chose to run was following an encounter with an adult black bear in Montana one summer, after I had gotten out of its sight. I had climbed a dry, steep, rocky stream bed to discover a spring dripping over a wide ledge, and above it sat a bear, twenty-five feet away. We surprised each other, my quiet footsteps having been covered by the flow and drip of the water. This bear stood its ground, and after one look at me, vocalized a myriad of high and low pitched sounds. My immediate reaction was to freeze, and my heart beat so hard I wondered if it could sense my fear. I knew not to run, and I stood momentarily hoping my nonverbal communication of "It's your place, but I'm not afraid of you," would be understood. I then did a painfully slow backward stalk down the hill. I suspect the surprise meeting created ambivalent feelings in it. Although wary of humans, it didn't want to leave its special, cool place and so was in sufficient conflict to keep it from running. When you find a bear that does not run from humans you have immediate potential trouble. This bear no doubt became less frightened as I receded from view down the slope at that slow pace, and my slow departure might have kept it from charging. It then grasped a big fir it was beside. It gave one shuffle up, then later one more—the better to view me, no doubt, as I disappeared downhill. When I was finally out of its sight (an eternity later), I ran! Unfortunately I stepped on fresh bear scat a short piece ahead. I stopped for breath, only to hear a bear cough ahead, so I changed direction again. I considered it unlikely, however, from the behavior of the bear I had seen, that this bear was the same one. However, friends whom I was visiting thought it was possible. Later we all returned to the spring. The claw marks on the tree indicated it had not climbed higher than when I had last seen it. Apparently it stayed to enjoy its domain. I was not at all unhappy that it had.

I have come across bear tracks that were just too fresh for me to want to track. I stayed at Thierrault Lakes in northern Idaho one July. On my walk one day I noticed freshly torn bark from trees near their base. When I went on it did not surprise me to find black bear cub tracks extremely fresh, likely within the hour. The tracks were too small for this cub to be wandering around very far from its mother. I did not check it out. I went back the way I came.

That night I slept in my van, enjoying its comfort and protection. Two nights later I was awakened in the middle of the night by the rocking of my van. In my drowsy state I thought first of bear. Then the van was still. I was processing the possibility that I had dreamed the movement. I also considered that an elk might have brushed against the van in passing. Then the rocking began again, and I heard the scratch of claws on the side of the van as a bear lowered itself down. I slung the curtains from the window but all was black. Perhaps the bear! I felt the front of the van shake. I looked out, then slapped the sides of the van. All was still. I never saw the bear. After a while I fell asleep.

The dirty paw prints on the van told the story. Sow and cub had paid me a visit. The sow had put her front paws on the top of the side rear of the van above the window where I slept. She also did so on the hood of the vehicle. The cub had put its paws on the driver's side door and the front of the van. The muddy prints were there. So now I had tracked bear on a car. They weren't hard to track, and I aged them perfectly. Their tracks went around the campground, and they visited a few other campers. A friend with whom I was traveling said one of the bears put its paws on the screen of his rear camper door and he wondered why she hadn't come through. These were without doubt the sow and cub whose tracks I had found a few miles away earlier. With their lack of concern about humans, I was pleased not to have met them in the field.

Glacier Road Seven inside the park is a fascinating road going from Fish Creek Ranger Station to Polebridge Ranger Station. It is known as the inside road, and I often saw bear there. It is barely two-laned, curved, and, with overgrown trees and brush, the sensation of being in remote wilderness is enhanced, for you are driving through wilderness which is accessible by trails from this road.

One day I was driving north on the inside road and had not gotten as far as Dutch Creek when just as I made a sharp turn a bear stopped on the left side of the road. It quickly climbed a tree at the edge of the road. It went up about ten feet and, hugging the trunk, stayed there and looked at me. I tried to see whether it was grizzly or black. It was small enough to be a young grizzly, which can climb trees very easily, but I could not see whether it had a hump. As I tried to assess whether this was a griz or a black, I noted its cinnamon color. Its claws were in shadow, and its ears looked a little peaked for a grizzly, but a young griz's ears might be of that shape. As I looked it over well, and as I thought about it later, I think it was a black bear. As it showed no indication of leaving, I honked the horn, and although that startled it, it stayed. I even got out of the car, staying close to the open door just in case its sentiments changed. It stayed. I watched it for a long while, but it never left the tree. Perhaps it was a sow, old enough to have a cub, and did not want to leave the area for that reason. I left it in the tree. (What else could I do?)

Another black bear I saw on this road was passing through a meadow I had already checked for tracks. I was on the road looking around, when a very large black bear appeared on the far side of the meadow, moving away from me, and climbing the slope of ground beyond. It moved very rapidly. Its coat of hair shone in the light so I had no doubt about this being a black bear. The grizzly coat would not have reflected the light in that way. The area was thick with vegetation, as Glacier is, and I waited for a while before I wandered over to look for tracks. There was no bare soil, but the vegetation had been pushed down where it had gone through. I did not follow it. I was rather happy I was not where I had been a short while earlier, right near its path.

Black bear tracks are even evident in trees. Near my home in Montana there were claw marks of bears that had climbed alder trees, leaving permanent tracks in the soft bark of the trunks. It was fun to follow the climbing movements of the bear, identifying the front and rear tracks, and to trace its route as it climbed. I have never tried tracking going up a tree, however!

I found bear scat in an unusual place in Glacier National Park. I was looking at a very old two-story cabin which had been occupied a long time ago, but not since. There were newspapers showing the sinking of the *Titanic* on the walls. I was so engrossed with the setting that it was not until leaving that I scanned the floors for other interesting features. I could not believe my eyes. In the corner of an upstairs room was a pile of bear scat. It was intact in natural fashion, for I had to consider if rats had carried it up. Considering the position of the segments, I think they did not.

In 1982 I had visited Glacier, and near Akokala Creek had found black bear track when I was walking in snow. I also found a tree that had been freshly clawed by this bear, no doubt, and I photographed the markings. In 1987 I was there, and again located and photographed the tree to illustrate the aging of the scratches. It was clearly the same tree, and I studied the differences. The color of the older marks was dull, and the tree had sealed the injuries. Photos each year illustrating the aging process would have been great.

Black bear swim, of course, but a surprising sight I had was when my husband and I were boating in British Columbia's Gulf Islands. Somewhere among those gorgeous islands we were making our steady way across a large channel and noticed a prominent rise in the water off to one side. As we came abreast of the object, although perhaps a quarter of a mile away, it was evident that we were seeing the head of a black bear which was swimming between the mainland and an island, heading toward the island. I watched as we proceeded, wishing that we would have been able to watch the bear finally beach. I recollect that the distance between the island and the mainland was more than a mile. It made me wonder what could possibly be in that bear's mind to make such a sojourn.

When I lived near Swamp Creek one winter in northwest Montana there were many bear, some of which came up to the house. The house was only a couple of miles from some other houses, but there was a profusion of wildlife everywhere. Many evenings I would walk down the road, but one evening I turned back as two black bears crossed the road ahead about 100 yards. I found bear scat along the side of the house sometimes, and saw a bear from the kitchen window while eating dinner. I also walked behind the property in heavy timber, where I frequently found bear track.

One day I was tracking a black bear which had very recently passed. It meandered on and off the old, overgrown bulldozed path and into the brush, through some mud puddles, and on toward an area near a highway. As I was tracking it near this area, I heard one shot ring out ahead of me quite close. I was some distance from my house at this time, but I turned and headed home. I thought some hunter shot at that bear from the highway and soon I might expect a wounded or frightened bear to appear charging in my direction. I don't know if he came back or not. I wasn't willing to check it out for a few days in case it lay back there somewhere, wounded.

Another day in Montana I rode my trail motorcycle 100 miles through back roads north of Thompson Falls. Near Fishtrap Lake my riding companion preceded me along the road. On our left was a steep hill, when suddenly a black bear cub dashed down the slope ahead, and ended up just ahead of the first bike on the road. It became confused and ran along the road in front of the bike for some time. It ran as fast as it could, frightened, its hind legs reaching out forward of its front legs as far as they could in its attempt to outrun the motorcycles. I could see it panting as I caught a few side views of it as the road turned. Then, just as suddenly, it was gone, leaving us laughing and delighted at the event. Top speed on those bikes is about forty-five miles an hour. I think it might have gotten close!

***

Despite its name, the black bear can wear many colors, from black to cinnamon, brown and even near white in Alaska. Its face is generally brown, and it sometimes has a white patch on its chest. Its weight varies tremendously depending upon the food supply. In the Pacific Northwest it may weigh from 200 to almost 500 pounds. In some areas it may reach 600 pounds or more. The male continues to grow as long as it lives, but the female reaches a maximum, although variable weight, in adulthood.

The black bear will be about two to three feet. Its tail extends from three to seven inches in length.

The black bear is a solitary animal, except during breeding season and when the sow is raising her young. The male may destroy the young cubs if the female does not fiercely defend them. The sow and her one, two or three cubs usually den together for the first winter of the cub's life. Occasionally they may disperse before denning time. A sow is reported to have had six cubs under optimum conditions, and sometimes four are seen. Bears mate in June or July in as isolated an area as possible, and the young are born in the winter den in January or February after a delayed implantation, and a gestation length of around seven months.

There is an old Indian saying: A pine needle fell. The eagle saw it, the deer heard it and the bear smelled it. A bear's smell and hearing are exceptional. Its sight, although reported to be poor, is not, but it relies more on its other, keener, senses. It is omnivorous, and although classified as a carnivore, it has adapted to a primarily herbivorous existence. It will kill anything it can, including man, but it cannot digest plant cellulose and protein, and must confine its vegetarian intake to the early growth of plants that its digestive system can break down to liquid form and assimilate. It enjoys a wide variety of food, including berries, bugs, roots and carrion.

Hibernation varies for black bears. In some parts of the world where food is available all year, and the climate is mild, it does not hibernate. However, in the Pacific Northwest it hibernates from two to seven months. It may rouse for mild periods, in which it does not need food. Dens are more often in lower elevations, though they vary. In any given area, however, all black bear dens are found at the same elevation and compass points. It travels in a certain territory, moving when warming temperatures open new possibilities for food. Its home range may vary from five to fifteen miles and on up, but the female usually travels less distance than the male. Some individuals have covered hundreds of miles, however.

The life expectancy for a black bear can be more than thirty years. Hunting and injury are the primary causes of death. Although cougar sometimes may kill a bear, man is really the only creature he must fear. Bears are capable of discriminating between people who behave or dress differently. Some claim they are intelligent enough to confuse trackers with their backtracking expertise, having been know to jump sideways off a trail to lose a pursuer.

The black bear is highly unpredictable. It should never be thought of as other than a very wild creature, quite capable, with no known provocation, of aggressiveness toward humans. There is no way to predict what specific situation might interact with an individual bear's experience and personality to make it suddenly dangerous to a human. Two different strategies of responding to an aggressive bear are suggested, depending upon the sex of the bear, the situation and the preparedness of the human. If caught between a sow and cubs, playing dead may be the thing to do. On the other hand, a bear who casually walks into camp may be frightened away by shouting and somewhat aggressive behavior. There are records of humans saving themselves by fighting a bear. A black bear is also capable of ambushing humans, so anyone in bear country should be very careful, and take the time to learn about its behavior.

GRIZZLY BEAR
Ursus arctos

The legendary grizzly is a spectacular creature in size, appearance and behavior. Having once roamed prolifically in the western U.S., probably less than 1,000 exist in the lower United States at present, although Alaska holds an estimated 40,000. About 16,000 live in B.C., 50 percent of all grizzlies in Canada, and 25 percent of the total number in North America. The population in the Yukon is 5,000 to 9,000 bears and the Northwest Territories have about 4,000 to 5,000 bears. Alberta has a population of about 800, an estimated 200 of which reside in the mountain national parks.

The Native Indians called it "great-grandfather" and would apologize when they killed one, but their fear of it was keen along with their respect, and relief came after the kill. For the white man it was the terror of the frontier, a threat to peaceful existence, and a mechanism for machismo and heroic tales over campfires and in bars. The philosophy was to eliminate the beast of all beasts, and walk on it as a rug. Meanwhile, although there were encounters, often initiated by rifle shots, the largest carnivore of the west ate flowers. The demise of the grizzly in the American west came about through shooting as they were pursued without mercy. Now its critical habitat has been invaded by ranching and they can exist only where agriculture cannot, and where man protects them in the northwest of Montana, northern Idaho and Yellowstone. And the struggle continues. Man seeks to destroy what he fears and cannot understand.

The microenvironment for the grizzly is coniferous, heavily forested areas with high elevations for denning at 6,000 foot levels. There must also be dense vegetation and severe winters, for the grizzly depends upon carrion when it first begins to eat after a week or so from denning. It has a variety of seasonal food needs, so it may be found from lower grassy areas to high alpine areas with glacier lilies. When the huckleberries ripen, it is there. In grizzly country it may be anywhere.

I tracked a bear along North Fork of the Flathead River one summer, and cast and photographed the tracks. The bear had stepped on tiny new growth beneath low brush willow and the tracks are difficult to discern in the photos. The casts of one front foot look definitely grizzly, and the other cast looks like a black bear track. The size indicates it could be either a black male or a female grizzly. The rear tracks were not good for casting. I tracked the bear as well as possible from the mud where I cast the tracks, across some dried understory debris, certainly not the place for a good definition of a track. In this area both black and grizzly can be found. The cast reflecting the more horizontal line of toes seems to have the toes spread apart, like the black bear. As you measure the other cast with a ruler, from below the big toe across the top part of the heel pad of the front foot, the toes do not fall entirely above the ruler, as is characteristic of the grizzly, but rather the ruler cuts the smallest toe in half. It will remain an enigma.

On the other hand, a grizzly made wonderful tracks in damp earth on a road near the Canadian border. It was unmistakably grizzly. The tracks were recent, and I could feel its immensity and power as I followed the broken bushes and soil crushed beneath its weight. It is scary tracking behind a grizzly who has so recently passed. The light was failing in the early evening and rain was imminent, so I didn't track for long. Perhaps it was fortunate, who knows where the bear was?

This occurred one October afternoon south of Moose City, Montana in 1986, with clouds hanging heavily over the land. The dark swells and knolls in the sky moved precipitously fast, rolling like the heavy smoke of a forest fire and coming as fast. A heaviness in the air gave me a sense of uneasiness. Perhaps it was premonitory, for as the thick tangle of Montana downfall threatened to trip me, my eyes focused upon a muddy grizzly track that looked recent. Lying across a fir log, belly higher than my head, I reached down and felt the track. The ground here held moisture a long time, since the sun only briefly penetrated the thick canopy. The weather for the last few days had been dry and 40–60°F, although dampness remained in protected areas. This hind track was almost wet, bespeaking of more than rainfall. It was a swampy edge, making the age of this track difficult to calculate. If I could find another track in drier ground, it would be easier to age. I pulled myself up and climbed over the debris. The track was cluttered heavily with low, green growth. The growth in the track had sprung up. I tested my own foot beside the indistinct track. The stiff growth slowly began to rise, succulent enough not to break. I watched it slowly, slowly rise. In twenty minutes it appeared nearly erect. Nearby vegetation was covered with muddy blobs thrown from the track. The underside of the leaves still retained moist earth which had not had time to dry. The track in the damp green growth was probably a maximum of five to six hours old. I went on. There ahead a rough, overgrown, bulldozed road showed a line of tracks. The road was firm with a clay base and a skiff of occasional dry dirt cover. I knelt. The tracks were depressed enough to reach the damp underlay and no real drying had occurred in the sticky bottom. The day's sun had only slightly dried the top surface of the soil. I calculated that the open areas would have received occasional sun until the last couple of hours when the clouds rolled in. I checked a half dozen tracks more, with little difference. Here I could assess some known variables: the soil, the probability of the sun's presence for a few hours, and fifty degree temperature for about six hours. I made a tentative calculation that the tracks were about two hours old. The first track I had found could not have told me that since the ground had been so boggy there. I would have had to step in the same ground, time the seep entry in the track, and try to estimate the difference in weight to give me an initial idea of the age. Difficult—to say the least. Plus I needed to know a lot about the consistency and aging of mud in this soil. I could only have obtained a very gross estimate. The tracks were large enough to be a male grizzly.

I glanced up at the now rippling trees, feeling cold slaps of wind against my body. I had been bushwhacking a semicircle through the brush. I was not going to try to track a grizzly at this time of day in this weather. Besides, he could be close. Tomorrow I might be able to return. I slipped and sloshed back to the van through swampy land. As I walked the main road I stopped short at one tight curve. More grizzly track on the shoulder of the road. I glanced at the sky, and rushed to the car for plaster of Paris to cast one front track. The light made it impossible to photograph. I blocked off the cast from any passing car with logs as best I could and covered it against the weather. Then the rain began in earnest. I left a survey ribbon and noted the odometer reading on the car, and drove off. Overnight it rained quite heavily. I worried how the cast was faring, and if I would be able to find it. I held little hope. I returned the next day and found the tracks with water standing in them, making interesting photos. The cast was solid. The brush, however, was far too wet for any further investigation. I was content to have come that close to the grizzly, and no closer.

A friend, Rosalind, a Glacier Park naturalist, and I went looking for adventure west of Glacier one year. We followed Trail Creek far upstream, and came to a high embankment above a very swampy area. It appeared as though there was enough wet ground down there to find tracks should something have made some. I was looking for lynx tracks primarily, and the ground had been so hard everywhere else, I was willing to make the long descent. The steep slope below us was about an eighth of a mile or so, and we negotiated it, thinking of the climb up. When we got down there and started for the creek, we soon came upon vegetation sign indicating feeding, and there was a trail through the grass which looked too wide for any deer. We looked at each other knowingly, and presently came upon bear bed, used not very many hours before, if that long. Scat was also present very close, corroborating the freshness of the visit. I was ready to retreat, but we decided to continue. Rosalind was used to this. We followed the stream and surveyed every piece of wet ground, and came again upon fresh bear sign, torn logs and another bed, and then another. Apparently the bear had been using the area for some time, and we felt he was still close. Nevertheless, there we were, so we enjoyed the stream and the day and finally climbed back up. We felt the bear was griz, judging from the size of the beds and our intuition. But no firm ground tracks were in evidence. I was happy to have had company in that spot.

From the Going To The Sun Road through Glacier, many bear can be seen. I will always remember one view. High above the road in thick, tall brush, a blond grizzly sow had three large cubs near a steep but narrow rushing stream. She had been in the brush trying to keep cool, but the day was becoming increasingly hot, and so she wandered out of the brush and into the stream. My patience waiting below finally revealed the three cubs, at times visible all at once. They also were blonde and reddish, and put on quite a show getting into the stream. Binoculars clearly revealed their grizzly identity.

On the road going from Apgar campground to Fish Creek Ranger Station one passes McGee Meadows, a large swampy area of grass. One day an exceedingly large bear of gorgeous, deep reddish color was lazily feeding on the grass beside the road. It ignored the line of cars watching it. I had a marvelous view. From car windows people were conversing about whether the bear was black or grizzly. Its ears looked grizzly, and it was so large it appeared to have a hump, but its head was always low as it was feeding, and in this position even a black can appear to have a hump. Its claws were dark, so one could not be sure of its origins from that, since most grizzlies having white claws. Its face looked dished or concave, but I did not see it full face to see whether it had a crease in the center top of its hair on its skull, designating griz, nor did it have a noticeable fur ruff at the base of its skull. Its coat was fairly smooth, but in the sun it did appear to shine, characteristic of black bears. I puzzled over the diagnosis a lot, and the next day I returned to the area to pick up tracks.

This bear had noticeably crushed the foot high grass beside the road, and I backtracked it in some dirt along the meadow edge. Here it had overturned rocks looking for insects. In one place it had left a pile of loose scat, showing sign of a grass diet. I tracked on about a half mile until it left the road area and went into the brush. All this time I was tracking on thick grass. Only once did it put its feet into a dry dirt area of loose soil, where the shape of its foot was indistinct. The photographs did not reflect what the eye could ascertain, but the track mark, although somewhat enlarged due to the condition of the soil, appeared very large. There seemed to be more indications that this bear was grizzly. It seems incredible to be so close to a bear and not be about to make a definite determination. However, let me tell you how difficult that really can be.

A Fish and Game man in the Kootenai National Forest near Thompson Falls, Montana, showed me slides of tranquilized bears he had trapped in a grizzly study in the Cabinet Mountains in northwest Montana. Apparently even some of the experts were not able to identify whether some of the bear were black or grizzly. Many of the bears had confusing features. Here I was viewing slides taken a few feet away from bears, and I had all the time in the world to evaluate the features. It was terribly difficult to impossible in many instances—a real education. And I don't want to wait until the bear is close enough to tell me whether or not it has white claws to be able to identify it as a grizzly! This wildlife biologist put a "cubby," a trap, where I was staying to see if a grizzly would find it.

This is a trap built with logs which has a snare in it that will not harm the leg of the bear. It is baited and the traps are checked quite frequently. No bear found it, however, not even a black bear.

Another day I tentatively started up a little-used trail just south of Logging Creek off Road Seven in Glacier. I do not go far on these trails alone due to the grizzly population and the black bear habituation to people. Being alone, I do find more tracks on the overgrown trails which others ignore. I am in conflict at various points along the trail as to whether to continue or turn back. I feel my way, looking at all the sign evident, fresh trails which could be bear, bear scat of any age, and I listen frequently as I progress slowly. In some sense this is a disadvantage, for one can be too quiet. I do wear bells which announce my presence in bear country, but you have to be moving along to initiate the bell, and I get very engrossed in what I am seeing, so at times I just ring the bell. I took one trail, ambivalence bothering me. My intuition had kept me out of trouble up to this point, and so the lure of the fascinating trail ahead was in direct conflict with my feelings. I came upon bear scat which was old. I went on, each turn beckoning me, and each turn telling me it should be my last. I found other bear scat, still older, and further bear scat which age I could not really determine. I thought the signs were sufficient, and I turned and left. Although you might be disappointed in this story, as I found nothing more, the important part is that nothing happened, and I am here writing this. It is important to rely on the inner senses, my sixth sense in this case. I felt I made the right decision, even that I had pushed it further than comfortable. I cannot prove it. Perhaps fortunately.

Avalanche Lake in Glacier is frequented by grizzlies. At the time I was there the trail was posted as having recent grizzly activity. On the trail I found a bear tree. This tree is large, but not enormous. The bark on the trunk some fifteen feet up is shredded by the use of many bears, probably to clean and sharpen their claws, and perhaps to leave scent for the other users. How this particular tree in among all the others came to be significant for bears is unknown, but it probably started when the first bear used it, and the next one found it, and the next, until this day. It will undoubtedly continue to be used by the next generation of bears.

***

Whether the grizzly is brown, black, cinnamon or a light blonde-white, white-tipped hairs give it a grizzled appearance. It can reach six to seven feet in length, stands four and a quarter feet high at the shoulder, and when upright reaches almost nine feet. Its tail is only three inches long. Weight can vary from 300 to 900 pounds, but some protected animals have grown to about 1,100 or 1,200 pounds. They are often difficult to distinguish from black bears. Diagnostic characteristics are a concave facial profile, large and often white claws of four to six inches in length, muscular cheek-jaw muscles, a fur ruff at the base of the skull, a crease in the center top of the hair on the skull, a high shoulder hump, wide and conical shaped ears, silver-tipped hair, and a grizzled, not shiny, coat of hair. However, these indicators may not necessarily all be present, or they may appear ambiguous in some individuals.

Home ranges are greatly variable, some individual bears cover up to 1,500 square miles. Some stay all year at river bottoms, but most follow the maturing food plants up to the higher elevations and down again for berries in the fall. They cannot digest cellulose except in liquid form so they eat plants only in their early stages. Grizzlies are omnivorous. Their diet is 90 percent vegetation and 10 percent animal. They will eat insects, carrion and any mammal. They can consume ninety pounds of food daily. Just before hibernation they feed for twenty-four hours daily to store fat for the winter denning.

Absolute size of the grizzly home range is determined by the quality and availability of the food. Actually, home ranges should be considered as widely separated activity centers where the bear does much of his hunting and denning. In between these activity centers exists plenty of "dead space" that all the bears in the area utilize. These bears need a sufficient amount of dead space to survive. Social accommodation is utilized to give them their needed space.

Grizzly are solitary in nature until breeding season. The female may be able to mate for the first time at five to seven years of age, but she is not sexually mature until eight to ten years. At best she alternates breeding years, and usually breeds every three years. Thus, every four to five years, two or three cubs may be born. By fifteen to twenty years of age, should she live so long, statistically only six female cubs may be born, giving the grizzly a very low reproductive rate. The female may mate with more than one male, or a pair may stay together for three weeks. After breeding, there is a delayed implantation of seven to eight months, and then for two to two and a half months the fetus grows, and one to four cubs are born in January to March in the den. The cubs weigh only one pound at birth, nearly naked, and their eyes open in ten days. They weigh ten pounds at about three months. They stay with their mother for two to three years.

Cubs have been known to den together for the first winter after leaving their mother.

Dens are most often at very high elevations, on steep slopes with good drainage, and in heavy snow-accumulating areas so the snow will not melt and deprive them of insulation. Usually this is in an area where trees can be scarce, but the soil is held together by root systems. Grass and limbs are used for bedding.

The physiology of denning is unusual. Scientists suggest that when the grizzly's fat cells reach a certain size they may emit some trigger substance that induces hibernation. Bear hibernation is decidedly different from the hibernation of other animals. The true, or deep, hibernator experiences a suppressed metabolism during which it cannot be aroused. However, periodically it awakes on its own to eat, drink and eliminate. If it did not do this it would die. During this period of awakening the heartbeat speeds up again and the body temperature rises. Bears, on the other hand, have little change in their temperature, and although their heart beat slows, it rises for a period every day. Bears can be easily aroused from their hibernation, but they do not spontaneously waken to tend to physiological needs. The bear's system essentially recycles waste products. A 400-pound hibernator uses 8,000 calories a day with a loss of only fat, not lean body mass. When the grizzly emerges from its den almost all of its area is still deep in snow. It needs some time for its digestive system to activate and so it does not need to eat immediately, but continues to rely on its fat accumulation.

Grizzlies are excellent swimmers. And although we hear that they are not good tree climbers, they can scramble up a tree by grabbing the branches to a good ten to thirteen feet, with a record of a thirty-three foot climb. The young are well able to climb. Compared to the black bears, however, grizzly claws are better adapted for digging rather than for climbing. Some of their principle food, such as roots and tubers, lies underground. Bears are exceedingly keen in their senses of smell and hearing.

Temperamentally, grizzly are unpredictable, and they can be very aggressive. Males will eat young cubs given the opportunity, but the female is ferociously protective.

In the wild they have been known to live fifteen to thirty-four years, and have survived forty-seven years in captivity. They are generally healthy into old age, but arthritis, liver problems or loss of teeth may occur. The worst dangers they encounter include hunters, injury, other grizzlies and the threat of starvation.

The tracks of the grizzly have diagnostic features, but are not always distinguishable from large black bear tracks. The size of the adult grizzly tracks can exceed that of the largest black bear tracks, but those of the female grizzly cannot always easily be distinguished from the adult black bear on the basis of size. The claw marks of the grizzly extend much further from the toe pad than do the claw marks of the black bear. Front claw marks are rarely less than 1½ to 1¾ inches distant from the toe pad; they are most often between 1½ and 4 inches. Hind claw marks are from about ½ to almost 2 inches from the toe pads. Grizzly toes are straighter across and their toes are closer together than the black bear's. The black's toes form more of an arch and thus a straight rule across the leading edge of the heel pad and base of the large outer toe will cut above the center of the small inside toe, but fall below the center of the inside toe of the grizzly. In the hind foot of the black bear, a wedge frequently shows in the instep, which is absent from the grizzly foot and track; and the grizzly registers a more pointed heel.

The speed of the grizzly can be fifty meters in three seconds (or thirty-seven miles per hour). It can shuffle at six miles per hour, and over rough terrain has been known to cover twenty-one miles in an hour. A subadult has been known to go thirty-six miles per hour.

ANTELOPE

1. Split hoof of the Pronghorn in soft soil near Millican, Oregon.
2. The heel pad of the Pronghorn is wider at the base than the Mule Deer.

CARIBOU

3. Caribou tracks in Gakona, Alaska.
4. Caribou tracks. Note the unusual dew claw marks.

Photos: Author

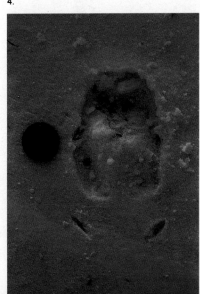

BADGER

1. Badger track in mud in the Ochoco Mountains of Oregon.
2. Badger track on roadway showing claw marks.
3. The five-toed badger marks on soft Central Oregon soil.
4. A badger peers from his den on Big Prairie in Glacier National Park.
5. A partial badger skull.

Photos: Author

BEAVER

1. Front track of beaver at Smith Rocks State Park, Oregon.
2. This track shows movement in the toes of the beaver.
3. The rear track of beaver in mud.
4. A beaver raised and slapped his tail down as he pushed a log.
5. Beaver-felled tree in Montana.

Photos: Author

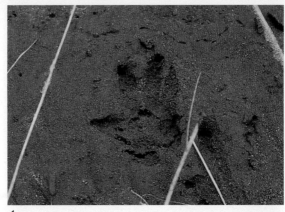

1.

2.

3.

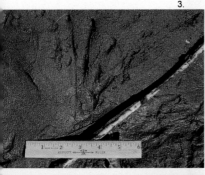

4.

5.

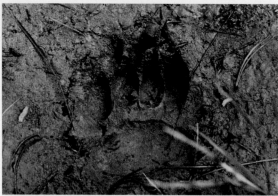

BLACK BEAR

1. Left front track of a black bear.
2. Front track of a black bear.
3. Front and rear tracks of a black bear.
4. Right hind track of a black bear. Note instep notch.

Photos: Author

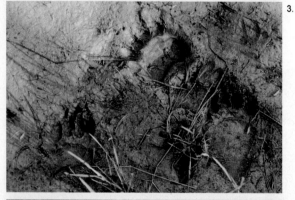

GRIZZLY BEAR

1. Grizzly front track in Montana.
2. Grizzly front and hind tracks in Montana.
3. Cast of a Montana grizzly track.
4. Grizzly skull from West Glacier Ranger Station, Glacier National Park.
5. Grizzly bear claws on display at St. Mary's entrance to Glacier National Park.
6. Tree used by grizzlies for generations, Avalanche Lake trail, Glacier National Park.

Photos: Author

1.

BIRDS

1. Canada goose tracks in mud.
2. Chukar tracks in snow, Eastern Oregon.
3. Chuckar tracks along the John Day River, Eastern Oregon.
4. Bald eagle casting below a nest.
5. Ruffed grouse tracks near Sisters, Oregon.
6. Pileated woodpecker work, British Columbia.
7. Pygmy owl which drowned in my stock tank.
8. Quail track in my roadway.
9. Wild turkey track in Central Oregon.
10. Chukar tracks in snow along the John Day River, Oregon.

Photos: Author

2.

3.

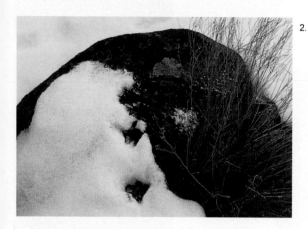

4.

5.

7. (above) & 8.

9. & 10. (below)

6.

COUGAR

1. Careful placement of the cougar's feet in dust.
2. Cougar track. The scallop on the posterior of the heel pad does not always register.
3. Cougar scratch, likely a scent spot.
4. Walking tracks of a cougar near Sisters, Oregon.
5. Cougar claws where it climbed a Ponderosa pine.
6. Cougar scat at the edge of its territory.

Photos: Author

4.

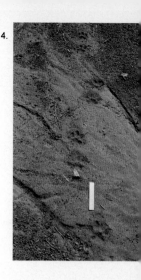

1.

5.

2. & 3. (below)

6.

1.

4.

COYOTE

1. Coyote track in the clay riverbank of the North Fork of the Flathead River, Montana.
2. Coyote track in Central Oregon dust.
3. Coyote track in snow.
4. Coyote dens near Wildhaunt.
5. Rocks provided the den for the coyotes where I saw the pup with the white-tipped tail.
6. Typical twisted coyote scat.

Photos: Author

2. & 3. (below)

5. & 6. (below)

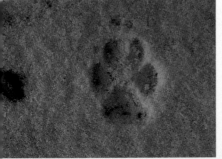

MULE DEER

1. Drag marks of the mule deer in deep snow. Note the wide straddle.
2. A mule deer bounded here. Note the globule of snow thrown forward from the left rear foot in the direction of travel.
3. A doe mule deer track. Note the rear track marking on the front track, and its outward position.
4. Running tracks of deer in moist desert sand.
5. Mule deer track showing the dew claw marks in soft soil.
6. Deer mouth marks as it stopped to eat snow.

Photos: Author

4.

1.

2.

3.

5.

6.

1.

4.

ROCKY MOUNTAIN ELK

1. Large elk track in Montana.
2. Elk track in dust in Central Oregon. Note the smoothed soil which reflects the sun and creates shine.
3. Elk track in moist desert soil.
4. Photo reflects the rear foot position imposed on the front track.
5. Elk biting on the alder tree in the Ochoco Mountains of Oregon.
6. Elk scat.

Photos: Author

2. & 3. (below)   5. & 6. (below)

GRAY FOX

1. Tiny gray fox track in mud at the head of the Little Deschutes River south of Bend, Oregon.

RED FOX

2. Running tracks of a red fox on hard-packed beach sand, Washington. The extension of the toes and claw marks indicate the running gait of this red fox.
3. Four feet come together in the gallop of the red fox.
4. Red fox track on Fort Worden Beach, Washington.

Photos: Author

2.

3.

For its size, the lynx has large feet. Its broad, furred paws are an important adaptation for snow travel; these "snowshoes" enable the lynx to travel over deep snow in search of food.

Compare the size of your palm to the paw print of the lynx and see how it "sizes up" against those of America's other native cats.

1.

LYNX

Lynx track from a lynx at Northwestrek Wildlife Refuge near Eatonville, Washington. This track was made by a captive lynx in Washington. Chart indicates the relative sizes of the wild cat family.

MUSKRAT

Muskrat track at Cherry Creek, eastern Oregon.
Muskrat track beside coyote tracks, John Day River, Oregon.
Muskrat tracks, John Day River, Oregon.

Photos: Author

4.

BOBCAT	LYNX	COUGAR
Although the lynx is only slightly larger and heavier than the bobcat, the paw prints of the lynx are double the size of the bobcat's tracks.		The tracks of the lynx rival those of the cougar—a cat which is 6 to 7 times heavier than the lynx.

6.

5.

MINK

1. Running track of a mink at the edge of Suttle Lake, Oregon.
2. Mink tracks in mud at Smith Rocks, Terrebonne, Oregon.
3. Tiny mink tracks show their busy comings and goings.
4. Mink scat, in its usual location.
5. The tiny skull of an unfortunate mink.

Photos: Autho

MOOSE

1. Moose track in deep mud near Libby, Montana.
2. Moose track showing the dew claws in Montana mud.
3. Moose track at Downie Creek, British Columbia.
4. Tracks of moose at Tok, Alaska. Note the crisp, frozen snow.
5. Winter moose scat in Montana.

Photos: Author

3. & 4. (below)

6.

MOOSE

6. Cow moose at Northwestrek, Washington.
7. Cow moose and calf at Northwestrek, Washington.

Photos: Author

7.

1.

PORCUPINE

1. The rear track of a porcupine overlapping the smaller front foot track. The wider part of the track is at the front, and soil has fallen into the claw marks.
2. The rear track of a porcupine at the top of the photo, and the front foot track below.
3. Porcupine and deer track in snow.

2.

3.

PORCUPINE

4. Porcupine track in deep snow. The direction of travel is to the right.
5. Albino porcupine mount at the Fossil Museum in Oregon.
6. Fleeing porcupine racing up a Ponderosa pine, Ochocos, Oregon.
7. Winter porcupine scat shows its woody composition.
8. Porcupine skull, retrieved after a predation, Central Oregon.

Photos: Author

1.

RACCOON

1. Raccoon tracks in mud Central Oregon.
2. Front foot track of raccoon in Eastern Oregon.
3. Rear track of raccoon near Mitchell, Oregon.
4. Front and rear tracks of raccoon in usual position, Yosemite National Park.
5. Raccoon and deer track near Corvallis, Oregon.
6. Raccoon front track

Photos: Author

2.

3.

5.

4.

6.

SNAKES

1. Gopher snake, Oregon.
2. The rattler that made tracks on Green Ridge, Sisters, Oregon.
3. Rubber boa, Wildhaunt.
4. Common garter snake, Priest Lake, Idaho.
5. Rattlesnake track, Green Ridge, Sisters, Oregon.

Photos: Author

SQUIRRELS

1. Gray squirrel tracks of a running squirrel. The long, rear tracks mark forward of the front tracks.
2. Gray squirrel tracks in snow.
3. Snow tracks of the gray squirrel show the larger rear tracks preceding the front foot tracks.
4. Chickaree tracks are smaller and more closely grouped than the larger gray squirrel tracks.
5. Red squirrel in snow.

Photos: Author

3.

4.

5.

1. & 2.

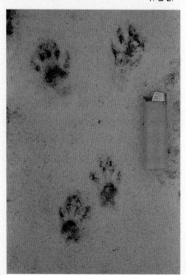

LONG-TAILED WEASEL

1. Bounding weasel tracks show the larger foot tracks behind the tiny front foot tracks, and the tail drag. The weasel was going to the left of the photo.
2. Long-tailed weasel mount in Fish and Wildlife offices, Bend, Oregon.
3. Weasel scat in a prominent location, typical of the weasel family.

Photos: Author

4. & 5.

WOLF

1. Front track of the black wolf I saw near the Montana/Canadian border.
2. Wolf track five inches long.
3. Front and rear wolf tracks in British Columbia.
4. Wolf track in mud showing the smaller rear track at the top of the photo.
5. Wolf pup in a wildlife refuge in South Dakota. Note the blue eyes.

Photos: Author

1.

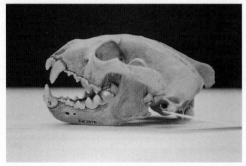

4.

5.

WOLVERINE

1. Wolverine reverse cast.
2. Wolverine cast imprint in desert soil. It is two and three-quarters inches wide and long, a small wolverine track, seen on the banks of John Day River, Eastern Oregon.
3. Wolverine cast imprint showing the size.
4. The feet on this adult wolverine mount are only slightly over two inches wide, but their tracks would mark larger in most soils.
5. Oregon wolverine skull. This wolverine was killed in a government trapper's coyote snare. It was within a few miles of the wolverine track I found at the John Day River, and within a month or so of the discovery. I believe it to be the same wolverine.

BOBCAT

1. Track in Central Oregon sand, note the leading front toe.
2. Bobcat tracks in clay, front track is on the bottom.

Photos: Author

1.

2.

1.

OPPOSUM

1. Opposum track, Corvallis, Oregon.
2. Opposum skull.

RABBIT

3. Front foot track of a jackrabbit.
4. The two front foot tracks of a jackrabbit.

Photos: Author

2.

3.

4.

Chapter Five

The Deer Family
Cervidae

MULE DEER
Odocoileus hemionus

The mule deer's large eyes watch you with absolute, undivided attention. This docile and curious deer inhabits a variety of terrain where browse is available: from wooded and mountainous areas to desert, chaparral and grassland country. If you are fortunate, they may graze near you for awhile before bursting off, bounding beyond view very quickly.

The microenvironment for the mule deer in the Northwest is in both heavily forested coniferous areas and in the high desert more than 3,500 feet. As with most ungulates, cover is essential for survival, and even the fairly open deserts of Oregon and Washington have sage and rolling hills where mule deer survive.

Although mule deer can jump ten feet or more, you learn the ground cues to watch for this, their individual ways, and how they browse on the bitterbrush and juniper boughs. It is exciting to find fresh deer track. Feel the freshness of the track with your fingers. One deer is easy to track, but three or four test any tracker's skills. Pick one deer's track out of four where they walked together, following each other. The buck's track differs from that of the doe. His heavier chest is broader than his hips, and he carries antlers most of the year. This is reflected on the ground by a set of front tracks that are broader apart than the rear tracks. This, with the added weight of his antlers and chest, causes his feet to splay outward. The bucks with the heaviest antlers have the greatest outward pitch. The doe, on the other hand, has hips broader than her chest area, and she registers greater width between her rear tracks than between her front tracks. This can be seen, however, only in the normal walk on level ground, for slopes and fast gaits change this. Deer have individual walk patterns as do humans. In Oregon, I tracked a mule deer doe whose right rear hoof splayed out with a distinct, abnormal pitch, probably from some injury. It was during a workshop. The group had been evaluating track measurements, age and sex differences. One observant student noticed the unusual pitch to the right rear track of a mule deer, so we continued to track the doe for a distance, noticing the consistency so we knew that we would know this deer again. We were also able to evaluate the rear hoof placements on the outside of the straddle. In one instance on another deer's tracks we were able to ascertain that front foot pitches were made quite consistently on level ground and that we were certain that we were tracking a buck. The difficulty comes with young buck who carry light-weight antlers. Where I see these and track them, it is a fine judgment call on the sex as far as the pitch of the front tracks. Once the hooves pitch out sufficiently to distinguish the buck from a doe, they seem to carry the pitch during the months when the antlers are shed as well. I encourage each student to make their own observations on this. My experience cannot be totally comprehensive and each tracker can learn some new cue, and contribute to the fund of information.

Early on sunny midwinter mornings in the Tumalo Winter Deer Range, with new laid snow crisp and sparkling, I walk to scan the white expanse, eagerly anticipating what I shall find. The maze of deer tracks cross and criss-cross in a myriad of directions, deep into the snow, the drag of deer hooves marking the snow before sinking to make a definite track. The feel of the deer's presence is active in the snow, the freshness of their tracks impinging upon my senses, and I walk among them pleased to be where I am. From the flat ground I can glance up and often see them on the slope of the ridge where they take one or two main trails. Sometimes they are bedded in certain places in the sun to chew their cud. They are used to my presence, and if I do not move too quickly they do not move, but look at me expectantly. If they do startle it is just for a few feet, and then they turn to stare to see what I will do next. I might say a greeting and pass on looking for coyote track next. Early in my experience I was tracking three deer for about half a mile in soft Oregon ground, managing to discriminate one deer's tracks from the others where they crossed and overlapped. The tracks were indeed fresh, and as I tracked I began to realize how fresh. The last tracks I saw I certainly did not have to feel, and

I felt as though the deer were there. It was such a definitive judgment, I slowly raised my head to glance ahead. There they stood, less than fifty feet away, looking at me. Closeness to the track gives you a view of its life, its creation, its experience and its age. It tells you when the animal was there, what it did, where to go to find the creature, and a rough idea of how long that might take. These fresh tracks glowed with their immediacy. The deer moved on, and I relished the opportunity to be so close.

One recent evening as I sat on my deck I heard a loud, long wheeze, much louder than a doe warning her fawn. Some movement became apparent through the juniper at a salt lick. Another loud wheeze came and then another. Suddenly from somewhere, about 100 feet away, a doe bounded across my view and all was still for a short while. Then suddenly loud stomping came from the lick, and within a minute another doe bounded across my view at the very same place as the first. I cannot tell you what was going on, for I puzzle still. Was the lick activity prompting the bounding of the deer elsewhere, or were they all unrelated? It was the noisiest and busiest evening at that lick that ever occurred. I suppose the dominance display of the noisy deer had ramifications all over a far area!

A mule deer met her death on the edge of my property one winter. I had tracked this deer in ice and snow, a solitary doe. At this time of year most deer are in groups, and I pondered on this. I do have an occasional lone doe, one which is never accepted for some reason or another by the other does. As I tracked, snowshoes crackling noisily as my weight broke through the crusts, I never expected to see the deer in spite of the freshness of the tracks. At last I did glance up to see her barely 150 feet away, browsing. I stood very still to observe, and she was quite unaware of my presence. After a while she lay down under a juniper, and a little later rested her head on the ground. I began testing my stalking skill, a real endeavor on snowshoes in this type of snow. As the snow was in slow melt, my standing on the snowshoes had partially frozen the shoes to the snow, and lifting them up made considerable noise. I kept my eyes on the doe. She never moved. I moved on, cautious, and to my astonishment she never moved. She dozed on and off, occasionally opening her eyes. As I found myself within fifty feet of her she just appeared to look at me, and closed her eyes again. I continued to move closer, concerned and puzzled. Within twenty or so feet she must have really noticed me, rose, bolted away, and off in the distance stumbled at a wire fence. Then my heart sank. She was alone for a reason. She was unable to keep up with the other deer due to her weakness. I felt ashamed and guilty for disturbing her.

Two days later I found her partial carcass where coyotes had found her the prior night, an eighth of a mile from where I had left her. Tracks revealed she had not had the energy to run. I am very careful now not to crowd lone deer into expending survival amounts of energy. However, it was apparent that this deer was well on the way to her demise.

One morning I was awakened very early at home by one of my dogs' barking. As I listened I determined she was standing still, but beyond the yard fence. As my dogs are fenced in, I was concerned as to how and why she was out. I reached the scene as soon as possible to discover that the dog had climbed the fence (an ability of hers), obviously at the sudden appearance of the doe I was viewing. The doe was standing, but barely, and heaving, on the verge of collapse. I called the dog to me, who was not out of breath, so I knew she had not run the deer. We stood off further from the doe, and she then felt safe enough to lie down. I believe I watched her for a half hour, and took the dog home to lessen the stress on the deer. In an hour I slowly ventured back, and she was gone. I tracked her slowly, wanting to be sure she was alright. Her tracks at first staggered and dragged some, and then her breath must have returned, for she continued on in a normal walk, browsing along the way. I cut for coyote or dog sign in a circle for an eighth of a mile but did not find any. Something had pursued her, and she survived another day.

After tracking and observing wildlife over the years, one develops keenness in catching the intent of the creature. I glanced out of my window one day recently to see a buck and doe approach my stock tank for water. I did not recognize the buck, and paid little attention to the doe, as I was learning the configuration of the buck's antlers should I see him again elsewhere. The doe I instinctively knew had been here as she was already to the water by this time, unafraid. But I was interested in the buck's behavior. I knew intuitively that this buck was on new ground. He was extremely alert and cautious, even more than bucks usually are. He behaved suspiciously, looking at his surroundings as though he had never seen them before. He stood, too unsure to approach the water to drink, tense, his eyes searching for any movement. He jerked once as though to flee, and then something, perhaps the flap of a small tarp or a sudden bird flight unnerved him totally and he bolted, the doe following. The next day I found his tracks, marking well as buck; his gait had been steady for a quarter of a mile up to my house, then beyond. He and the doe were en route somewhere else. I was sorry he had not gotten water.

I have nearly been run down twice in my lifetime by mule deer. Once while planting seed on my place, I heard crashing through the trees and looked up just in time to avoid being in the direct path of a running doe. She seemed bent on going as fast as she could, and she quite took my breath away as she passed within five feet. My son had been up further on the ridge and no doubt startled her enough to give her a good deal of concern, and thus my experience.

Another time I was tracking bobcat in Oregon. My dog was with me, only twenty feet or so away, and I heard this sound of hooves and crushing brush behind me. I turned in time to back up a little as a buck passed in front of me about three feet away. He was going as fast as possible, and I suppose that my dog may have worried him out of a day bed, and he took off, not even realizing some other creature was there. I really wondered if he had seen me at all.

Both of these deer gave me the impression that they were looking only forward, frightened, the only thing on their minds being to put space between them and the object of their fear. They made their way through the forest rather like a crashing airplane, obliterating the foliage as they went. I guess I was fortunate to have been able to avoid a collision.

One day I observed a mule deer buck for some time. He stood in ready anticipation of an enemy, eyes fixed upon the junipers but listening. Large mule deer ears pivoted, tuned to any unusual sound coming through the winds. His front legs stood taut, the tendons stretching in the first stage of flight. A hierarchy of points protruded from his head, rising into a symmetry of three-pronged antlers. Only his ears showed occasional motion. Heavy flanks under gray-blue hair bulged with the weight shifted to them in his readiness. The winds blew shiftily, swirling the cedars and pines, slapping scents against his wide black nostrils, and parting his hair like a spinning top. Finally, almost imperceptibly, his tenseness eased and he slowly strode forward to the water, and sank his mouth down to drink heavily. Unlike the edgy does of this rut, who sprang easily at the flick of a chickadee wing, this buck held his head down for long draughts of water. Then he raised his head. Satisfied he was alone, he again dipped deeply into the water. When he finally raised his head again, water dripped freely from his mouth, and he sensed all around him before backing away. No quick movement alerted friend or foe as he was absorbed into the foliage.

After he was gone I waited an hour, and then tracked him. His front tracks characteristically splayed out more than his hind tracks. He left the area very slowly. There was a slight rise in the ground and he took the usual deer trail for a short distance. Then he continued to meander through the brush, off the beaten trails to the south on lower, flatter ground, keeping within the brush. After a while I stopped tracking so I would not interrupt his tranquility by coming upon him at rest.

It is not so easy to come within twenty feet of a buck and I cannot boast of such prowess, for I had watched this buck from my cabin window as he drank from my water tank. It detracts from the mystique of the wild to admit this. I have many deer come up to the house for water, since I live on deer range. Twelve to nineteen does bunch together and then split repeatedly all winter, and in the summer those that stay are in small groups. I spend many hours observing them, and when they are away from the house I track them, cherishing their dignity and hoping they will always prosper near me.

Deer do unusual things at times, at least unusual to me. One day at a lake in northern California I had been observing a muskrat close to shore. It was at a point where a small stream entered the lake. I sat at the spot where I expected it to appear, and waited. I shortly thereafter heard a noise in the brush nearby. I watched and soon a doe appeared through the trees, cautious but not fearful. She moved in apparent ease, slowly, toward the little stream. It was overgrown with vegetation, and in her path a log lay at right angles to the flow of water, extending into the stream most of the way. It appeared to be a firm log about ten inches in diameter, covered with moss. It was undoubtedly wet and slippery. As this doe came on to drink there were numerous places she could have approached the stream from the bank to drink. However, I watched with amazement and some concern as she walked out onto the log, not gingerly, but confidently. She went to the end of the log and drank, and then quite gracefully managed to back off of the log and return into the brush. Those would have been a set of tracks to ponder over.

Another unusual behavior is the aggressive deer. In Sunriver, Oregon, outside of Bend, a deer made news in 1994. This deer appeared to be a doe, but could have been an antlerless buck. It attacked a woman in her yard. The deer was described as very ragged in appearance, and rushed the woman and knocked her down before she beat it off. Police searched for the deer without success, thinking they could identify the one. I was asked to assist the local nature center in tracking if another situation occurred, but nothing more came of it.

That deer can be aggressive and inflict severe wounds with their sharp hooves is well known. Many humans have experienced this in situations where deer have been cornered. But an unprovoked attack is quite unusual.

The Sunriver Nature Center director felt that the deer had likely been someone's pet which had been turned free. The poor condition of the coat supported this hypothesis, for the deer would likely have had an inadequate diet, malnutrition being reflected in an unhealthy coat.

Befriending wildlife by taking a young animal to raise as a pet is rarely helpful to the creature. It is inevitably a problem as an adult, and must finally be released. Not skilled in survival, it experiences the trauma of release, and will be easy prey for predators or starve. It is not always accepted into its own kin's fold. In the Sunriver case, however, the aggressive deer was seen with other deer.

A very long time after the dust has fallen into the tracks of a deer, there is another way I track them. I point my toes randomly upon the land, and search for shed antlers. They are in the thick brush and open sand, at the base of a tree or on a rocky outcrop, anywhere. I look for antlered trees where the bucks have rubbed, and near the beds where they have lain. I look along ditch banks and into manzanita thickets. When I find one, in my mind's eye I can see the buck, heavy in chest, worrying the antler by shaking his head, irritated by the shifting weight, pushing against a juniper trunk to rid himself of the bother. And there before my eyes lies the success of his efforts. There lies the antler where it fell upon its release. There was the buck.

The last antler I found was old, splintered and bleached. It lay face down. Rodents had gnawed at it for calcium, and the weather was disintegrating it. It was a thick antler, a four point. I looked for a little while, but did not find its mate. I stood where this buck had been many years before, and thought of the moment. His bones lie somewhere now, scattered, some eaten. He has gone into the earth to replenish it. The antler is his track.

I have taken a day now and then to search for nothing but antlers. They grace Wildhaunt, scattered among the forest debris. As I walk, my glances often catch the gnarled old sage trunks, and my heart gives a start, for they look so much like antler shapes and shine, my legs start to move toward them; then I realize it is the pseudoantler of the forest. One day I decided to look for a pair of fresh antlers, those dropped together, which are most difficult to find. I drove to an area where I had seen many buck through the years, and left my car. I made a large semicircle through the woods, meandering with the thought in mind that my feet and intuition would lead me to a pair of freshly shed antlers. I made almost a mile before I came back close to the road where I had left my car. I slowed, thinking that my fantasy had indeed misled me. I stopped within a couple of hundred feet of the road, and my disappointment surfaced. So I sighed, and looking to see where to step next, I glanced by my feet. There was a beautiful fresh antler, a three point. I joyously picked it up, and looked a few feet to my left, where lay its mate. It was an incredible experience.

Another time I found a pair of antlers was just off Wildhaunt's boundaries. Two very large antlers lay beside an old, fallen pine. One was quite unusual for a mule deer. It had one main beam, with tines running off it similar to the white-tailed deer, but the other antler was forked like the mule deer. This pair still lies in my yard, now weathered over a decade.

After a forest fire claimed twenty acres of Wildhaunt, I walked the ashes, in places still hot. I saw a blackened antler I had left there years before, and reached for it, happy to reclaim it. I lifted it waist high, and it crumbled in my grasp, splintered and powdered it fell again to the earth, now in full cycle.

***

The mule deer is reddish or yellow-brown in summer and a blue-gray in winter. It has a white throat patch, and the inside of the ears and legs are white, fading to a cream or tan on the legs. At the shoulder it is about three to three and a half feet tall, with large ears five to six inches in length, from which it derives its name. Its tail is five to nine inches in length, black-tipped and whitish above, against a white rump patch. This large deer weighs from 70 to 160 pounds if a female, and 110 to 475 pounds if a male. The buck can also sport antlers up to around 50 inches long. These branch equally on each side, and are covered with nourishing velvet with many blood vessels about five or six months of the year.

A buck's antlers vary in size due to age, heredity and nutrition. The light coming through his eyes stimulates the pituitary gland which releases testosterone into the bloodstream and causes the antlers to grow. In August or September the light diminishes and antler growth stops with the subsequent decrease of testosterone. Then in winter the antlers fall. Other factors interact as well. Older bucks shed their antlers sooner. Cooler weather may hasten the antler drop as well as greater breeding activity. Nonbreeding bucks have been known to carry their antlers into March and

April, whereas most lose theirs much earlier. Poor diet may also be responsible for late growing and late dropping.

Antlers usually grow seven or eight points, but may reach sixteen or so. Many abnormalities have been seen in shapes and the number of tines. Diet regulates the number of points, or tines, but young bucks usually grow spikes when they are young and start producing antlers at sixteen to eighteen months. Old bucks may again grow spikes, or not produce antlers at all due to deficient nutrition.

Bucks and does gather together for a breeding season of a few weeks in the fall, and usually are apart the remainder of the year. However, buck fawns may stay with the mother does into the winter and occasionally into the following spring. Some young bucks are isolate from other deer, particularly the older bucks. A winter group may number from a dozen to 250 or more deer. A doe bred her first year usually has one fawn, but older does may have twins, born about 196 days from conception, usually in May or June. The fawns walk quite promptly and weigh about eight pounds. The doe conceals her spotted fawn for the first month, and although she leaves it while browsing, its lack of scent, concealment and immobile behavior keeps predators from finding it. At the first year it is just less than adult size. Fawns recognize their mother by scent from her hind leg glands and find each other by scent from the toe glands.

Mule deer range from forty to 600 acres or more, depending upon food supply. They use common trails, and bed in sheltered places. They will feed on shrubs, twigs, grass, herbs, mushrooms and domestic crops. When they browse, they move slowly from shrub to shrub. They stay near water, although dew may supplement their needs for a day.

Deer are subject to predation by wolves, cougar, coyotes and bobcat. Winter snows, which hamper their movement, make deer vulnerable to large predators; usually the weaker deer are culled. A deer's hearing is extremely acute therefore its most protective sense. Its speed also provides a measure of protection, since healthy deer can outrun most predators over a distance.

In bad weather, deer may starve due to low temperatures and insufficient feed. After browse is gone, deer will ingest bark. Deer require ten to twelve pounds of browse daily but can survive on two to three pounds. They may not move for days if the temperature is severe, as their energy expenditure may exceed the nutritional value of the browse. After one-third of their body weight is lost, no available food can save a deer. Deer chew their cud as do cows. They have four sections of stomach. They have no gall bladder. In twenty-four to thirty-six hours food will pass through their system.

Deer have been known to survive an average of sixteen years if unmolested and have lived twenty-five years in captivity. Causes of death are man, disease and starvation.

WHITE-TAILED DEER
Odocoileus virginianus

The white-tailed deer has the widest range of American deer species, and is found, with the exception of some western states, throughout the entire United States and in Southern Canada. It is known by its long tail, the underside of which is white. When fleeing, the females hold their tail upright and wag it, thereby flashing a white signal. It is thought this signal alerts the fawns to follow and communicates the need to flee to others browsing in the area. The buck flashes his tail initially when taking off but he usually runs with his tail down.

The microenvironment for this deer is in timbered areas. They stay within five miles of water, and usually in hilly, mountainous terrain, with a lot of downfall. They use their speed as a survival skill, and they use secrecy, by hiding in dense cover.

My favorite place to track white-tail is along North Fork of the Flathead River in Glacier National Park. Patches of overgrown willows nestle among the sand and rocks along the streambank. I spotted some tracks in the damp sand and tried to ascertain how old they were. It is not always easy to age tracks, especially when the sand stays moist. I tracked one doe toward a thick willow clump. Instinctively I paused. She was lying in there. The tracks had appeared so fresh but I was not positive of their age. I went back and positioned myself when I had a view and waited several hours. Slowly, then, she finally appeared. My heart was gladdened. It was worth the wait, especially in such a fine setting, and helped me improve my tracking ability.

A white-tailed doe I passed one day in Montana exhibited a decided reluctance to leave. I would have expected her to flee at the nearness of my presence, but she did not. I was on a road and she was about seventy-five feet away, browsing in an open field. After I passed, I wondered more and more why she was so incautious, so I returned to see what she would do. She still almost stood her ground, moving only a little in an uncomfortable manner. I concluded that as it was fawning time, she probably had a fawn nearby and did not want to leave until absolutely necessary. Deer's behavior is always purposeful, and one must consider what those reasons are, for they are necessary for the animal.

A part of tracking that challenges me but is very sad is the last behavior of the deer before it meets its demise from a predator. This is usually difficult to ascertain, for the immediate kill spot is quite a mess, and the carcass of the deer is at times dragged some distance, depending upon the predator. In Glacier National Park a white-tail I found, which met her fate by wolves, was in an area with which I was very familiar. It was a favorite daytime spot for deer to bed, and I have only to assume that the beds there were in use at night as well. In the case of this particular white-tail, the kill spot was beside a tree in moderately high ground cover, but open for almost fifty feet around a small clump of trees. A few of the deer's tracks remained leading to the spot, and they appeared to be walking tracks, those made when the deer moved to the spot, probably to lie down. The wolves' tracks obliterated all other tracks in the immediate vicinity. I concluded that this deer was ambushed at her resting spot. She no doubt heard the approach of the wolves but it did not appear that she was able to flee any distance.

On the other hand, a mule deer in Oregon met death from coyotes. In this instance the deer was running for some distance. I tracked back almost a quarter-mile and she had been running before that. At the point where she was finally attacked by the coyotes, she must have been so fatigued she tripped on a single line of sagging fence wire and went down, not to rise again. The event had occurred the night before and her remains included only the tail, one foreleg and the bladder. I never found any other part of that deer, including the skull, although I made a search in a half-mile radius for a number of days, amazed at the rapidity of nature's efficiency.

***

The white-tail is smaller than the mule deer. A buck stands up to forty inches high at the shoulders and is ninety-five inches long. The color of their bodies is tawny to orange/cinnamon or reddish in summer, and gray brown in some winter areas. The underparts are white including the tail, chin, throat, muzzle ring and band around the eyes. Some white-tail have black on the top length of the tail as well, sometimes extending onto their backs. Their voice is the same as other deer, snorts, blows and bleats. The white-tail can run thirty-five to forty miles per hour, but sustains twenty to twenty-five miles per hour much better. Walking, it does three to four miles per hour, and it can trot continually at ten to twelve miles per hour. Although it can swim thirteen miles per hour for as far as five miles, it really is not a strong swimmer, and drowns easily. However, it has been reported to have been seen five miles out in the Atlantic Ocean.

The white-tailed deer frequents woodland edges, swamps, river bottoms or high country meadows, utilizing a great variety of habitats. It stays within a mile of where it was born, although in some areas elevation migration may occur, due primarily to adverse weather. This may even be ten to seventy miles. In winter weather they may group together, called "yarding," but stay within a quarter of a mile of cover. They are very reluctant to leave familiar territory even when very hungry.

During breeding, a doe of six to seven months or older comes into estrus twenty-four to thirty hours in mid-November or mid-December. If not bred, she cycles into estrus one or two more times, and may breed as late as February. A buck will service only three or four does during the estrus periods. Interbreeding with mule deer has occurred and the offspring are usually, but not always, infertile. The offspring will have antlers of one species but the body features of the other species, and the tail and rump areas will have confusing features.

In about May or June fawns are born, usually a single fawn to a first-bred doe, and twins to the older bred does. Triplets, quadruplets and quintuplets have been on record, although anything more than triplets is a rare event. The five- to eight- pound fawn comes to his feet about an hour after birth and nurses eight to ten times in a twenty-four-hour period. The doe makes the fawn stay down, and it instinctively remains immobile until the mother returns. Lacking scent, it is protected from predators to a large extent. However, at seven days it will run if discovered. The fawn is weaned in September and may stay with its mother the first year and sometimes into the following fall. At that time the mother doe breeds again and the fawns usually seek the company of their own sex. The doe fawns may regroup with the mother doe after her next fawning, but the bucks group with other bucks. In winter and spring, all ages and sexes will group together. Bucks are isolate for the remainder of the year, until the rut. Young bucks stay in the areas established as yearlings.

ELK
Cervus elaphus

Who has not been lifted in spirits and awed by the bugle of the elk, and stared at the sight of his majestic, uplifted head and towering antlers?

Who, in the densest of the steep mountains has not held his breath at every step anticipating the fresh track of elk, and glanced to see its maker?

The microenvironment for the elk is in fairly high elevation areas of timber or partly open areas. In Northwest Oregon they are found from 3,500 foot levels to the highest timbered areas. They also roam the high desert which is primarily juniper and sage growth, and quite open. As elk were originally plains creatures, that is not so surprising. Some elk were introduced into Oregon's southwest mountains, and Oregon has both Rocky Mountain and Roosevelt elk near the coast.

I enjoy tracking elk, since their large hooves mark clearly in most terrain, and I can track at a fast clip. Running behind an elk puts the tracker into the feel of the animal and I can almost become one with the elk, in some sense. These are the moments I love most and probably my strongest reasons for tracking. Most of the time when elk are moving on, I never seem to get to the end of their trail, and have to eventually discontinue, wondering where they are, wishing for more daylight.

I once tracked a cow elk who crossed my land. She had followed the fence line and paused many times to think about jumping only to back off. A heavy animal, an elk does not like to expend the energy required to jump a fence. When they do jump, they manage it with grace and ease. I have seen elk go back and forth for twenty or more minutes before deciding to jump. This cow went almost a mile along an old homesteader's barbed wire fence. In another quarter of a mile she found the wire down and so was able to avoid a jump.

This same fence line provided another tracking scene for me one summer. My dog, who was in the house with me, started up and barked, listening intently. Of course she often does this when wildlife pass near. I dismissed the incident, as I was expecting a visitor, and went down to unlock the gate. There in the dust were very fresh elk tracks crossing the drive. Excitedly I backtracked to see from which direction she had been moving, and then tracked forward. It was easy and fast across the sparsely vegetated sand. As she was climbing the ridge I could not make out for awhile that it was a cow. As with all the elk which come across my land, this one was proceeding purposefully, as though she knew where she was going. The tracks reflected a constant speed, and I was waiting, amused to see what she would do when she reached the three strands of wire fence on my north border. The year before a cow elk had come this very way and taken out the fence in a jump. I wondered if this could be that cow.

The cow reached the fence and, typically, did not want to jump it, though it was only three-and-half-feet high. I tracked her along the fence line, seeing where once she stopped to think over a jump, discarded the thought, and continued along the fence. By this time I was directly north of my cabin, and the dog's bark came back to mind. It had been the elk, 700 feet from the house. If only I had rushed out in the right direction and seen her.

The elk continued on, and I needed to return to the gate to welcome my guest. Later I tracked her on for another mile where she found a place with the wire down, and she headed north.

I had tracked an elk along the same fence another time going in the same direction, when I suddenly realized I had lost the track. I back-tracked a few feet and there they were, four feet digging into the dirt, and splattering earth around. It was a crowded spot, trees and brush, and taut wire. She had stood there on my side of the fence and jumped. I was totally surprised at her choice of spot, knowing the ease elk like. Perhaps she heard something which gave her no choice. This elk went north, also, into better elk habitat.

For years elk have come through my land all year. I surprised three elk once and was interested in their startled tracks. They jumped about a dozen times, revealing bounds like the mule deer. At times they broke this pattern and galloped, then jumped again. The jumps were nine and three-quarter feet in distance. There were many beds in the area. They never used my water tanks, however.

During the remaining four-foot snow pack of the 1992–93 winter in central Oregon, I had elk within fifty feet of the house and still find a profusion of scat everywhere.

One elk I tracked was near home in December, 1990. A fire had burned more than 2,500 acres of national forest and private land in July of that year, taking fifteen to twenty acres of my old pine and juniper. I had little time for tracking in trying to rehabilitate the land, but took an hour or two to walk west into the burn area one day. I was searching for wildlife activity in a burn area.

So this clear, cool and snowless day I hardly expected to find elk track. A mile from home they shouted at me from the ash. The ash was very black, and on the edge of the burn it mingled with the earth. It was here I first saw the lone elk track. As I tracked, joyous to see the elk return, I watched for front hoof pitch to assess whether this could be a bull. The ground was bare ash with scattered, charred bitterbrush stumps, dead crisp juniper and pine with rusty colored needles, and bulldozed roads from the fire crews. No one was around. The land which had been heavily wooded gave stark silhouette in its openness. As I tracked it soon became apparent I was following a cow elk. I bent at the first tracks and occasionally soon thereafter to look at the soil and the disintegration of the track. Crumbling and some drying had occurred from the night's humidity; there had been some dampness in the soil. The track edges were fairly sharp with little smoothing, and the crumbling was minimal from gravity, a light breeze and the morning sun; relatively no debris was present in the track. I felt some more of the tracks. Along with the contrast and shine in the line of tracks ahead, the earth was soft to the touch. This elk had been here within twelve hours at the most, and quite likely even six or so hours prior. A lot of the time I had from ten to twenty-five feet of tracks visible ahead of me, and where the sheen and depression were easy to see, tracking was quick. Depending upon my interest, mood and the time, I made an early decision as to one of several goals, to go as quickly and as far as I could on the spoor, to evaluate the age, sex and behavior of the quarry, or to leisurely enjoy the way and pick up all the detail possible on the tracks. If the animal is a denning predator I may go slowly to ascertain whether there are young, if the animal is hunting, passing through, marking the area frequently with scat, or various other interesting angles that might arise with the clues I find. This time I wanted to see where the elk had chosen to go, if I could cut sign of other elk, and what the elk had done as related to the burn area. I had not tracked wildlife in a fresh burn area before. I wondered if she would turn into the unburned sections.

So off I tracked as quickly as I could, forgoing the detail of aging. The large hooves cut deeply into the soil and her stride was quite consistent, indicating a steady pace. She was walking fast, with purpose reflected from her spoor. There were cuts of green growth she passed through, and her path lay primarily on the forest edge, not going into the greenery and not venturing far from it. I wondered if she was taking an old route which had relatively nothing to do with the condition of the area after the fire, or if she wanted to remain close to heavier cover. I had no idea if she had been in this area previously.

The terrain was primarily level in the first half mile or more, and then rose slightly as a beginning elevation rise toward the Three Sisters. It then leveled and rose in slight ridges as it began its slow climb. The elk had been taking a fairly straight course south. As I climbed into the second mile she was gradually veering southwest, all in steady pace, and she was moving out of the burn areas. When I track this far I begin to realize, with this kind of behavior, that I am in for a long trip. The elk had not browsed or attempted to graze on the edge of the green. She was going somewhere. She was not exploring or bedding, so why was she here, alone? I paused at a high point and scanned the mountains and the forests of trees ahead. I glanced at the probable trail the elk chose ahead. I wanted to go all day and the next day and really find out where she went and what she did. I knew it would be a long trail. I was not prepared. I looked long and hard in her direction before I turned. I even walked on a short ways further, hoping to convince myself if it would work to just go on and never stop. I feel that way when I track any wildlife. One day I am sure I will just go on.

So I turned back, leisurely, backtracking here and there for practice, working again on a difficult spot where I had had to spend some time. So I just enjoyed the remainder of the day. When I came to the first track I had encountered, I was only a mile from home and I had to backtrack awhile to see which direction she had come from. Then I went home. The mystery unsolved only engenders keener needs for the next time.

I have been fortunate to find many elk. In the Ochocos, in Oregon, I had just camped in the fall and walked out to see what next was in store for me. I came upon elk track very soon along a trail in thick trees. The tracks were both old and fresh. The Ochocos here are spotted with both small and large openings, and soon the timber thinned out on the edge of a small opening. I looked to the ground to see how fresh the tracks were, for I was moving with those fresh tracks. I stopped and waited to listen and watch, and think. I searched the edges of the break, but saw no obscured, whitish rump of elk, no flicking ear to throw a fly, nor heard brush snap, nor soft call. Nevertheless I waited, perhaps to outwait another creature, perhaps to rest, enjoy, to dream. Then I casually tracked the several elk into the opening, watching very little ground but mainly the trees and space ahead. Beyond the opening the trail went through another line of trees I stalked through. Elk will often walk and watch you in order to decide whether to leave. I proceeded slowly, stopping, watching, listening. The tracks were fresh enough to be shortly behind the makers. And as I stepped into a broken opening, there they stood, 100 feet ahead, a young bull and three cows. The bull and a cow looked at me, unconcerned, but observing. The other cows were feeding on brush and grasses, standing still. I stood until the bull and nearest cow put down their heads to graze. Then I began a stalk, but reconsidered. Near rutting time they all are more edgy. The bull could certainly become irritated. I wanted to go close enough for a fair photo. I moved in a natural and easy manner in their general direction, but not in a direct line toward them. And I moved beside the trees where I felt safer. The young bull noticed me again, and kept glancing toward me as I approached. I took several photos, the noise not bothering them. Then I paused. The two forward cows had moved on a little, but the bull and the other cow had hardly moved. I knew from their posture they were leery of the short space between us, and the glances from the bull made me wonder if he was considering coming my way. I stayed still, ready to retreat. The group moved forward in haste, up a ways on a steep rise and into the trees. I became braver and went on. By the time I approached that area, they were further into the trees and I left.

A close look I had of a spotted elk calf was also in the Ochocos one spring. I had walked through an area with large openings, and I saw a cow elk feeding in the opening. She did not move as I passed within 100 feet and that should have given me a clue that she had a calf near. I gave her space and walked on through a treed area toward a creek. I noticed the tree barks ahead had been bitten by elk, and I moved a little quicker to get to them for photographs. My attention had thus waned, and it was unfortunate, for otherwise I might have been alert enough to spot the calf while it was lying still in the foliage. But the sudden bolt of the calf was within four feet, and I did get a good look, so close, but not long enough. It would have been a great photograph—another one that got away. Some lessons need to be learned more than once.

In Montana, elk came to a salt lick of mine along with Jersey heifers. Pregnant elk cows crave salt. The tracks of the adult elk were absolutely indistinguishable from the heifers. Tracking to ascertain the behavior of the animal was the best way to make the determination. In addition, however, the straddle of the elk was narrower than those of the cows.

I have witnessed cows and calves migrating in the spring to the higher elevations of northwest Montana. The sounds and sight of these many animals calling back and forth is an event to behold.

One evening before dusk I was on my front lawn in Montana when some familiar sound reached me, the high pitched squeal of elk. I resided some miles from others, and elk were commonly around the house. I immediately became aware of more sounds, the sound of many animals walking through the brush. Not ten or twenty, but many. The hum of the approaching vocalizations made a background of constant noise from which the sharp, frequent notes of elk emerged. Along with the plodding of many hooves on the ground and bodies pushing each other, the din of noise grew. And then one by two by four, they appeared. They were walking slowly, grazing and browsing a little as they passed within 100 feet or so. The calves were collecting close to the bodies of their cows, bouncing between the larger cows, behaving like babies of any species. At times a few would nurse briefly before the cow moved on. The calves uttered their bawling and cries, and I stood transfixed at the scene. As well as I could estimate from the noise and numbers I saw, there could have been well over 100 elk. To have this pass before my eyes, right at home, was the most surprising wildlife event for me. The herd was in a symphonic, coordinated movement, spread fluidly across the forest. Calf bleats and cow grunts and high-pitched calling all blended into an artistic scenario. And then they passed through, the noise becoming fainter, until the last flanks of cow and calf disappeared, and the brush and trees were still. In awe I sat for sometime, hardly believing my experience. I finally remembered the tracks. Yes, of course, the tracks....

***

High in the mountainous northern country of the United States and some parts of southern Canada, including Vancouver Island, this larger member of the deer family is found. Elk dwell in semiopen forests, foothills, plains and valleys, and in the mountain meadows in the summer. Reddish brown hair with a pale yellowish white rump is their distinctive coloration. Their white tail is 3⅛ to 8⅜ inches. The bull also has a throat main, and sports large antlers, a record 74 inches of main beam, with 6 tines on each antler side at maturity. Bulls weigh 25 percent more than cows, reaching 600 to 1,089 pounds. They stand 4 to 5 feet at the shoulder and reach 6¾ to 9¾ feet in body length.

In the lowland during the breeding season in the fall, the bulls and cows congregate, a bull seeking a harem of up to sixty cows. Elk are the most polygamous deer in North America. The rest of the year the bulls are quite solitary, and cows may group in small numbers or with the young of the year. During breeding, the bulls fight for the cows until they are exhausted, never eating or sleeping while they defend a herd of cows. The bulls roll in mud, urinate on vegetation and toss brush on their antlers, all to spread their scent to attract cows, and possibly to give notice to other bulls that they are claimants to the area and the cows.

A female breeds at two and a half years. After a gestation period of 255 to 275 days, one to two calves are born in the spring. They weigh twenty-five to forty pounds, born in a spot away from the herd. In a week they rejoin other cows, and the newborn suckles for about nine months. In the spring, cows and calves herd together to seek the high elevations as the vegetation greens.

Elk use a territory of several square miles and migrate to and from upper elevations. The bulls rub their antlers on tree trunks to rub off the velvet covering in the fall or late summer, and to further spread their scent. They also strip bark from the trees to eat. Elk are grazers, eating grass, and are never far from water. They will also browse from trees at times. Their hearing is their keenest sense, and next their sense of smell, and then their sight. They stay away from humans unless it is to feed on domestic haystacks. Temperamentally, they are seclusive and fearful, but can demonstrate an aggressiveness if threatened or if protecting young. They may grind their teeth in warning. The bull's high-pitched bugle is well known, starting low and ending with low-toned grunts. The bulls bugle their presence and challenge to other bulls during the rut, and this spectacular sound can be heard long distances. Other sounds than the bulls' bugles are the cows' high-pitched squeals or barks, and the bull also has these calls. At times the cow even bugles.

Cougar, bear and man prey upon elk, and they may live fourteen years in the wild. In captivity they have survived to twenty-five years of age.

PRONGHORN
Antilocapra americana

Like a tornado, the antelope crosses the open plains of the west, appearing and disappearing among the gentle slopes that rise and fall in its habitat. Streaks of tan and white colors typify the running antelope, and it is a wonder that their numbers once reduced dramatically, for their speed should keep them from harm. Today we can see more of them, and they brighten the dull colors of the plains and forests where they are found. They also appear in the very southern tip of Saskatchewan.

The pronghorn is commonly called the antelope and achieves tremendous speeds on the open prairies and sagebrush plains and grasslands of the west. They also inhabit brushland and bunch grass areas. Their beautiful and striking appearance of rusty tan with a wide white chest and black horns mark well when they congregate in bands of different sexes, scattered in summer and in harems in the fall rut. In winter, 100 may compose a band. In the Pacific Northwest they are found in south-central

Washington, and central and eastern Oregon. They are also scattered around the western states in various places.

Once I was tracking and photographing badger tracks in the Ochocos of eastern Oregon when I noticed six or seven pronghorn enter the far side of a meadow about an eighth of a mile away. They were feeding briefly, and moving on, unaware of my presence. I carefully moved behind a large Ponderosa pine some feet away and, with it between us, peered carefully around the trunk. As they approached I was able to move to remain concealed. However, as they came directly toward me, I knew that if I moved I would reveal myself, so I had to become another tree, stock still. They were adult does with large fawns. As they came directly toward me, for a second or two I feared they would go on both sides of me before they picked up my scent and spooked. I simply did not want to interfere with my experience, so I stood my ground, breathing shallow breaths. They approached within twenty feet and still came on; fortunately they were all on one side of me. When the closest, a fawn, was about six feet away, she looked at me. Suddenly unnerved and uncertain about what she was seeing, she looked again, became agitated, then moved nervously ahead. The pronghorn next to her caught her fear, and then two more stopped and looked directly at me, the farthest ones oblivious of me. They decided I was not a tree, and they broke into a fast pace toward the shelter of pines ahead, contagion catching the others.

Knowing their number, it was not so difficult to sort out their tracks. The ground was scabby, many small rocks mixed in with the dirt, and the "pursuit" was fun. Where they had stopped to view me was evident, and where they had bolted forward the ground reflected it, with the earth thrown in both directions from their hooves in their quick getaway. They were not so frightened that they were anywhere near full speed, however. Their speed left distorted heel marks indistinguishable from the mule deer, so if I had seen only these marks I would have had to backtrack to be absolutely certain of their identity. Tracking over a distance, however, would show their continual movement while feeding, a characteristic of pronghorn over the more relaxed, stationary browse of mule deer. The total absence of dew claws in all tracks would also have been diagnostic.

Lone bucks are most fascinating to me. I have waited quietly with minimal movement in a spot where I thought a buck might appear. One day one did, and he came within 100 yards before becoming aware of me. He looked carefully at me and decided to leave, running quite fast, and disappearing across the horizon as he ran lower and lower below the slope where I was. Here were his tracks for me. I spent time assessing the slow natural tracks as he had approached me. I found the spot where he had become aware of me and just stood, and then with splattering ground burst into a lope, frightened, and headed out. The tracks clearly revealed his change of attitude. When tracking and finding this, one can be assured that something was amiss in the animal's life for him to have made such a drastic change of pace.

Long ago in my hunting years, a group of friends and I were in southeast Oregon hunting pronghorn. I had won a draw and so was the hunter in the group. Pronghorn tracks were all around, but I was not too knowledgeable on aging them at that time. Nor would that have been of much assist as the speed of the animal can take it very far very fast. So hunting consisted of sitting and waiting for the animals. When we tired of that we walked over a low rise and sat some more, for our movement would prevent any antelope coming within close range of us; and they would definitely move the opposite direction upon hearing us. Pronghorn were often in the distance but had not come our way. When we saw them we didn't move, for their keen eyesight would notice any movement.

Finally some pronghorn appeared rather suddenly, bucks as well. As one got close I shot but apparently only wounded him, and off he went. We followed, and fortunately he was not too far when we found him down. This was the saddest and most awful moment in my life. His large eyes looked at me, this gorgeous creature stared directly at me and I knew I had to kill him. It took all of my psychological strength to do that. And I have never cried so hard. I have his horns on my wall to this day as a reminder of my foolishness. I have never hunted since.

While on this hunt prior to the above incident, my hunting companions decided that they should move in a semicircle to try to move a herd of antelope in my direction. I was to position on the lower slope of a small rise with my head over the top to view the scene, and thus be in an advantageous position to shoot an antelope. They left me at the spot, and proceeded cautiously around to do their part. As I sat there, I realized that the pronghorn would not be aware of me, and I would be in direct line of their stampede. I reconsidered this maneuver, and vowed that my tombstone one day would read: Here lies Barbara, who was not trampled to death by a stampeding herd of antelope.

This little hunting episode was typical of the situations I found myself in, and it is no wonder I took to tracking. This way I can be fairly assured of being behind the animal.

Tracking pronghorn takes care. Their hooves mark very similarly to a deer, and their size is equivalent, but the rear border of their hind track is broader than that of a deer. The definitive distinction is the lack of dew claws in the pronghorn, which is an adaptation for speed. Thus, dew claws cannot mark on the ground in pronghorn tracks. Of course, dew claws do not always mark on the ground for deer, so tracking the animal is often necessary to establish which it is, pronghorn or deer. Strides of the pronghorn can reach twenty foot bounds, although a bound of twenty-seven feet has been recorded. The rear legs of this animal are paired most of the time, or more so than are the front feet.

In the wide open sageland of rolling hills and vast expanses, the pronghorn can easily appear or disappear, for as the land stretches out it is difficult to tell where it rises or falls until an object moves into or out of sight. Distances are hard to judge. Some of this sageland is also timbered, and pronghorn inhabit this, also, in semidense pine stands. Pronghorn are found in the Ochoco Mountains in eastern Oregon as well as in the wintering area of the desert plains east of Bend.

***

Pronghorn are long legged, 49–57 inches in total length, stand 35–47 inches in total height, stand 35–41 inches high at the shoulder, and in weight the males are 90–140 pounds, the females are 70–105 pounds. Coloration is a pale or reddish tan on their sides and upper body, with white on the chest, belly, rump and inner legs. They have black horns, with two lyre-shaped prongs. Bucks' horns are 12–20 inches long, and does' horns are 3–4 inches, usually without prongs. These horns have bone cores with horny sheaths of agglutinated hair. These are shed a month after breeding. Bucks have a short, erectile mane, absent in the female, and black lower jaw patches. Their coat of hair is hollow and this enables the animal to cool or insulate its body by flattening or ruffling the hairs against or away from its body.

The speeds of the pronghorn are phenomenal. They can maintain 30 miles per hour for 15 miles, and reach 70 miles per hour for 3 or 4 minutes. A buck has been clocked at 44 miles per hour beside a car, and a doe at 42 miles per hour. Their range is usually about 1–4 miles. In some areas they migrate between summer and winter feeding areas. Older males have more specific territories, but they are constantly ranging over their territories. They will scrape the ground and urinate there to spread their scent as a territorial mark. They number around half a million at present.

In September or October in the north, the doe of at least sixteen months and the slightly older buck breed, resulting in a delayed implantation of a month, and a seven-month gestation, 217 to 252 days. Births occur, depending upon location, in April in the south to June in the north. With a first breeding one kid is born; subsequently there can be twins and, rarely, triplets. The kid is 4½ to 9 pounds on the average when born, 23 inches long and 17 inches tall, and in a half hour will attempt to walk. The first week they lie still when the doe goes off to feed. Then the kids are situated 100 feet apart, and are odorless, to protect them from predators. They remain motionless. In one week the doe and kids join the band. Pronghorn are light feeders due to their need for speed as their protection. They graze on many plants, herbs, grass and cacti in summer, and in winter browse on sage primarily, about five pounds daily, and also on other plants. They may migrate 100 miles for food if necessary. They often seek wind-blown high elevations where plants are exposed. In summer, when moisture is in the green vegetation which they consume, pronghorns drink far less water, but when water is available they will drink a gallon every twenty-four hours. They can go weeks without water; however, if they are used to water they seem to need it regularly.

Pronghorn rely on all their senses, which are all acute. They have large protruding eyes which give them a wide arc of vision. They can notice movement four miles away. They are curious and a flag would draw their attention. Oversized hearts and lungs provide them with great stamina. They run with open mouths for greater oxygen intake. Their legs are ten times stronger than a cow's. Males erect their manes in alarm and both sexes flare their white rump patch as an alarm signal. They are also excellent swimmers. Their voice is a loud whistling when startled, and the doe offers a low bleat to her fawn, similar to sheep.

Although they become tolerant of human proximity, they usually stay as far as possible from humans. As they are diurnal as well as nocturnal, they can be seen near roads that cross their ranges. Man, disease and predators cause their death, but starvation often occurs just prior to the growth of spring grasses. They have been known to live fourteen years in the wild, but usually seven to ten years.

MOOSE
Alces alces

This large, stately ungulate elicits immediate attention as it silhouettes vaguely against the dark lowland swamps or clear sky of the high timberline, for it is at home in either place. In the vast wild where moose reside, a loud bellow may shatter the silence, and you know a bull moose is out there somewhere.

It is up to 9 feet long including its tail, and stands 6 to 7½ feet tall. Males weigh 900 to 1,400 pounds. The high, humped shoulders, long, gray legs, and pendulous muzzle are unmistakable. A large dewlap flaps beneath his chin, and he has large ears. Bulls have massive palmate antlers which are broadly flattened, with a spread of four to five feet.

The microenvironment of the moose is rather varied in elevation, although the areas are always heavily wooded, often wet and swampy (at least for part of the year) and always in areas with cold winters. Moose cross logged areas and feed there as well, but most of the moose I have seen have been in or very near dense cover.

Tracking moose lends itself to some difficulties, but is very exciting. Although the tracks are quite recognizable and for the most part easily found, moose go through considerable downfall. They reside in areas of such dense vegetation and utilize such wet areas, that it is difficult to negotiate in their habitat. When you do go through this debris, often you are tracking by vegetation breaks. This is difficult, for all kinds of twigs and limbs confront the tracker. Trackers are best in areas of familiar ecology, for as vegetation and soils differ, so does the interpretation of these. The age of the sign depends upon the condition of the soil or vegetation under various heat and moisture conditions; each condition is different. Tracking is attending to changing minutia, and it takes considerable time and constant practice in a lifetime to learn this.

Tracking moose can also be as dangerous or more so than tracking bear. They are as unpredictable and even more spontaneously aggressive and temperamental, particularly the cow with her calf. In heavy brush you may chance upon a moose much too close, for the moose is not that fearful a being and thinks of itself as the intimidator, not the intimidated, so seldom flees at one's approach. Sharp hooves can slash terribly. Early in my Alaskan residency I was introduced to the outdoors through hunting. I remember a moose hunting trip where some airline friends and I sighted a bull moose. We went to the spot where he had disappeared. This was a large and impressive bull moose with large and heavy antlers. The plan was to surround the animal and the nearest person to get a good shot would shoot. The men sent me into grass taller than even the moose, pointing out to me the path through this tall grass made by the moose. I rather questioned the prudence of this move, moved in less than fifty feet, heard movement ahead, and retreated, advising those brave male hunters of the probable position of the moose. To this day I can visualize the path through the grass, and find these signs quite quickly in the environment. One experience like that is worth several tracking books. Someone shot the moose. Sad as I feel about that today, as I reflect on that hunt, it was preferable than being chased by a moose. In that kind of situation, careful evaluation of the trail made by a dangerous animal is crucial. Tracking by vegetation can be more important at times than paying too much attention to the ground (rather than the action ahead of you). All situations are different. I never really did like hunting. My interest is in seeing the animal.

My naturalist friend, Rosalind, from Glacier National Park, and I were crouched over a wet streambank off Trail Creek west of the park one day in an attempt to identify a cat track that had been made during the night. We had followed a narrow trail along the very edge of the creek. We heard a muffled thud and I, being closest to the trail, stepped out upon it cautiously to see what had made the noise. Only fifteen feet away was a young spike bull moose, coming my way. We faced each other momentarily, with utter terror showing in his face, and he started, turned, but left only to go another thirty feet and stopped. Had he been older and familiar with people, the result might have been different. Regardless, he was not so intimidated that he really fled.

Another Montana moose whose tracks I saw on the road, I saw ahead of me off the road. A cow with a yearling calf caught my attention for a while as the calf had a large patch of hair missing from its shoulder. Curious, I approached closer very cautiously, wondering if it was injured. As I got within 150 feet or so I saw a young, newborn calf lying in the brush near the cow, the answer to my question. The yearling apparently had not wanted to leave the mother, who, because of the new calf, had been encouraging it to do so by biting it.

When I first tracked moose I lived in Alaska, but at the time I was not as interested in the tracks as in finding and seeing moose. Later when photographing tracks, near Yaak, Montana, I had not found suitable soil for photographs. From the top of a very steep and deep siding I saw enough through the trees to know there was a muddy, open area next to a pond—just perfect habitat for moose. Indeed, a moose had left many deep, sucking tracks there, nicely photogenic. To have tracked him (for the tracks were large enough for a bull) through the downfall and thick trees and around the water and mud would have been good experience, but the tracks were both older and fresh, showing me that the moose was spending a lot of time there, and was possibly quite near. To extricate myself from that tangle would have been too slow a process if I needed to leave in a hurry.

I have found that tracking moose first along a wide streambank like that beside North Fork of the Flathead River in Montana is a good idea. Then when you become more skilled you are likely to spend sufficient time looking ahead, as you have incorporated your skills and are less likely to be completely absorbed in the ground alone. Tracking with someone is a wise idea if possible.

Swamp Creek lies in northwest Montana in bear and moose country. The trail begins past private land, unmarked and obscurely located. It is thickly vegetated and encroaches upon the very psyche of the hiker. The dense thickness of the foliage emanates a mystery and an expectancy that from anywhere, at any moment, the unexpected will certainly occur. Old growth fir and pine dominate the canopy, and a myriad of varieties of vegetation intertwine among themselves in greens and browns, reds and yellows. They flow together as though fall-colored paint has spilled upon the world, shaping into leaves and trees.

The trail proceeds at first high above the creek, a narrow, almost precipitous trail with often a tenuous hold on the slope. Below, to the right, flows Swamp Creek, coming from the wilderness toward which you head. As you penetrate further and further into this maze, it draws you further. You become all too aware of how far into its depths you are moving, and how with every step you become further away from your secure world. Black bear or grizzly could greet you at any point.

I approached Swamp Creek from this high ridge, and the trail finally declined toward creek level. High banks on my left almost beckoned me to explore them, but my feet were too magnetically drawn toward the easier paths, and the excitement of distant discoveries beyond. Even the smells of the pungent growth changed as I proceeded, to a heavier, muskier odor.

I crossed a muddy area. On a broad flat, surrounding a narrow trickle of stream, there they were. Large moose tracks cut sharp edges into the firm mud and short green growth. They were perhaps yesterday's tracks, and they paralleled the trail in the direction from which I had come. The moose had then found its way into the thick brambles off the trail and gone into eternity. I could not find enough track to firmly establish the sex identity of the animal. From the size of the track it could easily have been a bull. But the tracks were not as round and blunt as a bull's.

Further across this dark, moist flat I stopped frequently to sense my surroundings, and to wait for nature to reveal what it would. My glances found bear scat, moist but not fresh. Breaking the scat, the black, formerly runny texture, long since dried, indicated the bear had eaten some flesh. It had no longer any identifiable odor. Had it been fresh scat of flesh origin, it would have smelled terrible.

Here the trail had led some distance from the creek, but further on it closed in toward Swamp Creek, and the foliage spread across the trail. The ground rose again and the trail inclined upward gradually. I was going slowly. Moose tracks appeared intermittently on the trail. Fresh! No disintegration in the tracks and very smooth of surface with sharp edges. Cow and calf tracks went in both directions, suggesting time spent here. They likely were close by. I paused to look around, staring in between branches for the familiar figures. I waited and listened and waited. Shortly I ventured up the now hidden path. Around a slight curve of the trail they stood, just off the trail, forty feet away. Cow moose, and right beside her, the calf. The cow was staring at me. Her mind was processing me in her ease. Placid, large brown eyes surveyed me almost with disinterest, yet her gaze was steady. Enormous jaws chewed protruding leaves silently and steadily. Her huge, almost awkward-appearing form stood large and impressive. The dark brown and black hair of the cow was somewhat jagged, spread over large bone extrusions. Her very size was so intimidating, it inhibited any movement on my part. Although calm, she was alert. I occasionally diverted my stare, hoping not to alarm her. The brush would be no deterrent if she was angered and decided to charge me. The downfall would have likely prevented any retreat for me. I stood, just breathing, enjoying my good fortune with half-faint heart. Then all at once she perceived me as undesirable company, and quietly she and her calf moved on. Their presence was totally obscured within a few feet. I did not track behind her. She was too close, and with calf.

A cow and calf moose I did track was along Akokala Creek in the Polebridge area of Glacier National Park. I pushed my way through thick vegetation across the creek into a still wet slough looking for tracks of wildlife. The ground was firm and damp, and cut into this area between growth were the unmistakable tracks of moose. It was clumsy and annoying to track through this tangle, but I did, following a lot of crushed brush between ground tracks. Along the way I found calf tracks, and their freshness concerned me some. Moose can push through very heavy undergrowth a lot more easily than I. I was struggling, getting slapped in the face and cut by sharp twigs. The tracks which I did find were far apart, as there was much thick, dry debris which had been trampled on by many wild feet; it made it difficult to track in places. Here and there sharp hooves had made fresh vegetation breaks, however, and I pursued the spoor. The calf moved close at times to her cow, and at times seemed to wander off. After a while I decided it was nap time for them and me, and I discontinued. It was a hard job, anyway.

North of the Vermillion River in northwest Montana, a friend's small, red Volkswagen bug lurched sideways to the left and right, as our speed impacted the rocks in the road. Suddenly a moose dashed in front of the car across the road, and we abruptly slowed to avoid collision. As we stopped, a young bull overcame his fright enough to stop on the far shoulder of the road, and then he wheeled around and stared at our smaller vehicle, assessing his foe. His breath came in quick, long gasps, and his eyes showed his unnerved agitation. He swung again across the road in front of us, and stopped with lowered head, legs spread-eagled.

My breath, too, came in gasps, but in shorter ones. I considered the possibility of being rammed by a moose, windshield shattering with large hooves driven by hundreds of pounds of moose flesh and bone. The standoff seemed to give both opponents a chance to reflect further. Neither the Volkswagen nor the bull moved; both caught their breaths. Then the bull moved quickly off into the rugged Montana land. Tracking was not on my mind at that immediate moment.

The ground was torn where he ran. His large hooves had slid and buried themselves in mud. The mud blobs exploded forward, to the sides, and to the rear of the tracks. His running stride was nine and ten feet. I did not go far in the thick brush in the direction of this temperamental animal.

***

In addition to Alaska and throughout Canada, the moose is found in western Montana, northern Idaho and western Wyoming. It likes lakes and willow thickets. It is capable of extended ranges but primarily ranges up and down in elevation seasonally. Moose meander slowly if undisturbed, browsing on leaves and bark, which enrich the cow's milk. Moose are solitary creatures, drawn together during breeding season primarily, although some small groups collect temporarily, probably by chance. They are not territorial. The bull scrapes a pit into which he urinates during the rut, the hormone scent exciting the cow. If she is not prepared to breed at his approach, she moans. The bull also wallows in mud and his own urination to spread his scent for the attraction of the cows.

The cow is in estrus for 24 hours, and after copulation has an 8-month gestation period resulting in 1 or 2 light-colored calves. The young follow the mother 3 days after birth, can swim in 2 weeks, and are weaned in 6 months. The yearling or older calf is driven off before or at the time of the birth of the new calves. The cow is exceptionally protective of her offspring. With the irritable, aggressive and unpredictable temperament of the moose one stays at a safe distance at all times.

The moose's hearing and smell are keener than its sight, but it is well able to see you. Moose are abroad in the daytime as well as at night. Their speed is very fast for so cumbersome an animal. They can run 35 miles per hour, swim fast, and can move at 6 miles per hour for 2 hours. Their vocalizations include low moos with an upward inflection at the end, low grunts, bleats by calves, bellows from bulls, and long bawling from cows.

Tracks of this large beast are cloven and pointed, bulls' front hooves being 6 inches long and 4½ inches wide, with the imprint of the dew claws making the track's print 10 inches long. Its stride is 3 to 5½ feet in a walk, and 8 to 10 feet in a trot or run.

Moose can live for twenty or more years, but are hunted and can possibly die from parasites, one of which can affect the brain, contracted from the white-tailed deer. They die from predation, even by a bear if the moose is old or diseased.

WOODLAND CARIBOU
Rangifer tarandus

The caribou must run, for the wolves are behind them, and also in front, so they must go fast to escape. Their long antlers and their speed must protect them, as many wolves run toward them.

I have seen caribou in large herds travel through the Brooks Range in Alaska. At an earlier time of my life I was a stewardess in Alaska. We flew into every area. The Brooks Range is a traditional migration channel for the caribou going to and from their summer and winter ranges. Northward they migrate to the Arctic slopes in the summer, and to calve there. In the winter they return south. From 1950 to 1952, there were far fewer passengers going to Barrow over the Brooks Range. Only local residents flew from Fairbanks north. Alaska was relatively unpopulated and undisturbed then. Many times there were no passengers in one direction, and we flew low through the Brooks Range to see the wildlife. We spotted Arctic fox, bear, wolves and caribou. I saw thousands and thousands of caribou from the airplane, in their seasonal movements. As we flew for what seemed like a long time over the vast sea of caribou below us, I was mesmerized at the immensity of the herds, the thousands of individual animals crushed together, speeding over the ground, noisy although I could not hear, hot and sweaty, driven by internal urges they did not attempt to divine, instinctive prompting. The flow of life below me was a sight I knew I would remember all my life. Had I been below, I recall thinking what unusual sounds would have come to me—the clacking of antlers and groans and grunts of pushed and injured deer, the thumps of bodies as they bumped, and the ground torn and pounded with no living remainders. And the tracks, I think now of the multitude of tracks, the maze and mass of countless tracks into infinity....

Later I moved to Fairbanks and went with friends hunting moose, bear, birds and caribou. We walked where caribou were known to pass. We saw more tracks of caribou than actual caribou, so I had plenty of time to familiarize myself with their tracks.

It is impossible in a herd, even a small one, to track one caribou, but when one or two travel the edge of a herd, then one can track. Their weight registers well in most soil and is evident even in the frozen tundra, for their hooves are sharp and their track is large. One way to see tracks is to attract the caribou with flags or ribbons tied to a tree or post, for their curiosity will bring them in to see what it is. Thus they have made tracks for you to study.

It was in this manner we hunted caribou primarily, for you cannot approach caribou by tracking. They are too alert. I was in a group of caribou hunters in the 1950s on the outskirts of Fairbanks. As I was never a true hunter, I did not carry a gun, but I was anxious to see caribou. We came to a spot to wait. One of the group put up long ribbons on posts to draw the curiosity of the caribou which were expected to pass near. And we waited. And waited. Then we moved on, taking ribbons and posts and positioning them strategically beside a rise where hunters in various positions thought they would have an advantage. And we waited. And waited. Eventually caribou did come along, but it is much like pronghorn hunting. There are long open spaces with rises and you wait, hoping the wild creatures will come your way. While my companions were alert to the horizon, watching for long antlers and lanky bodies in the distance, I was occupied studying the dirt. There were, indeed, a lot of caribou tracks on the ground. A great number of caribou had been there, indicating a route for them. I enjoyed being outdoors and seeing wildlife. Foolishly I thought the thing to do in that case was to hunt. And I hunt today, but only for knowledge about the animals, the sights and feel of their majestic or commonplace behavior, insight into their minds, and to see innocent glances.

The caribou did come. A few came close from the edge of a small group. They were moving toward the ribbons, rapidly, their breathing heavy from the exertion of running, their nostrils flaring in scenting, eyes large in watching the flapping rags, hair laden with sweat. Then they stopped to examine the situation. One or two came closer. And a hunter shot a caribou.

It was in the early 1950s that I tracked caribou in Alaska, but in the Yukon in 1986, I drove past Burwash Landing. It was a bright and sunny November day, but it was minus twenty-three degrees Fahrenheit when I saw a caribou cow cross the road ahead of me. We parked and after photographing the track, I both tracked and backtracked her in the cold snow for a ways. She was moving fast, holding a steady pace, for she was about two weeks behind the main herd going south. I could not imagine what could have detained her other than injury, but her tracks gave no indication of this. She could have laid up to heal, becoming separated her from one of the main herds. Her large tracks churned the deep, crispy snow with her fast pace dragging clods of snow forward in a thrilling review of her passing.

***

If the caribou is seen running against a barren background its speed cannot be judged as well as if it is seen speeding across tree-studded terrain, but it is one of the fastest animals in North America. It achieves speeds up to fifty miles per hour for short distances. If you hear it, it utters low-pitched snorts similar to a pig, and short grunts.

The male caribou is a striking animal with his semipalmated antlers measuring up to 62 inches long. His body reaches 4½ to 6¾ inches of tail. At the shoulder he stands 3½ to 4 feet high. Weight of the male is 275 to 600 pounds and the female weighs about 10 percent less. Brown, shaggy fur with a whitish neck piece and a mane characterize the male, with the belly, rump and underside of the tail of both sexes white. In the Arctic, the barren ground caribou is almost all white. The cow has a set of short, spindly antlers 9 to 20 inches long. The spread of the male antler is up to 60 inches.

In the Pacific Northwest there are only about thirty animals found in a specific area in the far northwest corner of Idaho and far northeast corner of Washington. This herd also ranges across the border into Canada between Salmo and Creston, B.C. Occasionally there is a sighting reported in northwest Montana. This isolated group, due to a lower and different environment, has grown larger and darker than the woodland caribou in the more northern climate, and they are more heavily antlered. The more northern brethren have a range and migration route in the Alaskan and Canadian country between seasons and go hundreds of miles. They use trails which have been used by generations of caribou. The selected terrain is among coniferous forests, muskegs, tundra, taiga and mountains. The barren-ground caribou have an extremely northern range, as far as the Arctic slopes, where they may group from 10,000 to 100,000 in late winter before the spring migration after calving and before the fall rut.

Caribou are browsers and feed on many plants, a favorite being huckleberry. They utilize mushrooms, sedges, fruit, flowers and twigs of birch and willow. Lichen is a mainstay, and when deep snows allow the caribou to reach the arboreal lichen on tree branches, they may find that their primary feed where it is available.

Caribou breed in the fall or early winter, and the female is three and a half years of age before she can produce offspring. The caribou have one of the lowest reproductive rates of the deer family. At breeding season the cows are herded into harems of twelve to fifteen animals. During the remainder of the year the sexes group separately, unless migrating. After breeding, a gestation of seven and a half to eight months produces one or two calves, usually in mid-May to early June. The pregnant cow seeks a solitary birthplace in the high snowy reaches, presumably far from predators. The calf may not survive the exposures. Only three out of ten calves survive. They are 11 pounds at birth, stand in 30 minutes, run in 90 minutes, and in 24 hours can keep up with the herd. Although it may nurse into the winter, it eats solid food at two weeks of age.

They are very curious animals and will investigate a ribbon fluttering in the breeze. Although docile in temperament, males do battle during the rut. Their hearing, smell and sight are excellent. They are excellent swimmers and cross wide and fast rivers during their vast migrations. Their longevity is really not pin-pointed, but death occurs from man, wolves, grizzly, wolverine and lynx, and golden eagles hunt newborn calves.

Distinctively rounded tracks of five inches with angled dew claws indicate a pace, gallop, bound, lope and trot.

Chapter Six

The Weasel Family
Mustelidae

BADGER
Taxidea taxus

Look at that sand fly! It is coming out from the ground like an explosion. What is making this huge heap of soil, and where is it? It is a badger, of course! Nothing else can act like machinery when excavating holes. Just try to get a glimpse of him when in action....

Although the badger has a fearful and ferocious reputation, it is not characteristically aggressive without provocation. It is a strikingly marked individual and, when seen, engenders great interest, even where prolific in numbers. It has the respect of humans and animals alike. It is grizzled gray to brown in color, with a white stripe traveling from the center of its head to its pointed nose. It has a short, busy, yellowish tail, white cheeks with a black patch, small ears, and large fore claws, with which it digs incredibly fast.

The immediate microenvironment for the badger is a hole beside a large mound of earth, with the badger inside. Actually, the badger does not spend that much time in its den, except for the females with young. Most badgers dig a new den every night, and may move good distances frequently. If a female takes a permanent residency in an area, the whole area soon becomes filled with her dens throughout the years.

Most badgers I have seen are gray, but I encountered a brownish one in the Ochocos of eastern Oregon. We saw each other at the same time, I think, and then the badger made a ninety-degree turn and lumbered off through the brush. I took up the tracks. The dry dirt and duff of the forest revealed its passage, and in not too long a time I found the den. Try as I could, I found no tracks departing the den. The loose sand at the opening of the den obliterated any definitive tracks, but as I sat by the den quietly contemplating the situation, the sound of a badger's breathing came to me. I smiled. I wanted to linger. But it was not my place. I left. The hill was riddled with dens from previous years, and further tracking later revealed cub tracks along with the mother.

In this area within a mile I also found a tree which was scratched in the fashion of badger use. I looked closely at the tree with keen scrutiny for a long time, and later came back to it. The scratches reached too high for a badger, but there was no other explanation for the tiny claw marks down below the bark and into the cambium layer and sap of the tree. They were not too old. I stood back from the tree and realized that an old stump beside the tree was the correct distance for the length of a badger, should it stand on it and reach up to the scratch level.

Another scratch I found in Oregon in the immediate vicinity of badger diggings was on a smooth log where the bark had fallen off in the past, and there was a track of badger, five scratch marks the very size of a badger paw.

One winter there was another badger I spotted, just a flash of gray disappearing into the ground. I crossed the intervening snow-covered ground, and peered into a large abandoned coyote den, old white scat beside it. The frozen ground was bare of snow under the trees. The hole was dark, but as I peered into it I saw a turn in the digging. I saw a young badger peek around that corner and, at the sight of me, disappear again. I stood back and waited. It was not long before the badger again poked its head out and gazed at me momentarily. It was young, but adult in size. Had it seen a human before? It ducked back. I waited for its curiosity to whet, and snapped a picture of its little face the next time it showed. I left so as not to worry it. I looked back when I was away from the den, and it was outside. It sniffed the air where I had been. I said good-bye. We have not met again, but its kin's tracks will be ahead of me throughout the years.

Another badger I saw in its den was in Glacier National Park. There were a lot of badger dens I found in Big Prairie, but the ground was hard and overgrown with grasses, so finding track was not easy. I did find some track on the road, and the badger I saw had dug a den with two entrances, or two dens close to each other, right at the side of the road. I walked one section of the road north of Big Prairie frequently, watching for deer and wolves, and as I came around a bend a badger scurried into its den, tail disappearing and then head pushed back up out of the den to gawk at me. It stayed there, posing for a photograph. The tracks nearby had been run over by autos for the most part, and the hard ground and its speed made them poor tracks, but there they were, and I could identify the owner and guarantee their freshness.

South of my cabin is an old logging road which I frequently walk. The country is sageland and juniper, ten miles from the Cascades. Tall, old Ponderosa pine are here in moderate number among the juniper. The ground cover includes bitterbrush, rabbit brush, granite gilia, fox tail, cheat grass, Russian thistle and Idaho fescue. I have found fresh badger holes almost yearly in this area, but they have been dug by transient badger and have not been female natal dens.

Late on one July evening I walked to the end of the road, and upon my return I caught quick movement from the periphery of my vision. I stopped and watched for something to reappear. A badger darted out, and looked around very alertly. It came to the road twenty-five feet ahead of me and stopped. It was adult in size, but did not appear to be an older animal. It sniffed the air and moved to smell a bitterbrush beside the road. It was one which I invariably brush against when on this route, and I had again touched it about fifteen minutes prior. The badger smelled my trail, and came directly toward me to within fifteen feet. It stopped abruptly, never really looking at me. I am sure it did not recognize my presence, but just decided it did not want to have anything to do with human scent. It then turned back to its original route and continued in its rapid pace through the brush.

I had seen its route clearly, of course, and so I tracked. On the sandy road I could readily find its imprint. The definition of its tracks was loose, the toes of its paws indistinct but evident. I was not able to see its long front claw marks, as the loose soil fell back into the tracks. The heavy pine needle and undergrowth debris was another story. In spite of the badger's weight, the thick, springy cover on the ground left no clear sign. I stooped, sat, lay on the ground and side-viewed for a sign. It was too mussed, and the badger had not broken the needles to leave even a ghost imprint of its foot. I cut for sign ahead on the hard, crusted patches of summer soil. Slight disturbance was not visible, and I could not find definite track or sign before the light was gone. In the morning I photographed the best track, but was still unable to definitely document any further track. It was frustrating. Had I decided to spend another hour or so cutting for sign, I might eventually have found an area to corroborate its trail. Such an exercise is a great learning experience. And it was to be a number of years before I saw a badger there again. I wonder if they know the route the one before has taken even after many intervening years.

One hot July day I set out for a high ridge near Sisters, Oregon. From there one can see Black Butte, Mt. Jefferson, Mt. Washington, Three Fingered Jack, The Three Sisters, Broken Top, Tam McArthur Rim, and the city of Bend. My dog came along with me on a lead. The old logging road we hiked on was gravelly and hard packed. I had been following fresh deer tracks cut into the harsh earth when I saw the badgers. Around a bend in the road, fifty to seventy-five feet ahead, a badger appeared, trotting in my direction. I stood still immediately, and the dog did likewise. Behind the first badger came a second, somewhat larger. They continued on until about eight feet away from me when the second one stopped to look at me. A second later it wheeled and ran down the road, rusty tail flipping back as it proceeded. The smaller badger had not yet recognized the presence of a stranger and continued on a couple of feet closer. My dog could not contain herself any longer and lunged on the leash. The badger arched its back, bristles fanning, and then a look of fright came across its face and it, too, retreated back down the road.

The fresh scuff marks they made while running in the road would have been identifiable by their stride, straddle and some claw marks. After they stopped running the tracks were clear in the dusty soil: elongated toes, claws marks and arched heel pad on the wide foot. The tracks split, but both went in the same general direction.

***

Weighing 8 to 30 pounds, the badger is 18 to 22 inches in length, with a 4- to 6-inch tail. It is found in much of the U.S., but since it prefers open grasslands, deserts, farmlands and forest edges it is not a resident of the east, southeast or north Pacific coastal area. However, it can be found in southern British Columbia and southern Alberta. It can and does live in city parks, however. Its home range is about three square miles. The most obvious sign of badger presence is its diggings. It will leave large mounds of loose dirt where it has excavated its den or in its pursuit of rodents. The den opens elliptically in the shape of his body. It also cleans its claws on trees, leaving the bark denuded. It can exude a musk from its anal glands when attacked, which has a noticeable odor. It buries its scat in cavities and covers it about five or six inches deep. It is capable of many sounds:

hisses, snarls, squeals, purring growls, loud yells and soft sounds. The young make a squeaking chatter. It can be provoked if threatened, and one must remember that it can readily use its thirty-four teeth. Badgers are very fastidious and keep themselves well-groomed. By nature badgers are shy and curious. They will retreat when possible and seldom pick a fight. A curious feature is their tree-climbing ability; although they cannot climb vertically they can climb trees at an angle. They have been known to attempt climbing up backwards when trapped in a pit.

Badgers may travel long distances for breeding, a considerable number of variable miles until a mate is found. They can breed any time of the year; however, late summer and fall are the usual times. There is a delayed implantation of sperm until January or February, when the female begins her pregnancy. This ends six weeks later with the birth of two to five young, born well furred and blind, totally dependent for three months, and then weaned in three months. Five or six months later they disperse to find their own territories. The dens may be complex burrows and tunnels with many openings. During severe cold, badgers can reach a state of torpor, but they are not hibernators.

Badgers hunt small mammals and carrion, invertebrates and rattlers and also consume a variety of plant life. Their sense of smell is excellent, and their hearing is next best. Badgers have lived twelve years in captivity, and their wildlife ends most frequently through accidents and injury, and predation by larger animals.

WOLVERINE
Gulo luscus

Of all the wildlife, the wolverine has a mystique with no match. Rare predator of the high country, the lore surrounding the wolverine is due in part to its scarcity and remoteness. Early trappers witnessed its ferocity when they came to remove kill from their traps. Extremely reluctant to give way, the wolverine would defend the kill as if it were its own. This competition probably enhanced its reputation; however, its aggressiveness toward man has been exaggerated. As an opportunist it has no match, and if it thought it could bring down a meal, no matter the size, it would try. There is still much to be learned about the wolverine for it remains quite inaccessible.

Wolverines are growing in population since the early part of the century when they were almost trapped into extinction in the lower United States. They are found primarily in Alaska and northern Canada and south in the west to northwest Washington. Northwest Montana has a strong population and reports of sightings occur in Washington, Oregon and California from time to time. Wolverines seek high timberline, but they have been seen, and one was even trapped, in the lower elevations of Oregon recently. Their range is up to 1,200 square miles, depending upon the availability of food and denning sites. The average range for a male in Montana is 165 square miles, and 120 square miles for a female. They go farther in winter than most mammals. One wolverine had been known to travel thirty-nine miles without rest. When pursued they can cover fifty miles in a night.

I wish I could say a lot about personal tracking of wolverines. I have to be honest. On the bank of the John Day River north of Mitchell, Oregon, in February of 1986, I was using water putty for casting a bobcat track. As I waited for it to set, I looked around the area. Something unusual about a track caught my eye. It looked at first like the distorted heel pad of a coyote, and yet I could not imagine how, say, stepping on a stone could have changed the shape so. It was not dog, bobcat, cougar or coyote track. I cast the track to study it further at home. For a year I puzzled over it. Later, when I planned to go to Montana to search for wolverines, I began studying the track. Something looked familiar to me, and I took out the cast. Indeed, it looked wolverine. I compared it with Department of Fish and Wildlife casts, and put my cast into the ground to produce a wolverine track!

I had done my research on this single cast before I came to any definite conclusions about the identity of this track. Single and partial tracks can be puzzling problems. They are for the most part discounted, as there should usually be other sign in the environment to support the identity of the creature. In the case of this wolverine, that identity was so far from my mind that I did not do a thorough search of the entire area. I would certainly have been excited enough to do so had the thought even entered my mind. In spite of thorough searching, a tracker might miss what is there, or what was there to support the evidence might have been weathered away, or so obscured by other creatures that no other sign might be recovered. But if there is only one track, all possible investigation should be done as to origin before coming to a conclusion. Photographs, casts and common sense should prevail. Not reaching a conclusion, even for a long time, as was the case with this wolverine track on the John Day riverbank, is a conclusion which is justifiable and reasonable.

To not be able to identify a partial or single track is alright. The mystery is a learning experience and may eventually unfold.

A wolverine was caught by a government trapper in a coyote snare in Fossil, Oregon, a most unusual place for a wolverine. The trap was along a small creek with willow and choke cherry growth. This was very close to the track I had found in February. The wolverine in Fossil was trapped in April. I have always felt this was the same wolverine whose track I had seen.

In the Ochoco mountains of eastern Oregon, in recent years, there have been a number of credible wolverine sightings. They have been reported to have been there years and years ago, also. They seem to move out of the Blue Mountains and the Wallowas into these areas. As these reports are so interesting in that they reflect the behavior and gait of the wolverine, I recount a few here. Bend Fish and Wildlife gave me the names of those who had contacted them with wolverine sightings. I contacted these people and spoke with them.

One man was driving a back road in the Ochoco Mountains when he saw a creature described as a wolverine standing beside the road not far from him. The man continued to drive past, and the wolverine just stood there and watched the car pass.

Another man was putting up hay in a field near the Ochocos when he observed a creature having legs too long for a badger, with too long a tail, and with a lope unlike a badger. It was running and would hit rows of hay; the man thought this was to scare out mice. After talking with a Fish and Wildlife man he concluded that he had seen a wolverine.

A local rancher near where I had found the wolverine track observed a wolverine through binoculars about sixty-five yards from him. He described the creature as being thick and heavy, with a mottled horizontal stripe, about the size of a coyote, but it sort of shuffled along fast and stopped and looked back in his direction before disappearing over a hill.

A man who was shooting ground squirrels west of the Ochocos saw a wolverine. He felt the wolverine was preying upon the squirrels. It stayed in his view for a short while and then left.

Another report described the wolverine as being large, dark, long-tailed and having a pale stripe on its side. Let me describe this in more detail.

About thirty-five miles from my home is exquisite Alder Springs, arising from an underground lava tube originating in nearby Squaw Creek. The water rushes in tremendous gushes from the bottom of a cliff and cascades down through willow and thick green grass to rejoin Squaw Creek.

In July, 1989, I was in the north Cascades searching for lynx when this occurred in Oregon. A man and his dog were with friends when they came to Alder Springs. The dog was ahead on the trail some distance and when the people came to the spring they noted an animal in the rocks below them. It was watching the dog nervously and did not seem aware of the people. Then it disappeared into the rocks. The man telling me of this incident described a wolverine and identified it as one. He took me to the site and pointed out the exact spot he had seen it. However, ten days had passed and a heavy rainfall had occurred since the sighting.

I spent the entire next day climbing over steep rocks looking for protected areas where the rain might not have washed away wolverine track. The only tracks I found were from the yellow-bellied marmot, not a likely candidate for the pale-striped wolverine described. The remaining terrain below the rocks was grassy, and although I searched for spoor in dirt patches, I found nothing, nor was there any sign in the sands above.

Tracks were found and photographed in the Ochocos in December, 1993, by National Forest Service personnel.

***

The wolverine is dark brown, often with pale yellow or whitish fur on the head and a broad stripe running horizontally along its body, sometimes yellowish or sometimes whitish. The largest member of the weasel family, it is about 3 feet long and weighs from 18 to as much as 60 pounds, although generally 40 pounds is large. It has a bushy tail from 6 to 10 inches in length. The wolverine's jaws are powerful and with 38 teeth it is considered the most fearsome fighter of all wildlife. It is persistent, ranges widely and rapidly, feeding on carrion or any mammal it can catch. It can go fast, but cannot catch a hare on the run. It swims well.

Wolverines are territorial in terms of space and regarding their kills. They mark their food with musk exuded from their anal glands. This spoils the food for any other animal, and so no one but the wolverine will touch it again. Sometimes they cover their food. Wolverines are known to bite and chew trees, perhaps with some territorial significance.

Wolverines may breed any time from April through September, and there is a delayed implantation until some time between December and March. This wide time span helps increase the probability that these very solitary mammals dispersed over wide distances have an opportunity to breed. The males breed when they are four years of age, and the female breeds at two years. She may breed yearly, if food is abundant. Dens have been found dug under twelve feet of snow and usually in March and April one to six young may be born. The solitary wolverines avoid each other when they meet, and they often fight, as well. The scent of humans will not deter them, but their reputation of aggressiveness has been exaggerated, for a wolverine will generally avoid larger, dangerous animals. However, they have been known to fight a bear over a kill.

The wolverine is curious, cunning and crafty, and fiercely independent, but it is primarily shy and elusive. In the wild they can live from eight to a maximum of eighteen years. Injury, old age, starvation and parasites are its killers.

MINK
Mustela vision

A sleek and glistening dark brown streak dove into the water, and some minutes later a little nose and small head appeared in the stream, moving easily toward shore. This expensive mink fur has little sense of its precarious existence, its life being the expense if caught in a trapper's device. On shore a fish would be the bounty from its dive, but the mink might move quickly into the brush or onto a rock to consume its meal. It delights in life, playing in the water and living by its edge. And it lives on the edge of existence, as predators abound in its world.

Mink are found throughout Canada and the U.S., except for some southwestern states. I have often seen mink, some distance from shore, hunting for small mammals. It will eat a wide variety of land creatures, some large, such as rabbit. On the forest edge at Suttle Lake, Oregon, I watched a mink one day some hundred feet from the shoreline. It had a reddish cast to its fur, and it rather slowly made its way across the fallen debris on the forest floor, looking and sniffing for its next meal. Its back arched up in a weasel-like hump as it moved across the ground, unaware of my presence. Even though I had to move occasionally to keep it in view, it meandered along unconcerned about danger. Finally it disappeared into the maze of undergrowth, and I did not pursue it. I had observed mink tracks at the other end of the lake in the muddy flats beside the water, along with muskrat.

In the Crooked River at Smith Rocks in Oregon, I viewed mink occasionally swimming in the river, and on the banks. Their tracks merged with beaver and raccoon in innumerable muddy spots. When seen in conjunction with other larger tracks, their tiny tracks can almost be overlooked due to the focus on the more obvious larger tracks. The very observation of their tracks gives us an immediate impression of the quick movement of which they are capable. Their tracks on shore are prolific, indicating their constant activity in and out of the water. I have taken photos of beaver or geese, and have so concentrated on those tracks, that when the photographs are printed, I find surprise at the numbers of mink tracks also in the pictures.

In the winter I find tracks in the snow. Mink live along the Metolius River in the foothills of the Cascades in Oregon. One day, at least a quarter of a mile from the river, I found small tracks, and as I was trying to identify them, I followed them to a hole in the snow. More detective work brought me to a definite conclusion—these were mink track, but I did not realize they would go so far from the river. In the winter when the rivers and lakes freeze over, the mink can swim beneath the ice and find broken areas for air. I cannot remember seeing mink tracks in the high elevation lakes of the Cascades, however, which freeze all winter.

In tracking mink at times you have to be a kind of master. Snow tracks are the best, of course. There are fewer competitive tracks, and they are easier to see. In the summer on the banks of the rivers, the ground is filled with an assortment of all kinds of tracks. The business of the mink makes its sequence of tracks an enigma. It goes back and forth repeatedly along some of the same trails and areas. In the brush, a two- or three-pound mink does not leave much of an impression. Here, with your nose to the ground, experience is the only antidote. Experience and experience. And then, do you know what? The mink will still elude you.

Along Cherry Creek in eastern Oregon I tracked raccoon, and noticed a great number of holes high in the bank of the creek bed just the size of mink. I examined them, but was puzzled as I found no mink track. As the dens were considerably higher than the water level, I surmised that mink had been there at one time, but departed the area.

The greatest surprise I had with mink was at my driveway at home. I walked a couple of hundred feet from my cabin one day in arid central Oregon and on a large rock I saw this scat. I looked at it with great interest. It was black, almost four inches in length, and segmented with a shorter two-inch length. It had a cylindrical shape, and was very narrow. It was not a familiar scat for my area. It was most like weasel, which would not have surprised me, but it was too large. I pondered on this for a while, collecting the scat, hardly believing that a mink could be in my area with no fresh water. I was trying to find some other explanation for this scat. I checked the measurements and photos and my recollection of mink scat, and could find no other explanation. I called a friend nearby who rehabilitates wildlife, and she stated it was probably a mink which escaped about a year prior. She was glad to know it was still alive. A great deal can be said for the improbable. When you know that what you are seeing is what you know it to be, there has to be an explanation.

***

Mink can be 28 inches in total length, their tail growing to 9 inches, but can also be only 20 inches totally in adult size. They weigh up to 3 1/2 pounds. However, a friend in Montana weighed one he caught and it weighed slightly more than 4 pounds. They are usually a chocolate brown to black, with some white spotting on the throat and chin and belly. They are found over most of the United States except the very arid Southwest. They inhabit marshy areas and lakes and rivers.

Males travel along the water's edge for perhaps several miles, the females taking a smaller home range. They use urine and scat to demarcate their territory, with more deposits around their den area. However, they do not defend their territory. They may utilize abandoned beaver lodges, rocky areas, logs, streambank diggings or muskrat burrows. Their dens are small, have a four-inch opening, and the nests are lined with fur, leaves or feathers when there are young. Nests are about a foot in diameter. Mink move often. They cache their food in their den. They sometimes even climb trees.

In breeding they are promiscuous. It is interesting that they breed on the same day each year, and give birth on the same day each year. Breeding time is midwinter, January through March. They breed by the time they are 10 months old. Their estrus period is 3 weeks long. The length of gestation is 39 to 76 days, usually 42 days, and the young are born in the spring, April or May. Up to 10 young may be born, however, it is usually 3 to 6. Young are born blind and naked. They open their eyes in 25 days, are weaned in 5 to 6 weeks, and stay with their mother until fall. The young of both sexes have been known to disperse as far as 31 miles.

Mink are solitary except for the family grouping before dispersal in the fall. They are shy in the presence of humans. Occasionally they are seen in the daytime, but they are primarily nocturnal. In hunting, they rely most on their sense of smell. They eat crayfish, fish, muskrats, rabbits, mice, chipmunks, snakes, frogs, turtles and birds. They will eat this food on the spot or cache it. They use their trails in hunting. Temperamentally they can be vicious. And they have thirty-four teeth.

Their causes of death are from traps and predation.

If you hear a mink, you will hear a hiss, snarl, screech or even a purr. It will discharge a strong musky scent from its anal glands if disturbed. Should you see it reflected in your flashlight at night, its eyeshine will be yellowish green.

LONG-TAILED WEASEL
Mustela frenata

Such a blurr—no color, no shape, just speed, hugging the ground. It is a weasel, for nothing else moves that fast. No creature can run from it. It pursues its prey with a tenacious killing instinct. Furtive and supple as it flows over rocks and logs and climbs trees, relentless in its hunt for a meal, no matter its size, this is nature's most efficient predator. If I look back after I have passed a weasel, I may see it peer at me with curious, piercing eyes.

Its domain is far reaching. There are few places in the United States it does not inhabit, but in Canada it is only found in some southern areas of B.C. and Alberta. The least and short-tail weasel are prolific throughout Canada however. Its microenvironment is where there are mice and shrews, rats and rabbits, chipmunks and tree squirrels and birds. It spends time in the poultry yard, too. So where is it that it is not? Only the hottest places, Florida and Arizona, a bit of the Southwest. And I wonder if we really looked....

I have caught sight of only a few weasel. In Alaska I saw the white-coated ermine, and in Montana and California I saw long-tailed weasels in their summer coats, reddish brown or tan, with white underparts. Most were streaking elsewhere, but a couple stopped to look at me for a while, their noses and eyes working furiously as they did.

I have found more than weasel tracks. Their scat is much more prolific than any view of them, perched on logs and rocks in prominent positions. And I did have a close relationship with one. Yet I never saw it.

Occasionally I had seen a weasel track or two in the mass of deer tracks at home the spring of 1995. That summer in my corral and surrounding area, just a hundred feet from my cabin, I found drag marks about three or more inches wide, and up to fifteen feet long. I spent many hours puzzled over this, but finally identified weasel tracks in the marks.

Scouting around, I found a den hole under a large boulder with weasel tracks at the opening. Either it dragged its prey consistently or they were anal drags. I opt for the latter, thinking this its attempt to leave its scent for other weasels, perhaps even its own identity. This activity went on for a month, then my visitor disappeared, and I remain in regret. My mouse population had diminished, and I felt lonely for weasel signs. I had become fond of this company. As I have no natural pond or creek nearby I was surprised that the weasel stayed at all.

On a juniper gate post at the corral I found many whitewash droppings only a few feet from the weasel's den. I assumed they were from a local great horned owl, and I do hope that had nothing to do with the weasel's disappearance.

The tracks of the weasel display an abbreviated bound pattern, the tiny front feet landing on the ground first, and the larger hind feet planting at times ahead of the front feet, or in the front tracks. The tracks may be beside each other in a twin pattern. Hind tracks measure three-quarters of an inch in width and an inch in length, and the front tracks are shorter, but may be wider. As a member of the weasel family there are five toes on each foot, but usually only four show in the ground due to the small size of the smallest toe, combined with the ground condition and the speed of this mammal. The heel pad is a typical weasel configuration, a curved, narrow one in the shape of an arc. The straddle is a mere three inches. The stride may be up to twenty inches.

Weasel scat is black or dark brown, long and slender, often curved, perhaps an inch long. The same spot may be used frequently, and so scat accumulates.

***

The solitary, long-tailed weasel is a long, slender animal with a brown upper coat and lower white hairs. Its brown tail has a black tip, and its feet are brownish. In northern latitudes it is entirely white in the winter, but for its black nose, eyes and tip of its tail. The males are almost twice as large as the females, up to 21 inches long, with a 6-inch tail, and weighing about 9½ pounds.

Weasels breed in the summer, and in early spring 4 to 9 young are born blind and naked in an abandoned den of another species, in a grass nest. By 8 weeks of age the young have dispersed. Females will mate in their first year, males in their second year.

Weasels are entirely carnivorous, eating small prey and even larger species. They demonstrate no fear of attacking any predator that annoys them. Their temperament is a feisty one, and the smell of blood can incite them into a killing spree at times. They seize the prey at the back of the skull, or the neck or throat. Hunting occurs between cycles of rest throughout a twenty-four-hour period. The metabolism of the weasel indicates a need for frequent feeding.

Home ranges for the weasel are fixed; long-tailed males may range up to thirty or forty acres, but are more nomadic than the females, whose home range is perhaps a third of the males' in size. Weasels will defend a certain core area of their territory.

Their vocalizations are many. They hiss, squeak, purr and make a throaty chatter typical of the weasel species. They release a strong musk smell when angry or excited in mating.

Coyotes, fox, cougar, bobcat, snakes, owls and hawks prey upon the weasel. Their length of life in the wild is difficult to determine, perhaps up to five years.

Chapter Seven

The Raccoon Family
Procyonidae

RACCOON
Procyon lotor

Inquisitive about everything is the raccoon, and agile in every way; it peers at me at night or in the day from its tree den, I shall know it. Its fancy face is a giveaway. And so is its tail.

This widely located creature has been a delight to many and a nuisance to others. Expressive in movement and possessing dexterous forepaws, raccoons seem so human that many observers feel a kinship with them. Easily tamed, they can live in close relationship with people, but are much more interesting as wild creatures with their natural ways uninterrupted.

This popular creature is hard to track for any distance because it lives near water and frequently uses it as its route, to the detriment of the tracker. It is not popular with ranchers since it can be a pest and destroy poultry. It is also something of a nuisance to homeowners if it leaves its wild domain.

Raccoons are a delight to watch and fun to track. They are nimble creatures and often wrestle with each other. I once had a raccoon living in a tree beside my house in California. At night it would descend to my porch to steal scraps from my cats' dishes. However, the cats soon figured out what was happening, and they took to stationing themselves at each end of the porch and rushed the raccoon on approach. Fortunately for the cats, the raccoon conceded the territory.

Although I have no natural water and associated foods which raccoon like, I am only five or six miles directly from Squaw Creek, where I have found raccoon track. Several times in recent years I have found raccoon track at my house; they were passers-through, however.

Raccoon also exist close to where a subdivision has formed a pond from a well. A neighbor about three miles from me kept insisting she must be seeing raccoon tracks and tried to explain their shape and size to me. It sounded more like gray squirrel track to me, as I discounted raccoon, being as far from water as she was. They had a pond, however. One day my friend excitedly exclaimed that the tracks had been raccoon, for she had seen the raccoon. I didn't know they had goldfish in her pond.... That would have gotten my attention. I wonder if they restocked the fish.

If we move into wildlife areas, we should respect their ways and accept them and not destroy their needs. Putting temptation in front of wildlife we know what to expect. Most people move into beautiful rural areas for the scenery and wildlife, uproot the wildlife's natural foods, and replace them with city vegetation. Then when this is attacked, the people want the wildlife removed. What an injustice all around. Keeping natural habitat intact and understanding wildlife behavior will prolong the existence of the wildlife, take less water from our resources and keep conflict at a minimum. Raccoons are not the only conflict. All wildlife seems to be.

In Oregon, Cherry Creek flows into the John Day River north of the Ochoco Mountains, a habitat for some raccoons. The wet ground accepts their tracks, and retains them a long time in its clay-base soil. I followed the tracks of one individual. Its hind and front foot tracks registered on the ground side by side as it walked along the almost bare streambank. The water level had been higher from a rainstorm when it walked there, and I could see where it had walked in what must have been shallow water. The tracks were smoother than those that had been made above the creek. The raccoon left the water and climbed an eroding bank where all I could see was crumbled earth. Higher up, the ridge was covered with flourishing vegetation. I had to search to find its tracks. However, the open areas revealed so many coon tracks going in both directions, I could not be sure which was the one I had been tracking.

A diversion stream from Swamp Creek in Montana was used by a rancher for irrigation. I walked across this occasionally where it ran beneath the road. It had muddy banks from the changing water levels and was surrounded by reeds and cattails. I noticed raccoon tracks there one day and tracked the raccoon along the water and up the bank where it seemed to head for some trees. This was private land and I did not follow. I went down that way more often to see its tracks and in hopes of seeing the raccoon itself. After a while I no longer noticed the tracks. An inquiry revealed that the rancher had trapped the coon in a leg-hold trap. I stopped walking there as the recollection was depressing.

Gibbs Lake lies on the eastern edge of the Olympic National Park. It is a small lake hidden in the forest, and one spring I spent a few days there at a tracking workshop of Tom Brown's. Mountain beaver, deer, coyote and weasel frequented the area, and raccoon also showed their presence. I was tracking raccoon along the edge of the lake in dense foliage, and it was difficult. It was at a point where I was not at all sure which way this raccoon had gone. It was then I heard some soft whimperings, and I stood up and looked around to identify the sound. I heard them again, and I followed the sound to a tall, old stump at the edge of the lake, and near a trail used to circle the lake. I went a little closer, with some trepidation, and identified a raccoon den in the stump, with young. We all took care to avoid going too close as we went around the lake.

Raccoons tame easily, but they have sharp teeth and claws, and can carry rabies. They should be treated as wild animals. Although raccoons were rabies carriers in a Pennsylvania epidemic in about 1986 and 1987, in the west there has been very little problem. In Pennsylvania, a banana-flavored vaccine was ready to be air dropped to the raccoons at that time, pending approval.

I accompanied a friend who rehabilitates injured wild animals when she released a raccoon. He had lived with her and was quite used to her presence; nonetheless, in the excitement of the long car trip and the strange new surroundings, he bit her.

***

The raccoon is a striking animal, with a reddish brown coat mixed with considerable black and gray. Its remarkable face has a black mask outlined in white, and its bushy tail sports four to six alternating black and brown-gray rings. On the average it weighs 15 to 25 pounds, but can reach 48 pounds. It stretches 18 to 28 inches in length, with an additional 7 to 16 inches of tail. It is fairly lumbering in speed, although much faster than a porcupine. It is an extremely vocal animal. It can whicker, issue a long, drawn out tremulous call similar to a screech owl, purr, hiss, whimper, whinny, growl or scream. The mothers have a large vocabulary of sounds they use with their kits.

The raccoon is found over most of the United States except in exceptionally dry areas, for water is its love. Streams, lakes and coastal beaches find its unusual tracks laid beside them. It is classified as a carnivore and is extremely adaptable to most environments. Its food habits are as varied as its voice. It consumes fruit, worms, dragonfly larvae, clams, juniper, small mammals, birds, muskrats, fish, frogs, eggs, nuts and crayfish. The raccoon likes to soak its food in water and kneads it with its flexible paws.

The nocturnal journeys of the raccoon can take it from about ten acres to two miles, with the boars roaming the furthest. Scratches on trees and scat below indicate its presence and sometimes its denning area. It can climb sixty to seventy feet, and usually lives in a tree cavity. Its dens may also be found in the ground, logs, rock or brush piles. In the winter it may sleep for several days or more in extreme cold, living off the fall's accumulation of fat. Both mother and young may den together in the winter.

The dominant adult male raccoon mates with all the females in his territory, but the female mates with only one male a season. Young bachelors may not mate at all until they establish their own territory. In the north, mating occurs in February or March and in the south in December and January. In sixty-three days, from one to seven young may be born, and there is only one litter a year. The furred young weigh only two and a half ounces at birth, and their eyes open at three weeks. They can hunt with the mother at two months, are weaned in the late summer and become independent in the fall.

The raccoon possesses a great curiosity and is also gifted with excellent hearing and sight. Its sense of touch is especially keen. It is docile until threatened but can become highly ferocious. It has forty razor-sharp teeth and is usually left alone by predators. However, dogs, man, bobcats, cougars and coyotes do attempt to kill the raccoon. We know that raccoons can die of distemper, rabies, encephalitis, fungal and protozoan disease, but have lived to fourteen years in captivity.

Chapter Eight

The Porcupine Family
Erethizontidae

PORCUPINE
Erethizon dorsatus

This unusual large rodent is known for its slow and waddling gait beneath a fan of about thirty thousand quills covering most of its body. "Porcupine" means "irritable back," and it easily meets that reputation. Folk tales depict the porcupine throwing its quills at predators, but the quills are just loosely seated in its skin and pull free easily when their barbed tips sink into something soft. The quills nestle among its softer hairs and are erectile so it can effect a threatening pose by lifting them high as protection.

The microenvironment of the porcupine is a tree. Well, it can be at the bottom of the tree, in the branches, or among the trees, but trees are usually nearby since the main source of its food is bark and young twigs. Once I was tracking a porcupine when I saw it ahead of me. I do not often see porcupine as they are mainly nocturnal, and occasionally travel several miles at a fairly good speed. Thus fresh tracks do not necessarily mean the rodent is nearby, unless you happen to be out at dusk or dawn. Porcupines can also be hard to distinguish up in a tree, even when you have definitely established by tracks that it is there.

This particular porcupine was in a field of spring wildflowers in the Ochocos in Oregon. I saw it, but it did not see me at first. It was hungrily devouring the lush vegetation, and I approached it slightly from the rear and without a lot of caution since it was so absorbed. However, when I was fifty feet from it, it suddenly froze, and I knew I had been heard.

Without turning to look at me, it charged toward a Ponderosa pine. By the time I reached it, it was around the far side of the tree and climbing, so my photos were not close. Two hours later it was still safe on an upper limb. I learned to stalk even porcupine.

In the winter of 1987 in the Ochocos, I was searching for wolverine track, and I climbed Wildcat Mountain in the Mill Creek Wilderness. The snow was about a foot or more deep, and I followed a snow-covered road for easiest access. Tracks of coyote and squirrel assailed my senses, and I hopefully scrutinized every trail of tracks in hopeful anticipation that I might be fortunate enough to actually find the spoor of wolverine. It was not to be, but the adventure was exquisite. Near the top of Wildcat I came upon a porcupine's two-and-a-half-inch tracks. Easily I tracked this little one for more than a mile for it, too, took an easy trail. For some periods it walked straight in the road, as straight as an arrow when the road was straight. It was able to walk on top of the dense snow, and its pigeon-toed trail showed drag marks into the tracks, and its rear feet were registering partially into the rear of its front feet tracks. Quill marks plainly showed as though you had taken a whisk broom and brushed it on the snow. In places its toes marked quite clearly, and in some places only the outer shape of the foot was indicated, snow having fallen into the tracks. Its straddle and track size gave me some idea of its size, being adult of medium size. At times it turned from the road into softer snow where its tracks were more blurred than on the firmer snow. It climbed over rocks in some porcupine plan to reach some porcupine goal. I followed this obvious trail up the hill and around trees, and it again returned to the road and crossed it to begin a downward trek into a deep, rocky and narrow canyon. Here it stopped to urinate, and went on. I had tracked far enough. My goal was the top of the mountain, not the canyon depth, and so we parted ways. Besides, it was some time ahead of me.

One evening my dog barked, softly and steadily. I looked out at the dim evening light. The dog continued with even beat and volume, giving notice that something was wrong out there. I knew what she saw. I grabbed a leather glove and found the dog and a porcupine with high-arched quills in a standoff.

I approached the young porcupine rather slowly. This one apparently had no frightening experiences with humans, for it merely turned its back on me, some of the 30,000 of its ivory-toned quills blending into its black body. It sat under a bitterbrush and dared me to touch it. I had been noticing tracks of a mother and a juvenile around my place for a few days and surmised this was the young one.

My years of capturing porcupine made this little creature more vulnerable than mother nature and mother porcupine had intended. I merely reached with my gloved hand along the ground to grasp its heavy, short tail with permanent bristles, and lifted it upside down. I was delighted to have it, for it had been destroying quite a few of the young pine on my place by eating the bark. I swung it gently into a live trap nearby. I threw some tomato into the cage. It continued to display a fan of quills. I searched for its mother who should have been within a few hundred feet somewhere. I did not find her, but her tracks the next morning indicated that she had come up to the trap to see her young. I felt bad separating them, but I transported the baby to a new area twenty miles away. It was certainly old enough to survive on its own.

In another incident, I had tried desperately to catch a mother porcupine and her young during a winter drought. They had been decimating my pines and staying near my water tanks. I took to looking out the window frequently during moonlit nights. One night I saw the mother at a stock tank. Her large body and quills shone in the moonlight, and she looked startlingly like an albino in the silver sheen. I was prepared. I threw on some slippers and grabbed a waiting laundry tub quietly, which I planned to put over her. It was a high speed chase, and she won, getting under the low, stiff, juniper branches and off to safety. I was totally defeated.

I have had a lot of experiences with porcupine. Another one at home which gave me problems I found on my road right at the cabin when I returned from an evening walk. It was huge and was sitting right at the electrical transformer. There was an opening under the unit under which chipmunks and who knows what went sometimes. I pretended not to see this porcupine and walked calmly by. Out of sight, I rushed in for my leather gloves. I returned, and that was when it got a little wise. I got the rear view as it raised its tail. However, I grabbed it and pulled. But it was too strong for me. It pulled itself under the transformer most of the way and hung on to something. I knew I could not get it out. So I went to get my trap and upon returning found the porcupine totally under the transformer. So I set up the trap with rocks around it to prevent it circumventing the plan. I baited the trap with mushroom, and when I finished it was dark.

In the morning I eagerly went out to find it. It had been out and gotten the bait but the door had not tripped, having hung up on a rock. Disappointinged, I put in more bait, corrected the problem, and checked several times during the day, knowing that it probably would not emerge until dark. I checked until bedtime, and the bait was still in there. I was a little worried, but on the following morning it was there. I had quite a carry. I think it weighed about thirty-five pounds. It found a new life in the wilderness far, far from me.

A porcupine I never saw or tracked left tracks of a sort on my cabin when it was first put up as a weekend shack. I visited almost every weekend, and the first year I found large holes chewed through the plywood, one about two or three feet in diameter. As I looked thoroughly at the edges of the holes, the pattern was clear. I put metal flashing on the bottom three feet of the wall and that solved further destruction. Porcupine like the glue in the plywood. I fenced the yard later, but porcupines came in and had encounters with my dogs' soft noses right in the yard. Now I have a smaller mesh fence and we all live in harmony.

One winter in Oregon there was no snow, and I drifted around my area on a walk, glad of the temperate weather. In winter, porcupine spend a lot of time in one tree when it is very cold and the snow is difficult to navigate, but here the dry ground lay littered with green pine needles and debarked tender twigs beneath a large, old Ponderosa pine. A porcupine had spent quite a bit of time in that tree. Its large, oblong winter scat lay prolifically at the base of the tree in among the debris, though I had to dig to find it, further evidence of the time spent above. I wish I hadn't missed it, but I looked, and it was elsewhere.

Besides tracks and tree disturbance, porcupine leave other evidence of their presence. In the summer I found the round form of a resting place pushed into a dead bitterbrush at the base of a fair-sized pine. It was porcupine size, and recently used, judging from the still careful shape. The porcupine had made a ground resting place. It had not spent much time there, however, for scat was not in evidence, and they leave a proliferation of that. Other times I have found old logs used as their haven.

One winter morning, while considerable snow remained on the ground around my cabin, I picked up the tracks of a porcupine. I tracked it through patchy snow and frozen ground for a couple of miles. During that trek it never once climbed a tree, although it did linger around the base of several. It was puzzling, for most of the time porcupine do not go very far before climbing a tree to feed. I finally discontinued the tracking when it went through a lot of slippery rocks in a fairly steep drop into a canyon. There was a porcupine with something on its mind.

The most recent porcupine I have seen was killed by a cougar near my place in 1996, only 100 feet from where it killed a deer. Often predators flip the porcupine over to reach its belly, successfully avoiding quill penetration in a vulnerable spot.

***

The porcupine is heavy-bodied, short-legged and clumsy, weighing up to a recorded 43 pounds. It is about 25 to 36 inches in total length, and about 18 inches high at the middle of its back. The porcupine is usually blackish with yellow-tipped quills. The hollow quills are attached to voluntary muscles beneath its skin and occur all over its body, although most are found on its back and tail. Usually docile and gentle in temperament, it is persistent and when threatened it raises its tail and slaps the intruder, leaving a multitude of barbed quills in the victim. Secure bristles grow near the tail, but the loose ones have a waxy substance which facilitate entry into the skin, and the body heat of the victim causes the quills to expand. Porcupines molt in summer, and there are always quills of varying stages of growth in its coat.

The porcupine is found over most of the continental United States, throughout Canada and Alaska, in woods or brush, and at timberline level. It ranges up to about four miles, but the male goes further in the rutting season. In winter, a porcupine may stay in one tree or log for an extended period of time if it is very cold or if there is deep snow. Several may live together during winter, but usually they are solitary.

This prickly rodent generally reaches sexual maturity at two or three years. Estrus occurs every twenty-five to thirty days, if the female does not breed. Breeding most usually occurs in September to December. One young is born in a sheltered location on the ground in April, May or June, although births have been reported in February and October. The gestation length is 209 days. Twins are occasionally born. The young are born furred, with open eyes, in a placental sac, head first. The baby weighs one pound, and has soft quills one-quarter-inch long which harden in a half hour. It walks in a half hour, too, and in a few hours it climbs and eats solid food. It is weaned in six to seven weeks, although it may not leave its mother the first winter. When traversing the woods, these nocturnal mothers usually keep close to their young.

Porcupines are vegetarians, eating twigs, cambium bark, leaves, a variety of green plants, flowers, clover, skunk cabbage, pine needles and mushrooms, all of it amounting to about a pound of food daily for an adult. Sound and smell are more acute in this rodent than sight, as it sees only a few yards. It makes a variety of sounds, from grunts and groans to high-pitched cries, sounding like a baby, and bleating like a calf. When threatened, it chatters its teeth.

Predators learn to flip the porcupine on its back and rip open its vulnerable belly. Along with snowshoe hares, the porcupine is a primary prey for the fisher, a large member of the weasel family. The fisher attacks the nose of the porcupine. Porcupine are also caught by coyotes, bobcats and cougars. Man's traps also reduce their numbers. They can be the only source of easy food for a lost human, as they can easily be killed by a blow on the snout. They survive seven to eight years in the wild.

Chapter Nine

The Beaver Family
Castoridae

BEAVER
Castor canadensis

Beaver! I hear their tails slap on the water as they dive. They work and toil all night with industriousness. Their dams and lodges take tremendous energy and determination to construct, a symbol for man's aspirations.

The beaver can be found in forested areas near waterways throughout Canada and the U.S. It is dependent upon trees for its food and for its building material. It will build a lodge on its dam in a stream or use a burrow in a streambank. It has been criticized for manipulating waterways to its own liking, occasionally flooding roads and ditches, and for damaging timber. However, in reality it provides standing water that nourishes fish and wildlife, and by clearing timber near its rivers, it encourages plant diversity. Let us hope we can help it maintain its habitat so we can always catch a glimpse of its brown head rising in a still lake.

The microenvironment for the beaver is along a running stream with sufficient current to flow well and sufficient depth so the water will not freeze solidly in the winter. Wet meadowland and marshes are liable to surround the stream, and trees must be plentiful.

At Smith Rocks near Terrebonne, Oregon, I found beavers along the banks of the Crooked River. I tracked primarily over short distances since they usually did not travel far to collect their timber. The tracks were very clear in the mud. They were busy, working hard, as the loads they carried were somewhat heavy. Their deep tracks reflected the weight they carried and the push they used in their work. Many tracks were made over others, and I didn't try to track any one beaver for very long. I did photograph the repeated slap of a beaver tail as it proceeded toward the water, showing each slap partially overlapping the preceding one. The slaps showed the definite round edge of the end of the tail, marking several inches to a foot apart, as it raised its tail and slapped it down over and over again. I could visualize the beaver as it pushed a limb into the water ahead of it.

I have found beaver habitat along the Metolius River in Oregon where actual tracks were impossible to find. I knew there were beaver there from the other signs, including crushed grass and evident drag marks. However, the vegetation was so complete I never found a partial ground track, or even one in vegetation.

I have found many beaver tracks in areas where it was impossible to track them. When I was teaching a group in Glacier National Park one year, I showed students beaver tracks in some soft earth on the edge of a stream, but the lush grass would reveal no more. Too many people had walked the area. However, older beaver tree cuts remained nearby as we followed the bank of the river, indicating their history there.

The same brief, tempting tracks were clearly on the soil of a bank of a small stream in the Ochocos one year. I looked around for other sign, but found none. It had apparently swum through from other origins, and decided not to spend time there after leaving the water and looking around.

These brief encounters with beaver sign are frustrating and only compound the frustration of the difficulty in really tracking beaver due to their overgrown habitat, and their back and forth movement on the same trails. A lot of vegetation sign is often the best that you can do.

The Willamette River runs north through the Willamette Valley in Oregon. Many beaver reside in and among its banks and waters. Many tributaries and other streams flow through the valley. The large amount of rainfall received here makes the vegetation very thick, and berry bushes are impossible to invade to reach certain areas. The land is privately owned, so access to beaver area can be a problem as well as getting through vegetation. Once I found myself under a bridge which fishermen used. The stream was narrow and surrounded with dense brush and tangled trees, and to go further one would have needed a machete. The ground was hard packed from use, but in the muddy edge track was there, two-inch, four-toed front, and five-inch, five-toed, rear webbed tracks.

Many beaver are trapped in this valley, as they are considered a nuisance. I once received permission from a farmer to follow a stream across his land looking for red fox tracks. Although I found no fox tracks, I found some trees gnawed below three feet and pondered on this. Beaver tooth marks are one-eighth to one-quarter inches wide—these were puzzling. They appeared smaller, and there was something different about the angle and pattern of the marks. The bark had been stripped and the tree gnawed—not as though it was attacked for cutting it down, but just for feeding. I couldn't find any beaver sign. I spoke to the farmer again. It was a nutria, an imported water rodent smaller than beaver, very similar, but with a round, narrow tail and webbing on only four of its rear toes.

In my wanderings, I have come across some large trees that had been cut down by beaver. In Montana beaver cut large diameter old growth fir, larger than I could encircle with my arms. In Glacier at River Campground, beaver cut a huge old fir. In Oregon, the trees I have found cut by beaver include large poplar trees, in addition to their preferred willow, alder and cottonwood. They have even cut juniper and pine.

It is often easy to see beaver in early morning or evening. One can identify the location of the beaver's lodge entrance by observing the frequency of its dives in a particular spot. I sat in Montana in a large swamplike reservoir watching beaver most of one evening. I "tracked" them by sight when they swam close to the surface and discovered their dives were always in the same place when returning with tender twigs. It was a giveaway for the lodge entrance. Beaver do much constructive work by keeping erosion in check, and they have been introduced into areas for this purpose alone. At the present time, the Fish and Wildlife Department in Bend, Oregon, are introducing beaver into an area south of Bend. Where increased growth has intruded into beaver habitat as the urban area expands, the "nuisance" beavers find themselves relocated.

***

The beaver usually weighs from thirty to sixty pounds, occasionally topping out at 100 pounds. The beaver has a small head in relation to its body, with small eyes. It has a large, flat, scaly tail shaped horizontally as a flat paddle. Its five-inch long hind feet are webbed for swimming and have two minor nail clefts, with which it meticulously grooms its hair.

The beaver has scent-marking glands that manufacture castoreum, a bitter substance with which it marks its territory. It deposits its scent on several mounds of mud it constructs around its territory. It also exudes scent from anal glands on sticks and grasses, probably with the same purpose. The scat of beaver is hard to find since it usually defecates in water.

Beavers dam streams and build large lodges so they can live in quiet waters. Their lodges loom above the water, up to ten feet high and forty feet wide. Their dams can be several hundred yards long, made of logs and branches, carefully cut and dragged into the stream. They caulk the interstices with mud and rocks. An underwater entrance leads to a bedding area inside that is above the waterline. One or more openings on top function as vents to release moisture. Beavers build and repair their dams through the spring into fall.

Beavers are as much at home in the water as on land. They can dive six feet six inches per second underwater, and go 2,500 feet in one dive. They can stay underwater for fifteen minutes.

Dam building provides the most frequent sign of beavers, as well as cut tree stumps bearing the marks of the animal's incisors, and the ring of chips around the felled tree. They eat the bark and transport the logs to their dam.

The beaver continues to grow all its life, as do its teeth, for it uses its teeth constantly. Beavers store their food in their lodge for winter use when it is very cold outside. They consume bark, twigs, plants and leaves. In winter, they emerge from their lodge daily until the water freezes. If ice completely covers the entrance to their lodge, they may not have sufficient food to survive. Beavers do not travel very far; they range within a mile of their lodge. Although the beaver is docile in temperament, it will defend its territory aggressively. It is a prey for felines and canines if caught unawares. Otter can also kill young beaver.

In January or February, the female of two and a half years will breed, and in 105 days one to eight kits are born, furred and with open eyes, weighing one pound. In a half hour they may take to the water. They are skillful swimmers in one week. The mother may carry the young on her back if they are tired. On land the young may ride on her tail or she may hold them in her forepaws. The young leave the parents at age two, or they are sent away prior to the birth of a new litter. They can build a dam alone in the second autumn of life. Beavers pair for life and live in a group of ten to fourteen maximum. If the food supply is short, the males will leave the area.

Beavers are shy and fearful of humans and have been trapped for their fur for generations. They live eleven to twenty-eight years in the wild, and nineteen years in captivity. Death can also come from predation and starvation, particularly if they become frozen into their lodge by ice in the winter and use up their food supply.

Chapter Ten

The Squirrel Family
Sciuridae

WESTERN GRAY SQUIRREL
Sciurus griseus

Captivating acrobat! Silver-tipped hairs mark this squirrel well against the green foliage of the forests. Balancing so expertly in the trees with its long tail as a rudder, sometimes its rapid bark pierces the forest in early autumn. Though two pounds of weight is considerable, it can travel almost seventeen miles per hour if it wishes. If it sees me, its bushy tail may flick, and I know that it is not pleased at my presence. If it chatters, I know it is very unhappy with me. If I look for it at night I will see no eyeshine.

It was over a year before I saw a gray squirrel at Wildhaunt after the forest fire in July of 1990 either took those in my immediate area, or they left. I had identified only several in the acreage surrounding me, certainly there were not many. Only two at a time had come into the feeders for seed, but primarily they are isolates, and usually only one at a time entered my yard. Their territory ranges from a half to about seven acres.

The resident squirrel was a large one, and its ability to climb and jump over the plywood buffers at the feeder meant to keep ground squirrel off was an admirable sight. As it spent a great deal of time on the ground, tracking it when it left involved some time. The ground lay covered with pine and juniper needles, and this squirrel's weight barely touched the thick, stiff understory. Thus I frequently cut for sign ahead, and back-tracked to maintain a sequence of tracks, to utilize an invisible trail through logical evaluation of the squirrel's behavior. At times I lost it as it climbed a tree and went from tree to tree. Fortunately there were enough open sand areas to be able to see its tracks, but tracking squirrels is very difficult.

Occasionally I found the diggings where the squirrel had buried seed and tamped the ground afterward. They found the seed again by smell, not by memory. Many pine seeds came to life through the negligence of a gray squirrel when it missed a buried seed. Another sign would be the muss in the dust where the squirrel bathed to try to rid itself of lice.

There were many roadkills in my area, and I took one of the killed squirrels home to study its feet and body. It is a beautiful creature, so unique in its coloration. Its long, full, soft bushy tail is gray, lined with black hairs and white tips on the edge. Beneath it is white, or buff. Its feet and toes are long and the claws long and sharp, and quite curved. The pads on its feet are large and bulbous, and mark well on soft ground or snow.

After the fire I saw a gray squirrel at my home one spring. It came to the feeder in terrible physical shape. I thought this was a female who was deplete because of the stress of a litter, being thin, with short and thinning hair. They do molt twice a year, but I wondered if this squirrel was failing. I never saw a gray in such poor condition again, and the next squirrel that came in some weeks later appeared to be a different one, so well nourished and sleek was it.

I would see the gray squirrel which I believed came into my feeder as far away as an eighth of a mile north, and also a quarter of a mile away from Wildhaunt. A half mile and more away I would see what I believed was a different gray squirrel in another direction, but I was unable to positively document this. It was also strange to me that south of Wildhaunt I never saw a gray squirrel in the forest for many miles. I thought that this specific area might have been too far from water, but in 1995 it became gray squirrel territory.

Chickaree once inhabited my land, but their stride and tracks are much shorter, and their straddle is an inch to two inches narrower. It was usually quite easy to distinguish them from the gray. The gray squirrel's pace is a bound, the rear feet registering forward of the front feet. With very poor or partial tracks, the only other possible distinction would be of rabbit, and this confusion could be quickly dispelled by the shape of the feet. In addition, the shape of the grouping is more triangular for the squirrel, and more oblong for the rabbit.

There are large California ground squirrels in the dry canyons north of me, and their tracks could easily be confused with the gray squirrel.

Tracking in the snow is much more rewarding, as the tracks are more visible, and one can ascertain the squirrels' habits more readily. Sometimes where they leave the ground and climb a tree, the slight scratches are visible in the bark. On the ground, however, they can run from their slow stride of about a foot to three feet.

***

This large and easily identified tree squirrel has a big, bushy tail up to one foot in length, as long as its body. The family name means "shade tail," as these squirrels hold their tail above their body when sitting. Its tail has bands of gray, white and black, particularly underneath. The tail is so graceful, and is used as leverage, cover from the rain, a rudder when swimming, lift when leaping and to slow its descent. Its gray color is beautiful, edged with silver tops of hair, with a white belly and dark feet. The backs of its ears are reddish brown, and there is a back stripe of reddish brown as well. It inhabits the Pacific states, Cascades and California Mountains.

Gray squirrels range daily for food, unless the weather is too bad. It buries its food for future use in a spot other than where it is found and pats the ground over it, finding it again by smell. It may girdle Douglas fir trees for food, as well. In the high desert I have seen tree bark stripped on juniper which I believe was done by squirrels, and not rabbits, owing to the height. Its territory is usually up to seven acres where the food supply is ample, and it marks its tree trails with scent. The male secretes a waxy substance from a gland to hold the scent. It has regular and elaborate tree trails, and trails along the ground, as well. However, it is not protective of its range. Squirrel densities can be from one in ten acres to two per acre. Interestingly, overpopulation was thought to be the reason for a very large migration in the east in the nineteenth century.

Gray squirrels breed in midwinter, the female coming into estrus in early January, with a second estrus cycle nineteen weeks later if not bred. There are three possible estrus periods. Males are sexually mature at eleven months.

Nest locations are in tree cavities or high twig nests in a tree. They are large, and quite visible in the winter in deciduous growth. Bedding might consist of leaves and shredded bark. The gestation length is more than forty-three days, and the young are born in March to June. One to five young constitute the litter, usually two to three, with one litter a year, except in the warmer areas where there may be a midsummer litter as well.

They weigh about twelve grams at birth, nurse for five to six weeks, and are ten inches long at five weeks of age. The female may move the young to and from different nests. The young stay with the mother about eight weeks, and although the mother will defend the young in the nest, they are on their own after leaving the nest, although they follow the mother for some weeks. Either the young or the adults may disperse upon the maturity of the young to seek other territory.

Gray squirrels are isolate in behavior, and tame enough to live near human habitation when not threatened. They are diurnal, abroad particularly in the early and late hours of the day. They are docile in behavior, shy and curious.

These squirrels need to live near water, and they feed on fruit, baby birds, cambium bark, eggs, fish, seed, suet, caterpillars, carrion, nuts and fungi. They can smell a nut under one inch of snow. They can ingest twenty-four ounces of nuts a week. Their sight and smell are used primarily, and there is little known of their hearing. Tactile hairs grow in their ears, and they have flexible ears, so sound must play some part in their survival.

Their front tracks are 2 inches long, their rear a half inch longer, with 4 toes in front and 5 toes in the rear. The trail width is up to 5 inches. A slow stride will measure up to 15 inches, but a leap can be 3 feet. Claws mark one-quarter to one-half-inch apart.

Predation upon these squirrels is from humans, canines, felines and snakes, owls, hawks, other gray squirrels and raccoon. Their longevity in the wild can be up to nine years. In captivity they have been known to live ten to twenty years.

Chapter Eleven

Snakes
Class: Reptilia

In some areas snakes are predominant and easily found and in others they are not. The use of certain techniques may increase your chances of finding track. Basic cues apply to the tracks and tracking of snakes, no matter what the species. Pressure ridges occur with the movement of the snake to indicate its direction; the ridges show to the rear of the push due to the backward pressure of the snake's forward movement. Snakes move their entire bodies with the aid of cross scales on the underside of the body, which are attached to the ends of the ribs. These scales oppose each other, providing a grip on the ground. The usual snake track is an undulating one, made by a snake when its entire body is flat upon the surface of the ground. The track waves from side to side, made by the body of the snake following its head. Thus the ridges left at the base of the curves are due to the pressure of the body against the earth. At times a straight line of the body registers in the dust. These are made by a snake when it is not in a hurry. The muscles on the underside of the snake move their scales in a wavelike fashion, pushing the body of the snake in a straight line. Desert snakes, such as the sidewinder, loop their body as to appear that they go sideways, a motion necessary for moving through loose sand.

A long stick can be used to overturn rocks and logs to find a snake or the beginning of his tracks. Also, the time for finding a snake under debris is in the heat of the day, for snakes are cold-blooded and cannot stand intense heat. They have no mechanism to control body temperature. In the evening, however, pavement or gravel holds the heat of the day longer than does the earth, and snakes can be seen in the open soaking up the last of the day's warmth. In the early part of the day, snake tracks can be found more easily. The afternoon desert winds blow and erase tracks, and the night is usually still, so early in the morning snake tracks are fresh and visible without the distraction of the confusing, disintegrating tracks of other creatures.

Snakes seek food by thermal sense. After a strike, smell finds the prey. With forked tongues and feelers, microscopic scent is sent into two cavities in the roof of the mouth. Scent is used in mating, as the sexes and different snakes have different scents. A nose is used, too. The garter snake emits very unpleasant secretions when bothered; the king snake emits a musky odor. So snakes make and follow scent trails.

There are four snakes and their tracks with which I am most familiar, and they can be used as a guideline for snakes in general.

RUBBER BOA
Charina bottae

This snake is found in pockets in central Oregon, and my cabin lies in one. The climate is dry and the habitat is high desert vegetation: rabbit brush, sage, bitterbrush, juniper and pine. The ground is open sand among the shrubs. I first came across this placid, nonpoisonous snake in my yard in the dark. I found several snakes at the foot of my steps. In my ignorance I thought they were rattlers, being uninformed about snakes at the time. Their tail is blunt, and in the light of a flashlight I imagined that it was a rattle. I tried to kill them, and I shudder at my stupidity to this day. They are the color of the sand, have no markings, and appear patterned with small squares. I have found them some years in the cover of my cistern where it is damp and dark. When I clean it out in the spring, I have found some, or their shed skins. Although most are small, ranging from one to two feet, one I found seemed almost three feet long. I believe twenty-nine inches is the recorded maximum length. They seem to like damp areas, and so it surprises me that they live in arid central Oregon. However, damp sand can be found, and the lava rock substructure holds a lot of water, places that snakes can find and easily go. They do live in coniferous areas, and so on that basis no wonder central Oregon near the mountains is home.

The rubber boa is nocturnal and crepuscular, but can be seen in the daytime. It can swim, and is a climber. It also moves its tail as though it were its head, while protecting its head in a coil. It has been said that it also uses striking movements with its tail, but I have never even seen one coiled. It is quite innocuous, and can be picked up and moved aside. It will strike, however, at prey, mice and lizards, but it kills by constriction. Three or four young are reported to be born. It burrows in loose soil. I find rubber boa tracks in my dusty road. Some years there are few, and other years I see more. I follow them as far as I can with no fear of being in jeopardy. A friend of mine was a herpetologist and had some snakes in glass cases at home. He always wanted me to find a rubber boa for him, but I could not bring myself to take such a quiet creature out of its happy abode. In fact, I have been reflecting on how I might attract more. However, since the forest fire on my place, I have only seen two. I cannot distinguish their tracks from another snake of the same size, but as I do not have rattlers right on my property, and have never seen a garter snake at home either, I feel I am looking at a rubber boa track when I see a snake track there.

PACIFIC RATTLESNAKE
Crotalus viridis oreganus

This species of rattler is the best known in the west and is a poisonous snake. Thirty species and subspecies occur in the United States. It can grow to slightly over five feet in length. It has variations in color from pale yellowish through gray, pink, reddish, greenish, brown or black. Blotches on the middle of the back, dark brown or black, are diamond shaped or bands as they reach the rear end of the rattler. There are rings on the tail which are light and darker near its rattle.

Spring seems to be a time when a lot of rattlers are abroad, as it is not too hot in the daytime for them. As the days get very hot in summer, they are more active in the dusk, dawn and at night. They emerge from hibernation in the spring when temperatures get seventy degrees Fahrenheit or more and go into hibernation about October in my area. They hide in rock shelters and in my area den a few miles away in great numbers. Their range varies, going either great distances, or remaining for years at the same location. They seem to travel from ten feet to a mile and a half a day. Young will be born in the fall, and may number up to fourteen. They can be found at up to 7,000 feet.

I saw some rattlers warming themselves in the evenings at the 6,000 foot level in eastern Oregon on Doherty Ridge. I got out of the car and approached them cautiously to see what their behavior would be. They moved to the side of the road, and some of them stopped and rattled. Actually, the rattling sounded more like a fine whistle to me. I have found rattles on the ground, also, where they have been shed.

In Dry Canyon a few miles from home there are a lot of rattlers. This canyon is very narrow and steep in places, although not very deep. At each end it flattens out. I hike there and once came across a female and her young one year on some rocks. I approached with great caution, nevertheless prompting not only the mother to rattle but the small young as well, and then a few of the young retreated. So did I, looking carefully as I went for others. As I left, scanning the ground and rocks carefully, I saw a large gopher snake spread out straight on the ground. It was about two and a half feet long, and gave me a start. I stood still and it did not move. I almost thought it was dead as I stood there, but I prodded it slightly with a long stick and it moved a slight way. I think it had eaten recently and was in a digestive state near torpor. I went on and in a short distance found another rattler, so I left the area. Sometimes there can be too many in one place.

In California one winter, I lived near a lake and rattlers were all around. I used to swim in the lake until I decided it might not be prudent. Rattlers cannot strike unless they are coiled, however, so a swimmer is less likely to be struck in the water—on shore when coming out of the water could be another story. However, their presence did not deter me from walking. I took the dog along and carried a long, hefty stick to handle any situation that might arise. I never did confront a rattler there, but I did find gopher, or bull snakes. Most people living in rattler country hardly ever see a rattler. They are not aggressive unless confronted or attacked, and will try to avoid people. Wearing boots to knee level is wise, however. That is about the height a rattler could reach. Then remember to be careful where you reach. At home I left three cats, and never did I find a rattler in my yard. Cats are quicker than rattlers, and keep them at a distance.

I chanced upon a rattler on a logging road on Green Ridge north of Sisters, Oregon, when tracking elk. This is in the foothills of the Cascades and is heavily forested. It stayed in the road and let me view it for a long time. It was apparently so comfortable it did not want to move, so I took some photographs. I wanted it to coil but it would not. There was a small stream just off the road where it was cool. I passed on and returned to find its tracks leading off toward the stream, but I did not feel like trying to track it in the tangle of brush, as I doubted if it had gone very far in its relaxed mood.

I once held a king snake a speaker had brought to an Audubon meeting. I had to decide if I wanted to hold it or not, in spite of the fact that I had picked up rubber boas. The king snake is immune to the poison of the rattler and preys on them. It is interesting that when a rattler comes upon a king snake, apparently it does not rattle or strike. The odor of the king snake results in a characteristic response; the rattler retreats while holding its head and neck along the ground, but raises the central part of its body, with which it may strike at the king snake.

This king snake was mostly black and four feet long. It was used to being held by people, or rather, holding onto them. So I braved it, and it was a different feel being held on to so close to my skin and clothing at every point, with the same pressure. I rather did not know what to do after a while. You don't exactly talk to a strange snake. Well, if I had met it in the wild, I might. So after about ten minutes I was ready for the owner to claim him. He had gotten involved talking to someone at the far end of the room, so I had to get even better acquainted with this snake than I had intended. I finally managed to give it back. It is too bad that humans are educated to be so uncomfortable around snakes.

At Smith Rocks State Park in Terrebonne, Oregon, a beautiful trail follows the Crooked River. It winds close to the river and among lush riparian growth, and one can find rattlers there except when they are in hibernation. Knowledgeable hikers take snake sticks, long sticks to probe ahead before they enter thick growth. There are many climbers in this park, and some of the trails lead up through steep rocks. You want to be sure that your handholds are not into a crevice where a rattler has sought refuge from the sun. Signs now post the area as rattler country. The only rattler I saw in the area was one swimming in the river, which came toward shore on my side. When very close it saw me and changed its mind. However, I have found many snake tracks there, and no doubt some of them were rattler tracks, but I have not pursued them to their makers. Although persistent in tracking, I am prudent.

Many of the highway viewpoints in Oregon and Washington overlook dry, steep canyons where people explore on narrow trails. These canyons are prime rattler habitat. I have stopped at one such rest area east of Ellensburg, Washington. It is posted for rattler presence, but most are not.

When I was planning a trip into the Trinity Mountains I spoke to a veterinarian about rattlers. He suggested that if I were struck, to cut each fang mark through twice at ninety degree angles, and suck out the mucous type substance rather than use a suction cup. Provided, of course, that one did not have any open cut in one's mouth. To date I have not had to follow his advice. Recent technique is to use an extractor which avoids cutting or sucking out venom, thereby lessening the possibility of infection.

Cryotherapy is also important in slowing the venom's course through the body.

GOPHER SNAKE
Pituophis catenifer deserticola

This snake is harmless, large and widely distributed in the U.S. Although of no threat, it is pugnacious. They will coil if threatened and behave in a menacing fashion. They will vibrate the tip of their tail rapidly, making a buzzing sound similar to the rattler. They may hiss and strike. They kill their prey by constriction. They have a mottled appearance, not too unlike the rattler, and can be six to eight feet in length. They are able to dig using their snout, and remove dirt by looping their neck against their body. They climb well, going high into a tree for birds.

I saw gopher snakes in California the winter I spent at Berryessa Lake visiting friends. The area was dry with grasses and chinquapin trees and, but for the low ground cover, open in many places. When I walked carrying my snake stick, I met some, and had a hard time at first distinguishing them from rattlers. I had to go up close enough to be able to tell that there were no rattles, and the thickness of the head differed from a rattler; whereas the rattler has a narrow neck the gopher, or bull snake, has the same thickness of head and neck. There is no pit along the side of the head as in the rattler. The snakes were a healthy width, and I saw some six feet in length. I was fortunate not to have any close encounters with any snakes which would have put me in jeopardy. Tracking snakes in these areas where rattlers are plentiful is a rather risky practice, for you are bending down or kneeling in vegetation where any snake might be obscured. Tracking in grass is totally impossible, as well.

Another gopher snake I saw of quite a length lay in the road north of the Painted Desert in Oregon. This is a rolling, treed and open area quite close to the John Day River. I stopped and tried to annoy it so it would leave the road and not get run over. I had already seen some snakes killed by automobiles along the way. This snake, too, did not seem the least intimidated, and did not want to leave its comfortable repose. Of course I did eventually get it off the road, but it did so under duress, acting quite defensive as though it might well attack me. I stayed a safe distance, but took stock of its tracks. Perhaps with enough study over time I might be able to say something about the differences between the tracks of the various snake species.

COMMON GARTER SNAKE
(Thamnophis sirtalis)

This snake can be found in the west and can reach four feet in length. As they like water, they are not found in the desert unless by a river. Their color can take many varieties, and they have a stripe of yellow color down the middle of their back, and may display red blotches on it. This snake has an aggressive nature and can bite if caught. Garters may produce a strong odor from anal glands. They are diurnal. Their broods have been reported to be very large.

While at Upper Priest Lake in Idaho after tracking elk, I was walking down a road and saw a flash of color in the grass nearby. I went over slowly to see if it was a snake. It was a beautiful garter snake with black background and bands of yellow. It moved a little more when I approached, but not very far. I had time to take out my camera and take a photo close up. Then it moved on to its snake world, after such an encounter with me. Although the brush was too thick to pick up any tracks where it went, I looked down the road a ways and found undulating tracks, which were likely his. They appeared to be fresh, but were rather faint in places as the ground was rather firm. Because of the brush, I could not track him to definitely verify the tracks were of the particular snake I had seen.

Humans stand taller than many other inhabitants in the Pacific Northwest, but can be tolerant of those who hug the ground more closely.

Chapter Twelve

Birds

Class: Aves

Some of the wild creatures most of us are fond of are birds. As birds are thought to spend most of the time in the air, they are rarely considered in tracking books. Indeed, tracking birds is a short-lived endeavor as most eventually fly up off the ground. However, there is much to be said about the tracks of birds, and some about tracking them. Many of the ground birds present the same type of tracking as do mammals, and their tracks where they take to flight are frequently evident. The perching birds who spend far less time on the ground present a much more difficult problem in identification. Making a tracking bed by smoothing out the ground and placing some seed in the center allows you to observe birds who come in. You might have to do this at a watering basin for the insect eaters and hawks. Then you can immediately go over to study the tracks and thus be sure of identity when you see them again. Some tracks are similar, and it may take a long time to be able to make certain distinctions. Bird tracks fall into two broad categories: the walking or ground bird, and the perching or tree bird. Tree birds pair their feet and hop to navigate, and ground birds walk, placing their feet either directly ahead of each other or diagonally opposed. The feet of birds can be categorized also. Some have three toes in front and one behind, which is most common. The owls and road runners have two toes in front and two in the rear, forming an X pattern. Some form a K shape, as with the flicker and some woodpeckers. Some form a Y shape, with two toes in front and one in the rear, as is seen with the three-toed woodpeckers. Even the weight of the bird may be significant in identifying its tracks, particularly if it is a difficult track.

Although my tracking has focused on mammals, in my roaming I have been in contact with certain varieties of birds, and their tracks also have been of interest.

PTARMIGAN
Lagopus lagopus

In Alaska from 1949 to 1959 I came in frequent contact with ptarmigan. They are an Arctic grouse about sixteen inches long. I spent a lot of time on skis in the winter, and ptarmigan tracks were in plain evidence. I learned to be very watchful in the snow, for otherwise I came upon the birds without seeing them and flushed them toward the next hill. They were always in groups, and the little bit of black on them in the winter was difficult to spot as it blended in so well with the vegetation. Whether I was seeing rock or willow ptarmigan or both on the outskirts of Fairbanks, I do not know. When they flushed, their tracks remained, and I could see how they had moved across the snow, and the wing marks in the snow where they had landed and taken off.

The ptarmigans' tracks in the snow were not as clear as in the summer, for their feet are feathered to protect them from the Arctic cold, and so the tracks were blurred. Winter was the time when I was close to them, for navigation on skis was less difficult than traveling over the rugged land in summer. Their foot is four-toed, the short rear toe hardly noticeable, and the center forward toe is thicker and larger than the outer toes. They mark in a straight line as the ptarmigan walks. In the summer their tracks resemble the other species of grouse, but in winter the feathering distinguishes them.

One day I was skiing near the top of a mountain about twenty-five miles outside of Fairbanks at a ski slope called Cleary Summit. I was already almost on top so I climbed higher for a view of the snow-covered world, and I came upon a flock of ptarmigan. This time I was alert enough not to flush them, and I watched them while they watched me. They stood there frozen in movement, waiting for the stimulus to take to wing, but I did not give them that. I was probably thirty feet away, and there might have been twenty birds in this flock. Their beady eyes stared at me without distraction. I waited as long as I could in the cold without moving so as to observe them, and I was hoping that they might accept me as a bush and go about their feeding, but I was not to be so rewarded. I could not take the wind and my limbs finally became cold, and I moved slightly. The rush of wings came suddenly and they flew over to the next hill. I decided it was still within my range of skiing and I went my fastest in deep snow, floundering once in a while,, but it was a sunny day and I was enjoying it. It was a challenge to find the birds. When I reached the top where I thought the ptarmigan might still be I went as slowly as possible, looking very intently at the ground so not to have made the hill climb in vain. I moved on and found tracks. It had not been the spot where they had landed, but I found where they had run. I peered carefully, but I could not follow the tracks as far as they went; and what would you expect? Of course. I flushed them to the next hill. Or perhaps the next? It was the end of that tracking.

But ptarmigans are fun to find. Their feathers turn brown in the summer, and they are in a transition stage during the change of season. The rock and willow ptarmigan are difficult to distinguish in summer plumage, but I remember black tails standing out against the snow. They are wary, and have all the advantage.

SPRUCE GROUSE
Canachites canadensis

I saw a great deal more of this grouse than the ptarmigan, for this bird is easy to find, and I could get so close it would have been a crime to shoot one. I spent many mornings getting up at four or five to drive outside of Fairbanks to see the wildlife and these birds were always there, either on a road or in the thick brush of Alaska. They are black or brown in color, the males being the darker, and with some whitish feathers in the tail, and they were considered so dumb to allow people so close to them that they were called a fool hen. Their tracks are much like the ptarmigan; however, they are not as fat as their quick-flying cousin, and their stride is slightly shorter, and they toe in some.

When I saw some spruce hens one morning I walked up to them and they flew up in a tree, almost as though it was an effort to do so. I walked around the tree and they stayed in the same limb of the tree. I really tried to extricate them by coming as close as I could, but one or two moved to another limb, and the others remained where they were.

I was looking at tracks of spruce hens one morning in the cold. They left the road and I tried to track them, but the ground was hard from freeze and made it very difficult. I continued on into the trees, with my eyes on the ground and nowhere else, and suddenly right in front of me on the ground was a huge pile of bear scat, still steaming in the cold air. I left as quickly as possible, and I always tell that story.

RUFFED GROUSE
Bonasa umbellus

While spending my days in the wilds of Montana I became familiar with the ruffed grouse. They have a fan-shaped tail and are reddish brown. I came upon them in their so-well-camouflaged state they always flew abruptly, making a loud whirring sound, and then they were gone. For months as I walked in the woods, I would occasionally hear what I thought was the sound of a far-off motor, like a generator, start and then fade away. I actually thought somewhere out there was some encampment, and they were having trouble with their generator. I could not reconcile this with the number of times I heard it in different places and finally had to face the fact that I was absolutely wrong. Yet I did not know what it was. Finally I thought to ask someone and was quite chagrined at discovering the answer. It just did not seem that it could have been a bird, but indeed, it was the ruffed grouse. Then I began to hear them closer, but could never stalk them to see them. Now every time I recognize the drumming sound of this bird, I smile to myself.

One ruffed grouse I did see, however, was near Swamp Creek. It was the nesting season, and I was walking slowly toward the creek to head up it when I flushed a ruffed grouse from literally beneath my feet. The reason for her waiting so long was clear. I think I counted more than twenty eggs in her ground nest; they were a pale tannish shade. I was sorry to disturb her, and as it happened they logged there the next week, and I am afraid of the fate of that nest.

The tracks of the ruffed grouse were very hard to find, living as it does in the thick brush in the Montana area. I know that the summer tracks register on the ground as much slimmer than in the winter, but the rear toe is so short it may not be easily seen. In the winter a fringe appears in the track from the front toes, almost like an incomplete webbing, which acts like snowshoes. This bird has a very short stride and toes in slightly. The winter tracks I saw were quite mussed and blurred, usually where the grouse had landed and taken off. I never saw tracks going on for any great distance. Sometimes in the severe weather they would make holes in the snow where it was warmer.

CHUKAR
Alectoris graeca

There are many chukar in eastern Oregon, and they are hunted. These birds are larger and fatter than quails, and have dark striping on their sides below the wing. They are light brown with a white throat and a black line demarcating the throat and eyes. Their legs and feet are orange, as is the bill. The tail is a rufus shade. I have tracked this bird many places, especially north of Mitchell along the John Day River. With a long middle toe, the tracks mark one ahead of the other. A small rear toe also marks. I have photographs of chukar tracks in snow which look almost like the webbed tracks of a small duck with a short stride.

Chukars run very fast, and spend a lot of time on rocky slopes where they are hard to see. Their tracks are plentiful on the ground where they do mark, however, and are distinguishable from quail and grouse.

CALIFORNIA QUAIL
Lophortyx californicus

This common bird is plentiful in my home area of desert shrubs, juniper and pine. They are about ten inches long and have the characteristic short-curved plume on the crown. Males are more colorful with black and white on their face and throat. The females are duller in color, both sexes being grayish.

The quail runs along the ground most of the time. The male often perches on a high spot to look around for danger. The female and her young run quickly across a field or road. The young when first born look so tiny and fragile as they run as fast as they can, I always wonder at how they can be alive being so tiny. Their little legs go so fast they just blur, as though in a comic strip. The tracks are easily found, and I have seen their tracks two and a half inches long in deep dust. I have found straight line tracks with as short a stride as the bird could make; and long strides of about four inches with a trail width of more than three inches. At that time there was drag of the foot between the tracks. After the forest fire on my land I seeded, and the quail moved in in flocks. It was the only time I walked where I had to walk without being too sad to move them on, for they consumed a considerable amount of seed. Some was left, fortunately. And the quail deserved what they got.

I watched quail drink at my water tank one day. Two of the young stayed behind, one finding the soft dust suitable to cleanse its feathers. The other one soon followed suit. The mother hen called from beyond and finally came back to see where her strays were. Several others returned and watched the proceedings, whereupon the original laggards bobbed up and left. All the rest finally dust-bathed in the same spots, kicking their feet and flapping their wings, then lying still, almost covered in the deep dust. I looked at the spots after they had departed, three deep holes and quail tracks.

Another early summer morning a clutch of twenty-six quail were hollering in my yard. As I went out to find out why, a goshawk swooped for one of them ten feet in front of me, missing it. The quail found cover in a fallen juniper, and the goshawk landed four feet up in another juniper, fifteen feet from me. The frightened quail continued to vocalize in protest as the goshawk awkwardly kept its balance on a swaying limb. It watched me a minute and flew thirty feet across the yard to peer at me from a better position for another ten minutes. Its awkward maneuvering made me think it was young although it boasted of mature plumage:S a blue-gray back and white stripe above its eye, pure white feathers underneath. Its four foot wing span gave it some disadvantage in the close quarters around the trees at my cabin. When it left its perch, it landed on the ground, leaving me wondering if a chipmunk had met its doom, but the ground cover did not reveal just what had occurred. Surprisingly it took the quail only twenty minutes to leave cover and go about their forage.

MOURNING DOVE
Zenaidura macroura

This slender brown bird, about ten inches long, with a pointed tail and some white spots bordering its tail, is frequent in the west. They come into my trees and spend a lot of time on the ground. When I walk in the evening I am likely to spook them into flight. Their tracks show all four toes clearly in the dust of my area. The slender tracks are one and three-quarters to two inches long and they walk in quite a straight line. Doves are hunted and seem to cycle in population. At times they are infrequently seen, perhaps due to hunting pressure. Sometimes there are a lot in my area and I can notice their tracks after they drink at my water tanks. I recently had a dove in my yard which refused to spook and fly. I thought it might be injured but studying it I decided it was a young bird who just liked the spot. It flew up on my roof when it did fly, and then finally off and away. Usually doves stay in pairs. I see them on the fence wires often in the evenings.

FLICKERS
Colaptes auratus and Colaptes cafer

These brown woodpeckers have some white in the rump and are very large and identifiable. The *Colaptes auratus* male has a black moustache and the *Colaptes cafer* male has a red moustache. Both have a red crescent on the back of the head. The four-toed tracks are paired and form a K on the ground. The flicker spends a lot of time on the ground, but is rather awkward when hopping. They have sticky tongues and consume ants, but I see them eating sunflower seeds in my feeder. The summer after the forest fire left burned trees on my land, a flicker used one of the snags to have her nest. The young birds were very loud and when I walked up to the tree, they immediately stopped cheeping. An old snag before the fire was used as a nest, also. When the birds left I reached into the hole but could not touch to the bottom. I find tracks at one water tank which is level with the ground. Thus I can smooth out the dirt and when I see a bird there I am able to look at its tracks when it has flown away.

PILEATED WOODPECKER
Dryocopus pileatus

This very large woodpecker has a very conspicuous red crest. It has a black and white body of about eighteen inches, and also a white under-wing which is noticeable in flight. It digs for insects in trees, and leaves oblong holes, excavating large amounts of sawdust at the base of the tree. It also attacks the lowest part of the trunk of a tree, which all woodpeckers do not do. I have seen very large piles of sawdust beneath the trees which they have excavated. It has a paired track formation, a K-shape from the four toes. The right foot has a reversed K. I have seen pileated woodpeckers in Montana, Oregon and B.C.. They are found in the Metolius area in central Oregon. They are large enough to be easily visible, especially as you are alerted by their red crest. They are rarely seen on the ground, so their tracks are very hard to find, particularly as they inhabit areas where the ground is littered with forest debris. They come into burn areas as most woodpeckers do, since the insect life flourishes there. I have seen them quite close, so they do not seem very worried about humans.

HAIRY WOODPECKER
Dendrocopus villosus

This woodpecker of about ten inches is white-backed and has white spots on its wings. The male has a red patch on the back of its head and has a large bill. It excavates square holes in trees looking for insects. Its tracks form a K shape, the inside lower toes registering on the ground shorter than the others, probably for leverage when holding onto a tree. At times I cannot distinguish it from the downy woodpecker which is smaller, and common in my area, especially after the forest burned. The familiar tapping is part of the daily background noise of the forest, and following the sound is a certain track to a woodpecker.

DOWNY WOODPECKER
Dendrocopus pubescens

This seven-inch woodpecker is a very pretty bird, with more white spots on its wings than the hairy. The male has a red patch on the back of the head with a smaller bill with which he bores small round holes in a tree. It marks a K shape in the ground when you can find tracks, and has a hopping, side-by-side pattern. The inner rear toes are shorter than the others. It often accompanies chickadees and nuthatches during the winter. It will bathe in my stock tanks, and its presence keeps other birds waiting.

GREAT BLUE HERON
Ardea herodias

I have been in enough wetlands to be very familiar with this bird. It is usually seen alone, or possibly with another in the water fishing for its food. At night it returns to a rookery. This four-foot tall, long-legged and graceful bird also has a long neck and bill. It walks most of the time in the water, lifts its thin legs with precision, and walks slowly, fishing. At times it stands motionless as though just resting. I have found its tracks in the mud. They are eight inches long, with the middle front toe extending furthest and the rear fourth toe being long and quite visible. There is a slight webbing and it toes in some when walking, which is noticeable. I have never been able to track a heron very much in the mud as the mud is usually too soft for me. When I come within 100 feet, most of the time the heron flies, so I rarely try to approach any closer and disturb its feeding. It is so majestic it is soothing to just watch this bird.

RED-TAILED HAWK
Buteo jamaicensis

This common round-tailed hawk, two feet in length, has a rufous color on the upper side of the tail which is diagnostic. I have recently had two red-tails come in for water, both at different times. They take a long time to decide to enter the water for a bath, and are very cognizant of their surroundings. Some of the chickadees and robins came in quickly for their baths, and were quite appalled at finding this hawk. Some of them sat there a little in shock, and others flew away immediately. Most of the time the hawks took up to an hour at the water, but very little of that time was wet time. They have the most interesting tracks of all the birds tracks I have seen. Their front three toes are slender and reflect the long talons which drag in receptive ground, showing their movement very well. The rear toe is long also, and marks very clearly. The tracks are four and a half inches long. When they flew away, they kept close in among the trees.

BALD EAGLE
Haliaeetus leucocephalus

I was able to accompany my friend Diana on her monitoring of bald eagle habitat for the Oregon Eagle Foundation. With binoculars it is possible to sometimes identify the sex of the bird, the female being larger. The well-known white head, white tail and yellow bill of the mature eagle are readily visible to the naked eye. The immature bird has a dark head and tail, and dark bill with whitish streaks on the breast and wing linings. The immature may easily be confused with the golden eagle, but there are distinct differences. Bald eagles are up to forty-three inches in size, with a wing span of up to eight feet. Although I have never found an eagle track on the ground, its size is five and a half inches long and just over three inches wide. Including talons, it could be six and three-eighths inches long and three and a half inches wide. Three toes are forward, the middle one extending about a half inch beyond the other two, and one long rear toe marks. Other track signs are infrequently in evidence. As with owls, regurgitated castings of greater size are indicative of eagles. Diana noticed a casting when I was with her that was two inches long and one inch wide, very light weight, composed of fine broken bones, fur and fine feathers. Feathers themselves may rarely be discovered and, if found, must be left, as it is illegal for anyone other than Native Americans to be in possession of eagle feathers in the U.S. Although at times a feather falls from a flying bird, I suspect that to see one fall from the majestic eagle would be a rare sight indeed.

GOLDEN EAGLE
Aquila chrysaetos

This familiar bird is thirty to forty-one inches in length, and spreads up to seven and two-thirds feet. Adults are dark below, with a possible slight lightening at the base of the tail. A faint gold may be seen on the back of its neck. The immatures, however, show white on their wings at the base of the primary feathers, and a white tail shows a dark terminal band. Golden eagles can be confused in the air with vultures, but the dihedral of the vulture's wings identify it.

I have glassed a golden eagle nest from some distance to see two white chicks, one distinctly larger than the other. The nest was on a rock ledge some distance from a canyon floor, a very large nest of sticks and limbs. When I returned a week later, I brought a road-killed rabbit to lay in an open space on the ground, not venturing any closer. Lack of disturbance during nesting time can be critical to the survival of the young. Many shoot this bird's prey for sport and thus impact the survival of eagles, which depend upon small rodents and rabbits for food.

At Glacier National Park I noticed three ravens closely chasing one eagle, the eagle for the most part ignoring the harassment, which occurs frequently. Further west in Montana I observed a golden eagle doing an inside loop, while its partner did other aerobatics.

Golden eagle tracks are almost as difficult to find as are bald eagle tracks, but they would be identical, only slightly smaller, probably not distinguishable.

GREAT HORNED OWL
Bubo virginianus

I am familiar with this owl as it is frequent in my home area. It can be two feet long, and it has ear tufts which distinguish it from others in my area, with well marked bars below. It sits in trees at times by my cabin, and I hear its voice frequently during the seasons it calls. Its feet are covered with feathers, and it has long talons. Its inner toe is shorter than the middle toe. It marks Xs on the ground where it might have captured its dinner. I rarely see any tracks on the ground, in spite of its hunting success. If startled, it will fly low but not very far.

PYGMY OWL
Glaucidium gnoma

This seven-inch owl has shared the same area in which I live all the years of my residence. Its whistle keeps me company many an evening, single hoos every two seconds, at times ending in a rolling trill. I sometimes see it waiting to drink, and once rescued one from drowning. I call to it occasionally, and we keep each other company.

A friend had come to help me decide what to do about a young bluebird with an injured wing. The rehabilitation center had not answered my call, so we tried to contain the bird in a box; but the bird would not settle down, beating its wings continually. A disposition for the bird had to be made. We decided that we should leave it near water. As we put it at the base of a juniper trunk and backed away, we were startled at the sudden whir of wings from an adjacent tree, the blur ending in a loud crack as a pygmy owl struck the base of the juniper at the bluebird's position. We rushed to find the bluebird in further shock, but only a small blue feather floated to the ground. A pygmy owl waited nearby. We went quite a ways to leave the bluebird. I am always wracked with ambivalence when I let nature take its course, but it has its own rules, and I have learned to respect them. The tracks from this incident are clearly in my mind, although they were not on the ground.

Pygmy owl tracks comply with other owls with two toes in front and two toes in the rear, forming the X pattern.

SPOTTED OWL
Strix occidentalis

This large, dark brown owl lives in old-growth forests. It can be nineteen inches long, with a puffy, rounded head. It has dark eyes, unlike other large North American owls. Underparts are barred and spotted. It can sound like a small, barking dog or make a series of rapid hoots. A friend and I were trying to locate owls for the Deschutes National Forest. We called one, two, then three hoos, and moved slowly through the old growth towering above the entangled forest floor. We were on the crest of the Cascades in central Oregon. We stopped and listened, looking into the high snags of Douglas fir for nests or cavities, or the silhouette of an owl against the still-light sky. It was late evening and a friend and I were volunteers on a spotted owl monitoring program. I had never seen a spotted owl, but my friend had been with the program all that year. We were looking for young. The National Forest Service wanted to know if a pair in this area had produced some young. We had found the adult female a little while previously.

The conifers were tall and the canopy dense. A dried stream bed was, nevertheless, damp beneath the area, for it was in shade all day, with only slivers of sunlight reaching the floor. A coyote's paw pads had left fresh tracks in single file across the stream bed, but into the fern and debris of limbs of the understory they could not be found. A smashed coyote-sized area of vegetation was there, however. Passing this, deep, regular holes in the vegetation caught my eye, and I bent down to feel the shape beneath. Elk.

We called again. No answer. This area was the second we had tried, having no success at the other. We scanned the leaves for the whitewash droppings left from a perching owl above. There was whitewash spotted on the understory leaves. I looked up. It was beyond the end of some very slight limbs. These were the tracks of a bird. Must have been a windy day. The limbs were frail. I thought a light-weight, young bird must have sat there, hopefully a young spotted owl. Shortly my friend exclaimed joyously as she bent down to retrieve a ball of regurgitation full of feathers and small mouse bones. Owl! This was another kind of track, found under a tree where an owl has spent some time in digesting its prey, then coughing up the indigestible residue. We went on and called.

There! Its distinctive pattern of hoos! It was a high-pitched hooting like a sharp dog bark. It was an owl, not us. It was upslope and within a quarter of a mile. We called back and were answered. We made our way quickly and as silently as possible, waiting for further location identification. It came, and we climbed on. Suddenly we were very close to the call of the male, and we strained our necks to see an owl in the heavy growth. Abruptly my friend sat down, grinning broadly and pointing. It was a young owl, much smaller than its nineteen-inch male parent who was looking down on us, too. Its dark brown body and puffy head encompassed large, dark eyes that peered at us with innocence and curiosity. The young owl uttered a shussss, and we saw a second young owl. It was a deeply satisfying thrill for me, not only to see this much-publicized, unusual bird, but to have been part of helping to find the young.

We sat a long time on the ground, talking back and forth to them in soft, hushed tones, looking eagerly to learn their color, their movements, to get to know them. They flew occasionally from one branch to another close by, getting closer and closer to us. Their underparts had begun to show barred and spotted markings.

It grew dark and we needed to leave. Sadly we made our way back, the young following us. We talked to them and told them not to come, but for a quarter of a mile one continued with us.

Not all tracks are on the ground. One will likely never find a spotted owl track upon the ground. A wing mark in the snow, perhaps, nest cavities in old growth snags, nests in tree canopies, a voice: hoo, hoo,hoo, hoo, hoo, hooo.... And a memory.

TURKEY VULTURE
Cathartes aura

This bird is nearly six feet, with two toned black wings. In soaring its wings are on the dihedral, appearing to be unsteady in flight. The adult has a red head, the immature has a black head.

One very hot day after many years of drought in central Oregon, a chipmunk drowned in a stock tank at my place. I threw its body aside a few yards away, and forgot about it. A few hours later I glanced out of the window, attracted by the spread of large bird wings. A turkey vulture had alighted in a juniper top, no doubt attracted by the odor of the dead squirrel. I got a long, good look at this bird, the best I have ever had.

It sat there indifferently, pruning an underfeather, and I waited to see what it was about. It must have been casually surveying the total situation before going to the ground to feed. It then flew to an adjacent tree lower of limb, and looked around. Its bare red head and neck and red eyes and wrinkled skin were evident in detail. Its beak curved with deadly precision downward. Its head swiveled in almost all directions. As it turned its head in profile, I could see straight through its nostrils. Its large body was black, but its wings were centrally brown, edged with black. Its long legs ended with formidable claws. When it showed its six-foot-long wingspread to float downward to the ground, all was very still at the watering tanks. The songbirds had hushed or flown away upon its entry. It was very placid. Once on the ground it was very careful in its feeding, unrushed and delicate in eating. It took it only a few minutes to finish the meal, and I saw its large wings puff out for the push and takeoff, and it was gone, a silhouette in the air, with silent, jagged wingtips, moving back and forth effortlessly as it scanned the ground for further sustenance.

I went out into the dry dust of the desert spot where it had fed, camera and ruler in hand. The ground was marred with depressions of its landing and its movement on the ground. Only two suggestions of tracks remained. What appeared to be a three-toed track measured three and a half to four inches wide, and two and a half inches long. Nothing else remained.

SANDHILL CRANE
Grus canadensis

This long crane can be three to four feet long and is long necked and long legged, gray, with a bald red crown. I have seen them in large flocks in southeast Oregon. Sometimes they hop and flap. The tracks in the wet bogs show the walking pattern and the four toes register. The rear toe shows a small mark, as the toe is higher on the leg than the foot. Due to the size, the toes are wide. An Oregon man, Dayton Hyde, did a lot of research on the sandhill crane, tracking by car as far as he could, the migration of a crane he reared. He wrote about this.

TURKEY
Meleagris gallopavo

We are all familiar with the turkey, domestic and wild. Males can be four feet long, and females three feet long. I have seen wild turkey in Montana, and Oregon has some introduced near my area. They stay in small flocks and return to a familiar roosting ground. The large-size tracks can be five inches long, with the stride of the gobbler about an inch longer than the hens, about eight inches, with the middle toe slightly longer. They have three fat toe marks in front; and the end of the abbreviated rear toe track shows to the side. It appears toed-in due to the inward curvature of the middle toe. Their wing tips might also mark on the ground. They have a staggered walking pattern. Not only have I seen flocks of these birds in the wild, but one afternoon in Montana I was sitting at a friend's house and we looked out the window at a flock of about a dozen turkeys making their slow, noisy way through the yard.

In March of 1996 I was walking about 300 feet from my cabin when I saw a large track in bare sand. I was flabbergasted to see strange track, and one with three toes. It was five inches long and as wide. A rear spur marked in a few of the tracks. The stride was two and a half feet. I stared in disbelief, wondering if some emu had gotten free somewhere. However, emus do not have the rear spur. I had not seen turkey track in many years, but indeed, these were wild turkey tracks. I tracked a half mile, following a pair traveling together. I called Fish and Wildlife to ask about this, and they told me they had released about thirty only six or so miles from me two years before. That I had never seen their tracks before was amazing. I remembered a neighbor had tried to describe such tracks to me, which she said were walking over a mile. I couldn't trust her description, but it sounded like raven tracks, although the distance would have been far. But one with an injured wing might have walked that far. I thought immediately of her story.

YELLOW-BELLIED SAPSUCKER
Sphyrapicus varius

This colorful nine-inch bird has a black back with white spots and a red crown and throat, with white and black on its head if a male. He also has a white rump with a few black lines on his tail. The female has a brown head and back, but carries the black and white wings and tail. These birds feed on the sap of trees, and their tongue has evolved into a brush to extract sap. They punch small, evenly spaced holes around the trunk of a tree. I have seen a lot of these sapsuckers in my area, and a lot of my trees show their sign. Their tracks are a K shape and are paired as they are perching birds. The red-breasted (*Sphyrapicus varius*) and Williamson sapsucker (*Sphyrapicus thyroideus*) are familiar birds in my area, and they both make the same type of pattern on the tree trunks, but the holes seem larger. They also have K-shaped, paired tracks.

ROBIN
Turdus migratorius

This most familiar songbird can be eleven inches long and has large eyes, and a slight, yellow bill. It has a brown back and brick-red breast. It is a combination of a perching and walking bird, for it not only walks, but hops. When alighting on the ground, it usually hops a few times and then begins walking, and these are good clues to watch for in tracking. The walking tracks are a single file line of tracks showing three long toes in front and a long rear toe, with some inward curvature typical of the perchers. When the juniper berries are ripe, the birds, and the robins in particular, eat so many they become tipsy from the juice, and stagger or fly into windows in unbecoming behavior. In a dry winter, without carrion, the coyote eats a lot of juniper berries, but I have not seen it in such condition.

STARLING
Sturnus vulgaris

This short-tailed, eight-inch black bird reflects greenish or purple close up. It has a yellow bill in the spring and is aggressive toward other birds. It was introduced into the U.S. and has been most unpopular. Its tracks are about two and a half inches long, with three long toes in front and one long toe in the rear. It has a walking gait. When the starlings appear at my bird feeders, they chase all the other birds away. In Montana, they attacked swallows in their nests under the eaves, but they seemed to leave the bluebirds alone.

STELLAR'S JAY
Cyonocitta stelleri

This cocky, lively bird of thirteen inches has a long crest on the top of its head. It is dark black on its head, shoulders and breast and a vivid blue elsewhere. It has a saucy temperament and is very attentive to human movement. It has become very accustomed to humans, and tolerates a short flight distance. It is a percher, and its tracks are typical, with some inward curvature, showing the long three toes forward and a long toe to the rear. I have seen tracks two and a half inches long. I had resident Stellars before the fire, and eventually one returned. I noticed it at my feeder, lethargic and not eating. I knew it was ill, and I felt quite helpless. One day I found it drowned in a water tank. I was in grief, for this bird and its kin had kept me good company for a long time. I took the bird, and found its lower bill had been broken off. Thus it had been unable to sustain itself. I hoped for others to come to stay. Two did come in at nesting season, but they were rather spooky and were absent for about six weeks, when just yesterday one came in ravenous, ate and left. I had even thought of trying to import some. Eventually they repopulated and I now have six. One built a nest in my eaves while I was away, but my return moved her.

COMMON NIGHTHAWK
Chordeiles minor

This is a very interesting bird, ten inches long, which is abroad mostly at dusk, but I see it during the day, as well. It is a sharp-winged, slim bird of brown with white on pointed wings, and makes an unmistakable sound in its dives. To me it sounds like a train whistle. I have only seen the tracks of one bird, and they were blurred, as they were mostly on the pine needle blanket of the forest. The shape of the tracks was indiscernible. The tracks of this bird are very difficult to find, for it really spends so little time on any bare ground. Just before the forest fire razed my land, I noticed a nighthawk sitting on a nest adjacent to a route I used. She was beneath old Ponderosa pines, and on the ground in lava rock and brush. I would sometimes forget and come too close, and flush her off the nest, so I did see her two eggs. When I returned from a trip and found the fire's devastation, I went to her nest area. There were two baked eggs. I picked them up, one breaking, but I took them home and they remain in a dish on my desk, a sad reminder of the event.

MEADOWLARK
Sturnella neglecta

This common field bird can be eleven inches long and is very colorful, with a yellow breast and a black V on its chest. It is brown-backed, and has a white tail band. There are also black spots forward of its wings along the breast. Its song is very beautiful and cheery. It has large tracks with three forward toes and one in the rear. It walks in an alternating trail. They are plentiful in an old barley field near me, and their tracks are two inches long. A slight curvature is noticeable at times.

CANADA GOOSE
Branta canadensis

This widespread goose has a black head and neck, a long neck and is grayish brown on the body, with a light colored breast, and can be three feet long. There are many varieties of Canada geese, small and large. The large webbed tracks are easily noticed and identified. The shorter rear toe marks on the ground owing to the weight of the bird, and there is noticeable curving in of the tracks. The tracks themselves can be three and a half to four inches long in the wet sand they frequent so often. As their legs are situated more in the center of their body than are those of ducks, they can walk with more agility on land. The stride is short, however, although greater than the mallard duck. Geese make very distinguishing tracks on the banks of rivers, and they frequent most water ponds.

MALLARD DUCK
Anas platyrhynchos

This well-recognized bird of about two feet in length has a green head and narrow white collar. It is gray with a reddish brown chest, and its white tail has an upcurl. Its bill is yellow, and its feet orange. Like the Canada goose, the rear toe is short, and the three front toes are webbed. Most of the time the rear toe does not mark on the soil, but in wet sand it might. The tracks have the inward pigeon toe. In good tracks, the toe marks within the webbing are clear. The tracks measure around two and a half to three inches long. I have tracked ducks on the river banks, and they walk as though they are going somewhere, and then wander around, sometimes going in and out of the water. The places where they rest could show one track, as they often lift one foot up when sleeping, but of course, they put it down when they wake, and so two tracks show.

RAVEN
Corvus corax

Everyone is familiar with this bird or the smaller crow. It is totally black and about two feet long. Its voice is harsh and loud, and very distinctive. It also has throat feathers noticeable when sitting on a limb. It is a walker, with four-inch tracks, and its rear toe track marking very long. They are found sitting in the trees by carrion. I can see them from quite a distance to alert me to predator or poacher kills, and thus find tracks.

***

There are many birds whose tracks I know only in the sky, or on a tree limb, because the bird itself is there. But at times I have held these birds in my hand. Some have been injured, some dead. Some have been young, some old. I remember them all. I remember the green-tailed towhee with its long tail which hit my window pane just after I lifted the blind. I held it in my hands hoping against hope this beautiful creature might survive, but it did not. I once fished a baby quail from my water tank, perhaps only hours dead. I have held woodpecker and wren in my hands, robin and sparrow. Nothing made me happier than when the Townsend's solitare still breathed and gained strength in my cupped hands, after the shock of flying against the house. There were many others who flew once again after being held, flew to fly another day alive and happy, singing their feelings, perhaps nesting again.

So when you have come to the end of the tracks of your creature, and it seems to have vanished in thin air, this is when your experience comes into play. When the track is invisible to others, it is your intuition which makes it visible to you. And may you track on beyond the end, into infinity.

Chapter Thirteen

Humans

Tracking is a skill, not a scientific practice, but objectivity must be crucially exercised in order to read the ground accurately, and where the tracks disappear, the use of logic is the answer. Search and Rescue trackers follow the trail by fitting together evidence which the ground and vegetation presents. Border patrolmen know that the invisible trail beyond the evidence is just as much a result of logic as the sense and wisdom that surrounds the finding of each and every track. In a process of elimination (checking to the left and right to make sure there is no sign, observing obstacles to passage, etc.), the trail can be continued, until sign can be found further on. The invisible trail is also where that individual would have gone, based on the facts collected through the prior tracking of that person, with the accumulation of knowledge of his habits or his known goal. Or where, as a human, would you have gone? Common sense is a reliable quality. Actually, a tracker is a predator of sorts, in the sense of not being persuaded from his course.

I experience a different kind of energy when I am on the track of one of my own species. Bonded as a human to other humans, is there an inherent knowledge deep within me which gives me some unconscious advantage in tracking man as opposed to wildlife? Whether this is so or not, the ground must be read in as objective a fashion as ever. One's subjective self must not intrude into that reading. Yet as I track a human, I feel I have a better chance, that I know this quarry who is so much like me, and yet, different. Each human is an individual and leaves something unique on the ground to be read.

Experienced trackers learn the behavior of those they track, a reflection of the quarry's personality. In what we do, should it be to pick flowers, look in rock crannies or climb every knoll, we reveal ourselves. The choices we make as we move through the forest or along a dusty road are based on our individuality. The treads on the soles of shoes are only what lead us to that knowledge. And in so knowing, when pavement or boulders are crossed, knowing the quarry's behavior will give cues as to where to cut for sign ahead, for you know his ways. You have an expectation of his behavior.

Tracking across rocks is not impossible. A heavy boot may scuff the surfaces, moss may be depressed, twigs broken, shale disturbed, leaves crushed, rocks moved. Whatever the scene, a tracker thinks of what would happen to the microenvironment ahead should a human cross it. And importantly, *where would a human go*, what is the best way to travel. These are the places you look for sign after the last track tells you the direction of travel, and there are no more track. One border patrolman tracker indicated he tracked an individual along cement sidewalks by the residue of dirt left from the soil upon which he had been walking.

The motive and age of the person tracked, and his knowledge of the environment in which you are tracking, is important. Is this a lost child? A fugitive? What expertise does this person have in the woods? I had a young man come to a workshop once whose primary question was how could you tell if someone walked backward? This is a novice question often asked in relation to how you conceal your movements. We know that the globules of earth or snow are pulled forward with the forward movement of the foot, thus showing that in walking backwards, the direction of travel is from the heel of the boot rather than the toe, as it moves backwards across the ground. In addition, walking backwards has its own problems which would be reflected on the ground. You cannot see as well, and if you are continually turning to see, this weight shift and foot position is reflected in the ground. The stride shortens, perhaps the straddle widens in order to stabilize the body which cannot see well where it is going. One would fatigue more quickly, and the tracks would reflect this. I wonder how far someone could really go walking backwards. It is in opposition to the normal functioning of our anatomy. Tripping would likely be noticeable. Many cues would surface, and quickly.

The basic stride of man is sixteen inches, but we walk with much longer or shorter steps, too. (Are we a woman in high heels? Are we a hiker? Do we have long legs?) The next track will be about six inches to the left or right, whichever foot is next.

We do need to distinguish the tracks of the right person from other tracks in the area. If we are tracking a person we need to know the track measurements and the sole tread. With boots, the center of the sole often has an emblem of the manufacturer. This center area is where breaks, wear and individual stress marks show most prominently. These are the essences of pressure ridges, pressure that the individual puts on his feet, and therefore his shoe, which mark him from any other individual. It is the fingerprint of that person's foot. Some people walk with weight toward the outside of the heel, toe in or present other characteristics. Each individual is built in a unique way, and thus his walk is unique and leaves its identifiable pattern on his shoe, and thus on the ground. Two people of the same height, build, weight, age and shoe size, wearing the same make of shoe, would put pressure on different parts of their soles, and thus identify themselves. Differing back, leg, knee and hip problems and diseases, put different stresses in different places on the body, unique to each person. This reflects on the ground as they walk. Very old people have a wide straddle and a short stride for their stabilization, as their senses and orientation diminish. A lot depends upon the length of one's legs, rather than height, when it comes to someone's natural stride. I hiked with a couple for awhile, the man being about six feet, his wife being shorter, but her stride was longer than his. Her legs were longer.

The faster a person goes, the narrower his straddle. Observe a jogger's tracks. They are almost directly in front of each other, and the movement in soil shows the explosion of the earth as great amounts of pressure is placed upon it, less in dry clay than moist river bottom soil, but just as extreme in relation to that density. Knowing your soil density and how it reacts to differing amounts of pressure under different moisture conditions will give you a judgment of how fast the person was moving, and how heavy the person was who passed. Test your own movements in soil under those exact conditions (which may be different at the time you are there). It will be your basic unit for comparison. But you cannot extrapolate from that accurately. You must practice over a period of time before you can rely upon it.

Familiarity with wildlife tracks will assist you in tracking humans. Knowing when certain animals are active will aid you in aging, as some species will mark across the tracks you follow, and you will know something about the time frame of passage of your quarry. Becoming familiar with the scents of nature may clue you in to the actual or former presence of humans. If someone has broken branches from a tree which gives off recognizable scent, this may alert you to a direction or a campfire. Smoke from cigarettes, cigars or campfires are ascertainable within certain time and weather frames, and remain on an individual's clothing for a long time, as may perfume. Food scents from cooking or discarded residue from food may do the same.

People who are lost or running from detection may be careless in throwing away food wrappers or lose clothing or articles which might be in plain evidence. Do not assume that this find was recent, or from the particular person you are tracking, however, and be sure to evaluate the circumstance so it will not put you off track. When a person abandons items of necessity for survival, his mental state should be in question. Is he becoming hypothermic or going into panic? Crushed grass where someone sat or lay may be visible. Evidence is not always on the ground. It may be above the ground on a tree limb, torn threads from a shirt, a bloody limb where it pierced skin. Feces may be in evidence, and this can be aged, as with wildlife scat, depending upon your expertise in this, the given weather, temperature, moisture conditions and whether it has been in the sun. Flies may be present on the scat, and are more numerous when feces are fresh; then there are fewer after a few hours, and likely none after a day, but the number may vary in different climates and seasons. If a person's urine is a dark yellow, he is likely becoming hypothermic. If orange, he is in worse shape.

Remember conditions may be different when you are there than what they might have been at the time your quarry was. The person might have responded to a noise, an airplane, an animal, thought they recognized some landmark or actually changed their mind about their direction, and made a change. But if sign is absent, you must use common sense and that probably will be to continue on in the direction the trail leads, and try to cut for sign ahead, for a change of direction would be less probable. In heavy brush the tracker may track by feeling the depressions of the foot in the ground beneath. Fatigue shows in tracks. If one tires, the drag into the track becomes more evident, and if a person is exhausted, drags in and out of both tracks show, for he is too tired to lift up his feet.

Knowing the hundreds of patterns of shoes would be helpful, but is not necessary, as long as you can draw well and communicate the patterns if essential. Knowing the category of shoes is important: flats, which have no heel differentiation, or heels, which do. Some work boots, tennis shoes and sandals are flats. Hiking boots and street shoes are considered heels. Other soles are divided into categories based on whether they are lugs, or are lightweight, such as sneakers, tennis or running shoes, or are western boots. Take measurements precisely. Note the soil type and condition in which they were measured, which makes a difference in length or width of the track. Tread pattern must be exact. As you track, look for regularity, a tread pattern from a shoe. Nature's way is to make things look irregular, so set your eye for regularity. Practice identifying track from different angles, not just in the direction of travel or backtracking, but from ninety-degree and forty-five-degree angles in each direction. One can pass by tracks because of a rigid mental set. Barefoot tracks are not necessarily another story, for pressure ridges and characteristic walking patterns can be identified, but if you are tracking someone who does not go barefoot regularly, you will probably find the tracks in places which are easiest on the feet.

Much seems to be said by laymen about the depth of tracks and their relation to the weight of the maker. A tracker will know about different soils, and depth of a track relates to this and the moisture content of that soil when the track was made. When tracks are fresh, trackers press their own feet into the soil for comparison and estimate the weight to be heavier or lighter than their own weight. A tracker must be aware of the recent weather conditions. But if you are inexperienced in aging track, and unable to judge the ground conditions at the time the track was made, further analysis of weight is questionable. You must have practiced with differing variables. People have also jumped from a stump to find their tracks nowhere approaching the depth of a track, and assume the track-maker weighed a great deal more than they. Again, one needs information which might not be available, or experiential knowledge which one might not have, for a proper judgment. I followed a line of tracks across my land early in my tracking days, an adult male in vibram boots. I am never pleased when someone crosses my land, as it is posted. So I wanted to know why. The man had parked near my gate, gotten out and deliberately passed some no trespassing signs, and cut across my land. It was a purposeful stride, but it wavered to some extent for a short distance, although still moving with a consistent bearing. As I tracked, I noted the stride, and made a judgment as to his approximate height and weight. I didn't know if I would be able to corroborate this. But by the time I had tracked a quarter of a mile to my southwest corner, I knew that this man was with the National Forest. For he set a corner post, and turned around and went back. He had known his directions, and wavered a little in finding the exact spot. I called the National Forest to find out who it was so I could ascertain my skill level on my estimate of his height and weight. Today I don't recall the measurements, but I was pleased, and he quite surprised, for I came within a few inches of his height and fairly close to his weight. One has to practice this a lot, however, and know the soil well.

There are finer discriminations we make in tracking. There are indications that lost persons inadvertently keep circling a certain direction, primarily to the right. Some have thought that carrying a heavy weight on the opposite side of the body, such as a rifle, may counteract this. I think the dominant foot or hand has a bearing on the circling direction, but I have not experimented with this. I think a person is right- or left-footed, just like right- or left-handed. There are people who are bilaterally dominant, where they are adept at doing things with either hand or foot, or cross-dominant, as being right-handed and left-footed. I do not know if or how this affects their walking behavior in the field, where they might not have orientation to their directions. A person without landmarks likely has some internal or anatomical mechanism which guides him. People have a feeling foot and a dominant foot. The feeling foot has a slightly shorter stride in a normal walk on level ground. A slightly longer stride of the dominant foot may eventually propel him in a certain direction. Many other variables are influential in differing circumstances, as terrain or distractions, to change the person's direction. Whether these would be only temporary deviations from a primary set toward circling in one direction would need research.

It is important to gather as much available information as possible about the individual one is tracking as it has a distinct bearing on the situation. Has the person survival knowledge? Does he need medication?

Aging track comes after much practice in every weather condition and in all types of soil. Accurate conclusions are dictated through many years of experience in reading the ground under all variables of wind, sun, moisture and temperature. You must watch the track disintegrate after each hour, each day, each week, each month, and there is no other way. Not all people have the perseverance to do this. Smooth the ground and put track there, or see what marks on it, and start the learning process. When you come upon a track, put your own track beside it to test the difference. You see what a fresh track looks like and make your judgment from it, after you have experience in aging the ground. Remember also, that our sun is on the southern slope, which will age track more rapidly than the northern slope. Also, temperature changes the looks of the ground. High temperature ages track fairly rapidly. It can restore the ground to uniform color within two or three hours. And gravity works constantly at its slow and steady rate.

Most trackers only track well in their home area, as differing ecologies have different climates and the rate of disintegration of vegetation and soils can differ greatly between them. In ecologies of heavy vegetation, one ages it primarily, for the ground is rarely visible.

Jack Kearney, a border patrolman, has taught many trackers. He has made astute observations of changes in vegetation under different conditions, and how weather influences tracks. With green vegetation, color change is the most important thing to notice. Tracks look lighter in short grass, darker in tall grass. A trail through vegetation tumbles the plants and the underside of the leaves are revealed, and so look for a lighter color. Green vegetation crushed beneath a shoe and hard ground will result in a dark, smashed wound. Sand grains may crush into the underside of the plant when stepped on, and turning over suspect leaves may show this. One must differentiate between human damage and cuts by hooves of wildlife or cattle.

With leafy plants, a recent injury results in unnatural positions. Broken branches and vegetation can indicate the direction of travel, such as grass lying upslope when a walker has walked up a hill. In aging, this plant will take less time to erect than the plant lying downhill, for it has fewer degrees rise to regain its upright position, as opposed to many more degrees for the plant lying downhill.

Lush vegetation returns to its normal position after awhile and thus destroys the visible trail, but a heel's indentation in the ground beneath might be found. Very tall grass will take longer to become upright again. A plant with poor footing, as in swampy areas, takes longer to right itself. Live vegetation begins its process of repair immediately. The fresher the break, the lighter the color. Compare a break by making a fresh one.

Heat restores attached green foliage, but increases withering of separated branches. Extreme heat, however, will increase withering so rapidly that a recent break only hours old may look like it was made the day before.

In dry grass, an older trail shows up as dark, as moisture during the night causes stems to expand and round, thus not reflecting light as a flat, injured stem would. Also, dust accumulates after awhile, and thus does not reflect light. So clean, freshly flattened stems cause better reflection of sunlight and create a slightly lighter color. High temperatures would restore this disturbance to a natural state in several hours.

Weather conditions are important. Wind erases sign quickly, but a track can be seen in damp snow or frozen ground even with a strong wind. High wind on top of new snow on a damp or powder snow trail will likely wipe out the trail. But with only high wind on damp snow, a trail would remain. Rain can completely destroy a trail; even a light mist can do a great deal. Rain does not impact on broken branches, but moisture on a track in dirt results in graininess with a more uniform color, thus obscuring the color contrast. People think that tracking in snow is easy, but with so many different types and amounts of snow, combined with differing temperatures, it can become impossible. Thawing distorts and enlarges a track, making it look old. Refrozen snow is a gray color. Fresh, compacted snow appears very white, but when older, becomes icy gray in color. Press the track to see how frozen it is. Powder snow is difficult to track in. Blow away the surrounding snow and you might see a configuration. A foot can pick up globules of snow which remain after the depressions of a foot have smoothed, or the snow around has melted. Thick sleet presents difficulties.

Remarkable tracking stories from the American West have captivated us all. One was of Pedro Espinosa, when, in 1819 at age nine, he was captured and reared by Comanches. At age twenty-eight he was able to return to his relatives, and assisted in tracking Indians for the Union men. From his Comanche upbringing he had developed keen powers of observation and logic, and had learned how to read every sign on the ground and age it, becoming expert about every wildlife habit. Knowledgeable about Natives as he was, he was able to find their trails in spite of their clever ruses to disguise their tracks. He knew how they moved across the land on horseback by the use of landmarks, and thus as a tracker knowledgeable of the habits of the Natives would not spend time on the painstaking doubling back of the trail, the searching for sign from a rocky creek bed, etc., which they used to throw off the tracker, but would go directly toward where he knew they would pass in order to get to their goal. In one instance Espinosa did this over 100 miles, where the white men could not ascertain what he was following. Another trail he followed by cutting for sign in a circle around a camp where the Comanches had burned the brush to throw off pursuers. Espinosa noticed sign and, on hands and knees, blew away the ashes to find the imprint of a horse. Enough tracks were found to indicate a direction of travel, which led him to the different directions of several horses. Moving forward for four miles, he found the same trails of the various horses, and then moved ahead again a mile and a half, to corroborate his expectation that they were converging. He noted that the direction of several of the horses pointed to a common center, and thus the problem was solved.

I track trespassers across the land, wanderers, trappers, horseback and ATV riders, poachers and adventurers in the National Forest beside my land. As their tracks reflect their behavior, I learn a lot about who has gone before me. Backtracking also tells me much about their behavior. One instance in which this was true was a trail of flats with a narrow straddle and rather long stride, about two and a half feet, and almost a twelve-inch track, with a narrow width. The track displayed tiny holes across the entire track, deck shoes with round protrusions. I came upon this about 200 feet from my cabin one summer afternoon. A person was walking along an old, unused logging road. As I tracked, I immediately realized the individual was walking with purpose, no variation in stride or speed, as though with a goal in mind. I did not know if this was a young adult male or a female from the tracks; even though the straddle was narrow, it could have been a male of slight build. The trail led me across my forty acres and up a fairly steep ridge to where there was a view, and a comfortable chair. The tracks passed this, and entered a neighbor's property. This neighbor was not a permanent resident, and there was no one home. The tracks went on across a gravel drive and toward other neighbors. I went back to the point where I had found the tracks and backtracked. The tracks had come across the forest, from the general direction of a main National Forest road which had very little traffic. The trail made me think of my own in that I come and go from that road, meandering a little as I take a fairly direct course. (Had the person knowledge of where he or she was? Had a car broken down and was someone walking for help? No one knocked on my door.) The stride and speed only varied as the terrain dictated. The person seemed comfortable and confidant in the woods, keeping the pace and direction steady. Was it male or female? I needed something to verify one or the other. It came, but it was not something I expected. At a stump I found facial tissue, wadded and bloody. The female had been menstruating. I didn't go further. To learn where she had come from was less interesting to me now than where she was going.

The next day I picked up her tracks again, headed in the general direction of a nearby ranch. I didn't pursue them. But the plot thickened. A neighbor a half mile away called to inform me that the woman at the ranch had been alone, and during the night she had heard someone trying to enter a basement door. Having no phone, she lay there afraid all night. In the morning she found that someone had spent the night there. I knew who, but there was nothing to do about it now.

The next day I had to spend in town, and that night the neighbor called again to tell me that the sheriff had come out to my neighbors' (where I had tracked across the gravel of the driveway), as their house had been broken into. Nothing was missing. Someone had used the bathroom. They thought the person had been injured as they found blood. I knew who was responsible, but not where she was. The sheriff would be doing his job. This girl was either a runaway or hiding from the law.

A complication came when I was called as a Mental Examiner for Circuit Court, as I am a trained psychologist. I interviewed the mother of a young woman who apparently wandered out in the woods and stayed there for days. Her daughter had mental symptoms, and her unusual behavior reminded me of the tracks I had found. I discovered that her shoes were exactly like the tracks I had followed, not a common tread. I evaluated the young woman, who indeed had a mental disorder. The judge ordered hospitalization in a psychiatric treatment center. She had arrived at the hospital because she finally got to a shelter, where they noticed symptoms, and subsequently she was scheduled for a mental hearing.

I relate this story as it was an unusual coincidence and has tracking value. From the behavior exhibited as I tracked her, she was comfortable in the woods. As her mother had indicated, she had spent much time in that setting, which reflected in her trail. The mental symptoms were not reflected to me from her tracks. She was functioning to an extent; she found her way around and provided for herself to a degree.

Another brief incident came when I was down with a bad virus. At night I heard my dog bark furiously outside, and I looked out the window to see a man at the yard gate. I opened the window to advise him not to come through the gate or the dog would bite him. He asked the way to Bend, as his car had been disabled on the logging road. I offered to call the sheriff for him, and he said no, so I gave him directions and he left. I did call the sheriff, however, and they told me they had been looking for two men, one of which was this man. The offer to call the sheriff always has interesting reactions. In the morning his tracks in the driveway indicated he was running at high speed.

Another spring evening it was pouring rain, as it had been all day. The dog was inside, and began barking furiously as I heard two sets of steps on the deck and a knock on the front door. I knocked on a window where I could see and talk to whomever was there. Two young men appeared. I could see bicycles leaning against the fence. I had no intention of letting them inside, no matter the rain. They asked how far they were from Bend. It was hard to imagine cycling twenty miles in such a downpour. I told them the distance and gave the directions. I made my usual offer to call the sheriff, and they looked at each other and decided that they had no phone because they had just moved here. I suggested the sheriff could drive them to town. They declined and left. I called him anyway to try to get them some aid. The next morning I did my usual routine.

The bicycle tracks showed where they left the property, and where they lifted their bikes over the locked gate, because they were made in deep mud. But there were none coming in from that direction. I found they had come onto the property from higher up my ridge, over a barbed wire fence, and to the drive, then up to the house. My house is not visible in any direction over a couple of hundred feet because of the tree cover. As I had had mountain bike tracks coming across my land from the logging road in the past from another direction, and someone lifting the bike over the gate, I felt one of these men might have been here before, and knew the house was there. Perhaps it was chance. Fortunately I never saw the tracks again. So many people have trespassers they never know were there. I like to know what's going on around home.

I came home from a vacation once to find adult male boot tracks at my yard gate. This bothered me, and I tracked them coming from and returning to the neighbors land before they built their house. The man had a distinct splay of both feet, and he did something few people do when walking down a country road. He walked in the sandy center, where most people walk in the tire tracks. I asked another neighbor who knew these people to ask them if they had walked up to my cabin. They said they hadn't. I later noticed the neighbor's tracks and identified him as the one who came onto my property. As I drive east of a morning, his tracks still shine primarily in the middle of the road. At one meeting with him, I mentioned the incident of the tracks which had concerned me, and glanced down at his feet to identify his shoes. His eyes followed mine, and he gave a sheepish grin.

I was among fifty-four Search and Rescue personnel participating in a weekend workshop given by border patrolman Joel Hardin at Camp Adair in Corvallis, Oregon, in 1981. It poured rain the entire night before our field exercise, after two men made tracks for two miles in thick brush and poison oak, each in different directions for two different teams. In the morning each team divided up in smaller teams of three, and we set out in periodic rain. It was very muddy, and the brush and we were very wet. The tracks of our quarry were identified, and their depressions were deep in the soft mud, and surprisingly not obliterated in such heavy and continuous rain. Vegetation gave us cues, but the problem was the tracks of the other searchers. Those fresh tracks of the searchers (who mark their boots to differentiate them from the quarry), were very distracting, not necessarily that there were many other tracks, but that these fresher tracks were lighter. Our eyes were drawn to them instead of the older quarry's track, and it took a little longer to set one's mind back to the image of the quarry's tracks. Both teams managed to find the trails made, and it was a real confidence-builder to realize what could be done under such conditions. Joel Hardin was asked whether he would rather have one man or a team of searchers looking for him should he ever become lost. His response was, a team. One man might make an error, and increase the search time, or even lose the trail, but with a greater number of people, this would be caught.

There are human traces that we can follow, although the shape of their footprints have disappeared. Ghostly wagon train tracks lie across the land. In Oregon I see them where the cheat grass waves, a signal from the soil that many have trod there, oxen, wheels and people. The ground impacts stay for many years. There is an old Indian trail across the Cascades west of Sisters, Oregon, along the north of the North Sister Mountain, where obsidian arrowheads still lie. I think the ground would tell me where. Perhaps I can follow it before my eyes close forever to those cues, the ones that lie somewhere between the old trees and past the new. Some day I may catch a sign that tells me the way—if the light is just right, that is.

***

There is another interesting issue on bipedal locomotion which has been around for centuries. The Sasquatch, a giant hominoid with full body hair, leaves tracks. The Pacific Northwest is considered its home. The tracking of a Sasquatch would be as simple as any other tracking, but the evidence presented for the existence of the creature is complicated. The gait and perhaps the anatomy of this creature is purported to be different from that of man. Some then hypothesize that its foot placements, straddle and tracks are different as a result. (There are a variety of supposed tracks, casts of tracks and theories to support those differences.)

Let us look at how tracking a Sasquatch must be similar to humans in basic ways, regardless of any differences of foot anatomy, placement or gait, knowing what we do of the way bipedal man walks on soil, and what happens to the soil as a result. I do not address whether this creature exists, nor what its gait is if it exists, here. But what we do know when any living creature propels itself across the ground, is what must happen to the ground. It is the same as man. Even if a creature might lift its foot in true vertical fashion as it takes a step (and Sasquatch buffs do not propose that a Sasquatch does this), there are still ground cues if the creature is to move from that spot. It cannot lift its foot so vertically that it does not disturb the ground and take grains of it with its foot, which of course must be thrown forward, if that is the direction in which it is moving. Even if it lifts its foot precisely vertical, and propels itself forward in the air, so to speak, then the other foot will show the movement forward. There is no avoiding leaving sign even if it flew the steps, and landed perfectly vertical upon the soil; that would show.

So we will see evidence on the ground that the Sasquatch moves forward, no matter its gait or the contortions its foot leaves in the soil, and it leaves evidence of this with globules of soil or snow ahead of the tracks, and must roll the earth as its foot leaves the ground.

Next, we consider the length of its feet, which must be beyond the normal length of a human's, and its stride must be at least at some points, beyond the capability of man, including the tallest, longest-legged of humans and the best award-winning fast walkers. If research indicates those known giants in our society rival the Sasquatch's tracks then must we in addition indicate that these people were not in the forests walking barefoot with their consistent stride for many, many miles, further than man tracks? (And man does not track far enough.) It does not. We already know that running tracks will obviously be different than walking tracks, as the contortions the foot makes on the ground are different. Ground explodes and the depth of the toes is radically deeper when man jogs or tries to simulate longer strides by running. So we must ascertain whether Sasquatch tracks be walking tracks or running tracks with even greater strides and proper cues.

The proof of the existence of a Sasquatch can be simply a matter of tracking, and we are not fooled even if some huge-footed man who holds track records made the tracks. For he will not behave like a wild creature, which you will learn when you track him. Not that this is a simple task, but it is **the** task. No one, of course, can prove a null hypothesis, that is, there is **no** Sasquatch, for you cannot look everywhere in the world in order to make that statement.

The clincher is, then, that in tracking this creature, we must have the experience to know how a wild creature behaves in the forest. It is a matter of survival for it, not a matter of man faking long distances of tracks, beyond which he thinks others will track him. If you have tracked wild creatures and man, you will **know** if you track a Sasquatch. If you have not done your homework, your guesses will have no basis. And I do not believe a man with sufficiently large feet and stride will be able to fool a tracker experienced in both wildlife and human tracking. If he carries a pack, it will be reflected in his tracks. If he lives off the land, it will show. Even if the perpetrator has this knowledge of tracking himself, I do not believe he can properly simulate wildness. Over a long distance he will reveal himself. Pursuit is the name of the game.

So, if, as an experienced tracker, you find there is a real Sasquatch out there somewhere, it is stupendous knowledge for you. I envy you. I want to know. Communicating this as proof of the Sasquatch to the rest of humankind is another matter.

Epilogue

The profusion of small tracks which bombard your eyes early in the morning come from many numerous creatures of the night and early hours. Mice, shrews, voles, moles, wood rats, rabbits, hares, lizards, skinks, gophers, marmots, muskrats, pikas, mountain beavers, insects, all and more have been busy while you were elsewhere. Work the puzzle if you can. See how these creatures relate to each other, who seeks who, and who runs from who. If you can do this before the wind blows away their traces and the sun sets again, you will have knowledge of a world few know. It may take many winds and many hours until many suns have set, but in a few yards many silent voices will speak to you alone.

There is another creature we can track. He is prolific in population in urban areas and now also in the wilderness. He is readily seen too often in wilderness habitat. There are problems for all wildlife because of his presence. It is man whom we track now. His footprints alone would not cause undue grief, lest he carry leghold traps. It is the wide caterpillar and tractor treads that cut into the green, erode the riverbanks and clog the streams that do the damage. You will know you are tracking him, for if he is on foot often his left foot sinks consistently deeper into the soil. This is the hunter with a heavy gun strapped on his left shoulder. When his toe marks deeper than his heel imprint he carries a pack. Should his heel mark make drag marks into his slow prints, he is tired. Should his toe also drag out of his track, he is near exhaustion. There are sounds, too, we can track that tell of this creature. The chain saw whine, the cracking of wood as the tree breaks, and the quick whistle of air before the crash as it falls, taking young trees and nests with it. The sound of ATVs and four-wheel drives are not difficult to track, only to eliminate. The vegetation signs are clearly there. And he leaves more than his tracks. His bottles and paper and plastic we will be able to track forever. When there are no longer tracks of wildlife, will there be tire tracks instead?

In hopes that this writing has engendered in you sparks of eagerness to find the evasive tracks of wild creatures, I leave you. I have only touched the surface of wealth that lies ahead of you in the wilderness. I would tread with you in your searches, too, but I still have my own. Many more fair-footed than man imprint upon the land, beseeching me to know them, beckoning me to find them, and delighting that I rarely do.

As I continue to track in the wild, my own tracks become inextricably intertwined with these wild ones. Of the thousands of tracks I have seen and followed, very few have brought me to the very last track of the animal. Yet the last track I often find first—those scattered skeletons. I sense their ghosts in the ever-pervading desert dust, and hear their calls still in the rustles of the pines. Their images are with me between the hemlocks and the firs in the high reaches, and I am there with them. Although the dust has blown from their tracks, may their spirits still be in the wind.

Appendix

Wildlife Track Data

Track measurements; distinguishing configurations; stride; straddle/trail width; jumps; gaits and other significant information.

BOBCAT

TRACK SIZE: Front—1¾–2¼ inches long and 1⅞ inches–2⅜ inches wide; rear—1¾ inches long and 1½ inches wide.
NUMBER OF TOES: 4 on both the front and rear.
CONFIGURATION: Round, claws register about 5 percent of the time. Three-lobed posterior scallops on rear of heel pad; split on anterior heel lobe.
STRIDE: 8–13 inches.
STRADDLE: 1–3 inches.
JUMPS: 8 feet or more.
GAITS: Walk, trot, bound, lope, gallop, pace.
OTHER: Directly registers rear foot in front track.

COUGAR

TRACK SIZE: Front—3 inches long and 3½ inches wide; rear—3 inches long and 3 inches wide.
NUMBER OF TOES: 4 on both the front and rear.
CONFIGURATION: Round, claws register 5 percent of the time. Three-lobed posterior scallops on the rear of heel pad; split on anterior heel pad.
STRIDE: Slow walk—12–16 inches; fast walk—21–28 inches.
STRADDLE: 6 inches.
JUMPS: 20 feet chasing a deer; 47 feet reported.
GAITS: Walk, trot, bound, lope, gallop, pace.

LYNX

TRACK SIZE: Front—3¾ inches long and wide; rear—3¾ inches long and 3½ inches wide.
NUMBER OF TOES: 4 on both the front and rear.
CONFIGURATION: Round, three-lobed posterior scallops on rear of heel pad. Claws show 5 percent of the time. Tracks wider than long when running. Foot is heavily furred. No anterior heel pad split.
STRIDE: Slow walk—12–14 inches; running—up to 50 inches.
STRADDLE: 5–6 inches.

JUMPS: 8 feet or more.
GAITS: Walk, trot, bound, lope, gallop, pace.

COYOTE
TRACK SIZE: Front—2¾ inches long and 2⅛ inches wide; rear—2½ inches long and 2 inches wide.
NUMBER OF TOES: 4 on both the front and rear.
CONFIGURATION: Oblong. Claws show 95 percent of the time. Outer toe pads register as larger than front toe pads.
STRIDE: Walkz—13–16 inches; running—15–50 inches.
TRAIL WIDTH: 5 inches.
JUMPS: 6–14 feet.
GAITS: Walk, trot, bound, lope, gallop and pace.
SPEED: Trot to 20 mph, 40 briefly.

RED FOX
TRACK SIZE: Front—2½ inches long and 2 inches wide; rear—2⅛ inches long and 2 inches wide.
NUMBER OF TOES: 4 on both the front and rear.
CONFIGURATION: Oblong. Claws show 95 percent of the time. Paws are heavily haired in winter. Rear tracks are more pointed than front tracks. Only canine to directly register rear track in front track. Makes a very straight line of tracks.
STRIDE: Walk—10–14 inches; running—18–36 inches.
TRAIL WIDTH: 3½–4½ inches.
JUMPS: Up to 20 feet.
GAITS: Half walk-half trot is normal gait. Bound, gallop, lope.
SPEED: 30–45 mph.

GRAY FOX
TRACK SIZE: Front—1⅝ inches long and 1⅜ inches wide; rear—1½ inches long and 1¼ inches wide.
NUMBER OF TOES: 4 on both the front and rear.
CONFIGURATION: Oblong. Claws register 95 percent of the time. Claws are long and curved.
STRIDE: Walk—8–12 inches; running—18–36 inches.
TRAIL WIDTH: 3¾ inches.
GAITS: Trot, walk, gallop.
SPEED: 28 mph for short distances.
OTHER: Readily climbs trees vertically.

TIMBER WOLF
TRACK SIZE: Front—4–5 inches in length and 4¼ inches wide; rear—4½ inches long and 3½– 4⅛ inches wide.

NUMBER OF TOES: 4 on both the front and rear.
CONFIGURATION: Oblong. Claws show 95 percent of the time.
STRIDE: Slow walk—16–18 inches; fast walk—30 inches; running—35–54 inches.
TRAIL WIDTH: 7 inches.
JUMPS: 8–10 feet from a sitting position.
GAITS: Walk, trot, gallop.
SPEED: More than 40 mph for short distances.

BLACK BEAR

TRACK SIZE: Front—4½ inches long and 3¾–4 inches wide; rear—7 inches long and 5 inches wide.
NUMBER OF TOES: 5 on both the front and rear.
CONFIGURATION: Front foot is laterally oblong. Rear foot has a long heel. Front claws mark on the ground 1–1½ inches ahead of the toe pad. The largest toe is on the outside of the foot. A wedge is seen in the instep of the rear track. Toes curve around the heel pad.
STRIDE: Walk—18 inches; running—2–5 feet.
TRAIL WIDTH: 14 inches.
GAITS: Walk, gallop, pace.
SPEED: 22.5 mph.

GRIZZLY BEAR

TRACK SIZE: Front—5½ inches long and 5 or more inches wide; rear—10 inches long and 6 inches wide at least.
NUMBER OF TOES: 5 on front and rear both.
CONFIGURATION: Front is laterally oblong. Rear has a long heel. Heel is more pointed than black bear. Front claws mark 1½–4 inches ahead of the toe pads. The largest toe is on the outside of the foot. Toes are in a straighter line than those of the black bear.
STRIDE: Walk—18–20 inches; running—3–9 feet; full gallop—17 feet.
TRAIL WIDTH: 18 inches.
GAITS: Walk, gallop, pace.
SPEED: 37.27 mph.

MULE DEER

TRACK SIZE: Front—3¾ inches long and 2⅝ inches wide; rear—3⅛ inches long and 2½ inches wide.
NUMBER OF TOES: A split hoof, front and rear.
CONFIGURATION: Oblong, heart-shaped. Dew claws.
STRIDE: Walk—21–24 inches; running—6–15 feet.
TRAIL WIDTH: 6 inches.
JUMPS: Record of 74 feet.
GAITS: Walk, bound, trot, gallop.

SPEED: 35 mph.
ANTLERS: Forked.

WHITE-TAIL DEER
TRACK SIZE: Front—3 inches long and 1⅞ inches wide; rear—2⅝ inches long and 1½ inches wide.
NUMBER OF TOES: Split hooves.
CONFIGURATION: Oblong, heart shaped. Dew claws.
STRIDE: Slow—18–21 inches; fast—6–9 feet.
TRAIL WIDTH: 6 inches.
JUMPS: To 30 feet. Can jump an 8-foot fence from a standing position.
GAITS: Trot, single-foot, gallop.
ANTLERS: Main beam with short tines branching off.

ELK
TRACK SIZE: Front—4¾ inches long and 3 inches wide; rear—4½ inches long and 2⅞ inches wide.
NUMBER OF TOES: Split hooves.
CONFIGURATION: Oblong, but more rounded than the mule and white-tail. Dew claws mark at times.
STRIDE: Walk—26–28 inches; running—6–9 feet.
JUMPS: 7½ feet high over fences.
TRAIL WIDTH: 8 inches.
GAITS: Walk, trot, gallop.
ANTLERS: Main beam with branching tines.

PRONGHORN
TRACK SIZE: Front—3¼ inches long and 2¼ inches wide; rear—2¾ inches long and 2 inches wide.
NUMBER OF TOES: Split hooves.
CONFIGURATION: Oblong. Rear heel width slightly wider than mule and white-tail. No dew claws.
STRIDE: Slow run—30 inches; fast—14 feet.
TRAIL WIDTH: 6 inches.
JUMPS: 20 feet. Record: 27 feet.
GAITS: Walk, run, gallop, bound. Rear legs paired most of the time.
SPEED: 30 mph for 15 miles, up to 70 briefly.
HORNS: buck—longer, pronged horns; doe—short, usually nonpronged horns.

MOOSE
TRACK SIZE: Front—6 inches long and 4½ inches wide; rear—5½ inches long and 3½ inches wide.
NUMBER OF TOES: Cloven, split hooves.

CONFIGURATION: Oblong, pointed. Dew claws often mark, increasing length of track to 10 inches.
STRIDE: Slow walk—30–33 inches; trot or run—8–10 feet.
TRAIL WIDTH: 9–10 inches.
GAITS: Walk, trot, run.
ANTLERS: Large palmate antlers. Antler spread: 81 inches.
SPEED: Up to 35 mph.

WOODLAND CARIBOU

TRACK SIZE: Front—4½ inches long and 5 inches wide; rear—4½ inches long and 4½ inches wide.
NUMBER OF TOES: Split hooves.
CONFIGURATION: Round. Dew claws could increase length of track by 2½ inches.
STRIDE: Walk—25–28 inches.
STRADDLE: 9¾ inches.
GAITS: Walk, trot, bound, lope, gallop, pace.
SPEED: Up to 50 mph.
ANTLERS: Bulls—semi-palmate with flat brow tines 20–62 inches long; cows—small, spindly, 9–20 inches long.

BADGER

TRACK SIZE: Front—2 inches long and 2 inches wide; rear—2 inches long and 2 inches wide.
NUMBER OF TOES: 5 in both the front and rear.
CONFIGURATION: Front—slightly longer than wide; rear—slightly narrower. Pigeon toed. Long claws on front feet frequently mark.
STRIDE: Walk—6–12 inches; running—1–2 feet.
STRADDLE: 4–7 inches.
TRAIL WIDTH: 9–11 inches.
JUMPS: May jump above sage for a view.
GAITS: Walk, gallop, pace.
OTHER: Badger can climb trees at an angle.

WOLVERINE

TRACK SIZE: Front—2½ inches long and 2½ inches wide to 4½ inches long and 4½ inches wide; rear—to 3½ inches long and 3⅜ inches wide.
NUMBER OF TOES: 5 on both the front and rear.
CONFIGURATION: Usually wider than long. Front foot has a split heel pad. Asymmetrical heel pads. Densely haired foot pads in winter. Smaller inner toe may not register on the ground.
STRIDE: Walk—16–18 inches; running—19–36 inches.
TRAIL WIDTH: 7–10 inches.

GAITS: Walk, trot, lope, gallop.
SPEED: Fast but cannot catch a hare on the run.
OTHER: Climbs trees well.

MINK

TRACK SIZE: Front—1¼ inches long and 1¼–1¾ inches wide; rear—1¼ inches long up to ¾ inches wide. With heel marking, 1¾ or 2 inches long.
NUMBER OF TOES: 5 slightly webbed toes on all feet.
CONFIGURATION: Round. Thin, elongated, horizontal heel pad.
STRIDE: Walking—9–20 inches; running—20–30 inches.
STRADDLE/TRAIL WIDTH: 2¼–3½ inches.
JUMPS: 10–30 inches between groups.
GAITS: Alternate walking, bound, lope. Rear feet may fall in front tracks or display a group of all feet.
OTHER: Semiretractible claws may mark accordingly.

LONG-TAILED WEASEL

TRACK SIZE: Front—1 inch long and ½ an inch wide; rear—1½ inch long and ¾ inches wide.
NUMBER OF TOES: 5 on each foot.
CONFIGURATION: Round.
STRIDE: 12–18 inches.
STRADDLE: 1½–3 inches.
JUMPS: Upward of 6 feet; 8 feet recorded.
GAITS: Bound.
OTHER: Two by two pattern, hind feet registering in front feet tracks.

RACCOON

TRACK SIZE: Front—3 inches long and 3 inches wide; rear—3¼–3⅞ inches long and 2½ inches wide.
NUMBER OF TOES: 5 in both the front and rear.
CONFIGURATION: Front—round; rear—oblong, long. Long toes.
STRIDE: Walk—12–16 inches; running—16–28 inches. Front and rear feet mark opposite each other when walking.
TRAIL WIDTH: 8–10 inches.
JUMPS: Short.
GAITS: Walk, pacer primarily, bound, gallop.
OTHER: Climbs trees.

PORCUPINE

TRACK SIZE: Front—1¾ inches long and 1¼ inches wide; rear—2¼ inches long and 1½ inches wide.
NUMBER OF TOES: 4 on the front and 5 on the rear.

CONFIGURATION: Oblong with a pointed heel pad in the rear. Long claws may mark. Pigeon-toed. Quills may mark on the ground. Tracks appear to have a pebbled marking.

STRIDE: Walk—6–10 inches; running—24 inches.

STRADDLE: 5–9 inches.

GAITS: Walk, pacer primarily, run.

OTHER: Climbs trees.

BEAVER

TRACK SIZE: Front—2 inches long and 2 inches wide; rear—5 inches long and 5 inches wide.

NUMBER OF TOES: 5 on both the front and rear.

CONFIGURATION: Front—round; rear—oblong. Narrow heel fanning to wide toe points. Claws and tail mark. Can walk upright on rear feet and tail.

STRIDE: Walk—4–6 inches; running—up to 2 feet.

TRAIL WIDTH: 8–12 inches.

GAITS: Walk, pace, gallop, bound.

SPEED: 6 feet, 5 inches to 6 feet, 11 inches a second underwater. On and under water 3 mph.

OTHER: Can dive to 2,500 feet in one dive.

WESTERN GRAY SQUIRREL

TRACK SIZE: Front—1⅜ inches wide and 2 inches long; rear—1¼ inches wide and 2⅝ inches long.

NUMBER OF TOES: 4 on the front and 5 on the rear.

CONFIGURATION: Oblong in shape. Claws show in track.

STRIDE: Slow—10–15 inches; fast—15–38 inches.

STRADDLE: 4½–5 inches wide.

JUMPS: At least 36 inches.

GAITS: Bounds, and hops with front feet paired.

Bibliography

GENERAL REFERENCES

American Wildlife and Plants, Guide to Wildlife Food Habits, by Alexander C. Martin, Herbert S. Zim, and Arnold L. Nelson (New York: Dover Publications, 1951).

The Audubon Society Field Guide to North American Mammals, by John O. Whitaker, Jr. (New York: Alfred A. Knopf, 1980).

Field Guide to the Mammals, by William H. Burt and Richard P. Grossenheider (Boston: Houghton-Mifflin, 1975).

The Mammals of North America, by E. Raymond Hall and Keith R. Kelson (New York: Ronald Press, 1959).

Wild Mammals of North America, by Joseph A. Chapman and George Feldhamer (Baltimore/London: Johns Hopkins Univ. Press, 1982).

TRACKING REFERENCES

Animal Tracks and Hunter Signs, by Ernest T. Seton (Toronto: MacMillan of Canada, 1958).

Animal Tracks and Signs of North America, by Richard P. Smith (Harrisburg, Pennsylvania: Stackpole Books, 1982).

Don't Die in the Bundu, by Col. D. H. Grainger (Landsdowne: Citadel Press, 1967).

Field Guide to Animal Tracks, by Olaus J. Murie (Boston: Houghton-Mifflin, 1954).

Field Guide to Mammal Tracking in Western America, by James Halfpenny (Boulder: Johnson Books, 1986).

"The Footprints of Extinct Animals," Number 1, Volume 248, January, 1983, *Scientific American,* New York, N.Y.

A Guide to Animal Tracking and Behavior, by Donald D. and Lillian L. Stokes (Boston/Toronto: Little, Brown and Co., 1986).

The Search, by Tom Brown, Jr., and William Owens (Englewood Cliffs, New Jersey: Prentice Hall, 1980).

Tom Brown's Field Guide to Nature Observation and Tracking, by Tom Brown, Jr., and Brandt Morgan (New York: Berkley Books, 1983).

"Tracking," Number 2, 3, Volume 2, Spring/Summer, 1983. *The Tracker,* Asbury, New Jersey.

Tracking and the Art of Seeing, by Paul Rezendes (Charlotte, Vermont: Camden House Publishing, 1992).

MAMMAL REFERENCES

Badger
Badgers, by Ernest G. Neal (England: Blandfor Press, Poole/Dorset: Facts On File, 1986).
"Miscellaneous Non-Game Mammals of Oregon," Number 16, Volume 1, 1978, *Outdoor Almanac*, Oregon Department of Fish and Wildlife, Portland, Oregon.

Bear
Bear Attacks: Their Causes and Avoidance, by Stephen Herrero (Piscataway, New Jersey: Nick Lyon Books, Winchester Press, 1985).
Border Grizzly Project Report, by Charles Jonkel, (Missoula, Montana: University of Montana, 1975).
Grizzlies of Mt. McKinley, by Adolph Murie (Seattle: University of Washington Press, 1984).
"Grizzly and Man: Can They Co-Exist?" Number 5, Volume 61, September/October, 1986, *Defenders of Wildlife*, Washington, District of Columbia.
The Grizzly Bear, by Thomas McNamee (New York: Alfred A. Knopf, 1984).
Grizzly Country, by Andy Russell (New York: Alfred A. Knopf, 1967).
"Homeless on the range: grizzlies struggle for elbow room and survival in Banff National Park," Number 1, Volume 117, Jan–Feb 1997, *Canadian Geographic*.
"How to Cope in Bear Country," Number 5, Volume 22, August/September, 1984, *National Wildlife*, Vienna, Virginia.
Killer Bears, by Mike Crammond, (New York: Outdoor Life Books, Charles Scribners Sons, 1981).
Man Meets Grizzly, by Francis M. Young (Boston: Houghton Mifflin, 1980).
"Montana's Million Dollar Black Bears," Number 2, Volume 15, March/April, 1984, *Montana Outdoors*, Helena, Montana.
Night of the Grizzlies, by Jack Olsen (New York, New American Library: Signet, 1969).
No Room for Bears, by Frank Dufresne (New York: Holt, Rinehart and Winston, 1965).

"Stalking the Great Grizzly," Number 18, November/December, 1984, *Equinox*, Camden East, Ontario.

Beaver

My Beaver Colony, by Lars Willson (Garden City, New York: Doubleday, 1968).

Three Against the Wilderness, by Eric Collier (New York: E. P. Dutton, 1959).

"Oregon's Furbearers," Number 3, 1978, *Outdoor Almanac*, Oregon Department of Fish and Wildlife, Portland, Oregon.

Bobcat

"Bobcat," Numbers 1, 2, Volume 58, March/April, 1983, *Defenders of Wildlife*, Washington, District of Columbia.

Bobcat of North America, by Stanley P. Young (Lincoln and London: University of Nebraska Press, 1978).

"Bobcat Populations, Review of Available Literature," Number 79-2, 1979, *Oregon Department of Fish and Wildlife Information Report Series*, Portland, Oregon.

"Bobcat Social Organization," Volume 38, Number 3, 1974, *Journal of Wildlife Management*, Bethesda, Maryland.

Bobcat Year, by Hope Ryden (New York: Viking Press, 1981).

Reproductive Ecology of Bobcats and Lynx in Western Montana, by Scott M. Brainerd, Master of Science Thesis (Missoula, Montana: University of Montana, 1981).

The World of the Bocat, by Joe Van Wormer (New York: J. B. Lippincott, 1963).

Caribou

"The Fight for Long Canyon," Numbers 1, 2, Volume 58, February/March, 1983, *Defenders of Wildlife*, Washington, District of Columbia.

"Last Chance for the Border Caribou?" Number 4, Volume 57, August, 1982, *Defenders of Wildlife*, Washington, District of Columbia.

Cougar

Cry of the Panther: Quest of a Species, by James P. McMullen (New York: McGraw Hill, 1985).

The Ghost Walker, by R. D. Lawrence (Toronto: McClelland and Stewart, 1983).

Puma, by Stanley P. Young and Edward A. Goldman (New York: Dover Publications, 1946).
"Stalking the Mountain Lion to Save Him," Number 5, Volume 136, May, 1969, *National Geographic*, Washington, District of Columbia.
"The What, Where, and How of the Kingdom of Cougars," Number 3, Volume 56, June, 1981, *Defenders of Wildlife*, Washington District of Columbia.

Coyote
Don Coyote, by Dayton Hyde (New York: Arbor House, 1986).
God's Dog, by Hope Ryden (New York: Penguin Books, 1981).
World of the Coyote, by Joe Van Wormer (Philadelphia: J. B. Lippincott, 1964).
"Yankee Coyotes," Number 5, Volume 56, October, 1981, *Defenders of Wildlife*, Washington, District of Columbia.

Elk
Big Game of North America, Ecology and Management, by John L. Schmidt and Douglas L. Gilbert (Harrisburg, Pennsylvania: Stackpole Books, 1979).

Fox, Gray
"Denning, Pup Rearing, and Dispersal in the Gray Fox in East-Central Alabama," Volume 49, Number 1, 1985, *Journal of Wildlife Management*, Bethesda, Maryland.
A Field Guide to the Mammals, by William H. Burt and Richard P. Grossenheider (Boston: Houghton Mifflln, 1976).

Fox, Red
A Guide to Animal Tracking and Behavior, by Donald D. and Lillian L. Stokes (Boston Toronto: Little, Brown and Co., 1986).

Human
Tom Brown, Jr., Asbury, N.J.: pers. comm.
"Man Tracking: Introduction to the Step-by-Step Method," by Roland Robbins (Montrose, Ca., *Search and Rescue Magazine*, 1977).
The Plains of North America and Their Inhabitants, by Richard Irving Dodge (Cranbury, N.J., Associated University Presses, 1989).
Tracking: A Blueprint for Learning How, by Jack Kearney (El Cajon, Ca., Pathways Press, 1980).

Lynx

"The Ecology of the Lynx in North Central Washington, Progress Report," December, 1987, *Wildlife Research Institute*, University of Idaho, Moscow, Idaho.

Reproductive Ecology of Bobcats and Lynx in Western Montana, by Scott M. Brainerd, Master of Science Thesis, (Missoula, Montana: University of Montana, 1985).

Mink

The Audubon Society Field Guide to North American Mammals, by John O. Whitaker, Jr. (New York: Alfred A. Knopf, 1980).

Field Guide to Animal Tracks, by Olaus J. Murie (Boston: Houghton Mifflin, 1954).

Moose

"Wolves Against Moose on Isle Royale," Number 2, Volume 123, February, 1963, *National Geographic*, Washington, District of Columbia.

Mule Deer

The Deer of North America, by Leonard L. Rue, III (New York: Crown, 1978).

"Oregon's Hoofed Wild Animals," Number 5, 1978, *Outdoor Almanac*, Department of Fish and Wildlife, Portland, Oregon.

Porcupine

World of the Porcupine, by David F. Costello (Philadelphia: J. B. Lippincott, 1966).

Pronghorn

"Oregon's Hoofed Wild Animals," Number 5, 1978, *Outdoor Almanac*, Oregon Department of Fish and Wildlife, Portland, Oregon.

"Windspirit of the West," Number 3, Volume 87, May, 1985, *Audubon*, New York, New York.

World of the Pronghorn, by Joe Van Wormer (Philadelphia and New York: J. B. Lippincott, 1969).

Raccoon

"Oregon's Furbearers," Number 3, 1978, *Outdoor Almanac*, Oregon Department of Fish and Wildlife, Portland, Oregon.

World of the Raccoon, by Leonard L. Rue, III (Philadelphia: J. B. Lippincott, 1968).

Weasel, Long-tailed

The Audubon Society Field Guide to North American Mammals, by John O. Whitaker, Jr. (New York: Alfred A. Knopf, 1980).
A Guide to Animal Tracking and Behavior, by Donald D. and Lillian L. Stokes (Boston/Toronto: Little, Brown, 1986).

White-tailed Deer

The Deer of North America, by Leonard L. Rue, III (New York: Crown, 1978).
A Guide to Animal Tracking and Behavior, by Donald D. and Lillian L. Stokes (Boston/Toronto: Little, Brown, 1986).
"Oregon's Hoofed Animals," Number 5, 1978, *Outdoor Almanac*, Oregon Department of Fish and Wildlife, Portland, Oregon.

Wolf

Dance of the Wolves, by Roger Peters (New York: McGraw Hill, 1985).
"L. David Mech Discusses the Wolf," Number 6, Volume 61, November/December, 1986, *Defenders of Wildlife*, Washington, District of Columbia.
"Return of the Wolf," Number 5, Volume 57, September, 1982, *Defenders of Wildlife*, Washington, District of Columbia.
"Where Can the Wolf Survive?" Number 4, Volume 152, April, 1977, *National Geographic*, Washington, District of Columbia.
"The Wolf's Song Returns to the North Fork," Number 3, Volume 59, May/June, 1984, *Defenders of Wildlife*, Washington, District of Columbia.
"Wolves Against Moose on Isle Royale," Number 2, Volume 123, February, 1963, *National Geographic*, Washington, District of Columbia.
"Yellowstone Wolves," Number 1, Volume 56, February, 1981, *Defenders of Wildlife*, Washington, District of Columbia.

Wolverine

"Ecology of the Wolverine gulo-gulo in Northwestern Montana, USA," Volume 59, Number 7, 1981, *Canadian Journal of Zoology*, Ottawa, Ontario.

"Home Range and Habitat Use by Wolverine in South-Central Alaska," Volume 50, Number 21, 1986, *Journal of Wildlife Management*, Bethesda, Maryland.

"Long Distance Movement by an Adult Wolverine," Volume 67, Number 603, 1986, *Journal of Mammology*, Provo, Utah.

"Notes on the Wolverine in Alaska and the Yukon Territory," Volume 36, Number 2, April, 1972, *Journal of Wildlife Management*, Bethesda, Maryland.

BIRDS AND SNAKES REFERENCES

Birds

A Field Guide to Western Birds, by Roger Tory Peterson (Boston: Houghton-Mifflin, 1941).

Tracks and Trailcraft, by Ellsworth E. Jaeger (London: Macmillan, Collier-Macmillan Limited, 1948).

Snakes

Amphibians and Reptiles of the Pacific Northwest, by Gayle Pickwell (Stanford, Ca.: Stanford University Press, 1947).

Amphibians and Reptiles of Western North America, by Robert C. Stebbins (New York: McGraw-Hill, 1915).

"Poisonous Dwellers of the Desert," Number 3, 1964, Southwestern Monuments Association, *Globe*, Arizona.

Reptiles and Amphibians of the West, by Vinson Brown (Happy Camp, Ca.: Naturegraph, 1974).

Tracks and Trailcraft, by Ellsworth E. Jaeger (London: Macmillan, Collier-Macmillan Limited, 1948).

Index

OTHER HANCOCK HOUSE NATURE TITLES

Alpine Wildflowers
J. E. Underhill
ISBN 0-88839-975-8

Backroads Explorer:
Similkameen & S.
Okanagan
Murphy Shewchuck
ISBN 0-88839-205-2

**Clancy & Tidepool
Friends**
Carol Batdorf
ISBN 0-88839-336-9

**Coast Lowland
Wildflowers**
J. E. Underhill
ISBN 0-88839-973-1

Eastern Mushrooms
E. Barrie Kavasch
ISBN 0-88839-091-2

**Eastern Rocks &
Minerals**
James W. Grandy
ISBN 0-88839-105-6

Edible Seashore
Rick M. Harbo
ISBN 0-88839-199-4

**Exploring the
Outdoors:** SW BC
Eberts & Grass
ISBN 0-88839-989-8

**Introducing E.
Wildflowers**
E. Barrie Kavasch
ISBN 0-88839-092-0

**Northeastern Wild
Edibles**
E. Barrie Kavasch
ISBN 0-88839-090-4

Orchids of NA
Dr. William Petrie
ISBN 0-88839-089-0

Pacific Wilderness
*Hancock, Hancock &
Stirling*
ISBN 0-919654-08-8

Rafting in BC
VanDine & Fandrich
ISBN 0-88839-985-5

**Roadside
Wildflowers NW**
J. E. Underhill
ISBN 0-88839-108-0

**Rocks & Minerals
NW**
Leaming & Leaming
ISBN 0-88839-053-X

**Sagebrush
Wildflowers**
J. E. Underhill
ISBN 0-88839-171-4

Seashells of the NE
Gordon & Weeks
ISBN 0-88839-808-7

Tidepool & Reef
Rick M. Harbo
ISBN 0-88839-039-4

Trees of the West
Mabel Crittenden
ISBN 0-88839-269-9

**Upland Field &
Forest Wildflowers**
J. E. Underhill
ISBN 0-88839-174-9

Western Mushrooms
J. E. Underhill
ISBN 0-88839-031-9

Western Seashore
Rick M. Harbo
ISBN 0-88839-201-X

**Wild Berries of the
NW**
J. E. Underhill
ISBN 0-88839-027-0

**Wildflowers of the
West**
Crittenden & Telfer
ISBN 0-88839-270-2

Wild Harvest
Terry Domico
ISBN 0-88839-022-X

**Wildlife of the
Rockies**
Hancock & Hall
ISBN 0-919654-33-9